CONSTITUTIONAL CLIFFHANGERS

CONSTITUTIONAL CHANGES

BRIAN C. KALT

Constitutional Cliffhangers

A LEGAL GUIDE FOR PRESIDENTS AND THEIR ENEMIES

Yale UNIVERSITY PRESS

NEW HAVEN & LONDON

Published with assistance from the Mary Cady Tew Memorial Fund.

Yale University Press books may be purchased in quantity for educational,
business, or promotional use. For information, please e-mail sales.press@
yale.edu (U.S. office) or sales@yaleup.co.uk (U.K. office).

Set in Scala type by IDS Infotech Ltd., Chandigarh, India.
Printed in the United States of America.

The Library of Congress has cataloged the hardcover edition as follows:
Kalt, Brian C.
Constitutional cliffhangers: a legal guide for presidents and their enemies/
Brian C. Kalt.
p.cm.
Includes bibliographical references and index.
ISBN 978-0-300-12351-7 (hardback)
1. Presidents– Legal Status, laws, etc.–United States. I. Title.
KF5051.K35 2012
342.73'062–dc23
2011022723

ISBN 978-0-300-23430-5 (pbk.)

A catalogue record for this book is available from the British Library.

For Benjamin and Jonathan

CONTENTS

PREFACE

Soon after I started writing this manuscript, I attended a reception for a prominent legal scholar. I was lucky enough to speak with him, and at one point the conversation turned to my work. I was about fifteen seconds into a description of an issue I was working on when he asked, with mild revulsion, "Why are you writing about that?"

This book deals with a lot of issues of that ilk: weird twists of constitutional law that might seem unlikely to occur. In short, I am regarded by some of my colleagues as, to quote Leo Rosten in *The Joys of Yiddish*, "the kind who worries whether a flea has a *pupik* [navel]."

But I do think that at least one of the six scenarios in this book—or something very similar—will come to pass someday. I also believe that if anything like them does happen, the fact that people thought and wrote about such things beforehand will help to raise the tone of the public debate. (To be useful on such an occasion, I have provided a thicker-than-usual layer of citations and discussion in the endnotes, which I have consolidated into no more than one per paragraph in the main text.) More broadly, I think it is worth pondering why these sorts of pitfalls arise, how to fix them, and why we often *don't* fix them.

Aside from all this, these scenarios are just very compelling. In addition to their superb dramatic possibilities, they provide an opportunity to think about important and interesting general topics, like presidential immunities, pardons, constitutional procedures, presidential succession, impeachment, term limits, presidential history, constitutional interpretation, and presidential power in general.

So that is why I am writing about this.

ACKNOWLEDGMENTS

Portions of this book have previously appeared in print as law-review articles. Some have been edited, updated, and paraphrased; parts have been used verbatim, without direct quotation or citation. Specifically, Chapter 1 draws heavily upon Akhil Reed Amar & Brian C. Kalt, *The Presidential Privilege Against Prosecution*, 2 Nexus 11 (1997) (with Professor Amar's gracious permission); Chapter 2 on Brian C. Kalt, Note, *Pardon Me?: The Constitutional Case Against Presidential Self-Pardons*, 106 Yale L.J. 779 (1996); and Chapter 5 on Brian C. Kalt, *The Constitutional Case for the Impeachability of Former Federal Officials: An Analysis of the Law, History, and Practice of Late Impeachment*, 6 Tex. Rev. L. & Pol. 13 (2001).

I would like to thank Richard Albert, Akhil Reed Amar, Kristi Bowman, Bruce Boyden, Brady Bustany, Adam Candeub, Sonia Fulop, Michael Gerhardt, Mel Kalt, Sara Kalt, Mae Kuykendall, Michael Lawrence, Gerard Magliocca, Lumen Mulligan, Michael O'Malley, Adam Pavlik, Frank Ravitch, Alice Ristroph, Ronald Rotunda, Glen Staszewski, and Ben Walther for their suggestions. Robert Bennett, Josh Chafetz, Joel Goldstein, Adam Gustafson, and Seth Tillman deserve extra recognition for their particularly thorough comments.

I would also like to thank the people who provided the truly outstanding research support for which Michigan State University College of Law is justly proud: librarians Barbara Bean, Brent Domann, Jane Meland, and

Kathy Prince, and students Jon Abent, Jordan Brackey, Nathan Cortright, Christy McDonald, Jason Murdey, and Sarah Pulda. With all the hard work they did on my behalf, I'm even more embarrassed that this book took me as long to write as it did. On that note, I'd like to thank my dean, Joan Howarth, for her patience.

Finally, I must give special thanks to Jorge E. Souss, who contributed more careful scrutiny, helpful comments, and clear thinking than any sensible person would ever have taken the time to produce.

Introduction

Electing, punishing, and replacing presidents can get tense. Ideally, the constitutional rules would be clear on such occasions, but often they are not. This book examines six presidential constitutional cliffhangers: scenarios in which the fate of the president or presidency is in doubt as politicians, courts, and the people argue over the proper interpretation of the Constitution.

The scenarios covered in Chapters 1 through 6, respectively, are:

1. a president is criminally prosecuted;
2. a president pardons himself;
3. cabinet members try to oust an allegedly "disabled" president, who in turn tries to oust them;
4. with the president and vice president dead, the secretary of state and the Speaker of the House fight for control of the presidency;
5. an ex-president is impeached; and
6. a two-term president attempts to stay in power.

As the title indicates, this book is mainly a legal guide to navigating these six scenarios should they ever occur. In the process, though, these six discussions shed light on how law and politics combine to settle cliffhangers, how the constitutional weak spots that produce cliffhangers can be patched up, why such repairs are nevertheless rare, and how best to prevent these weak spots from forming in the first place. Rather than clutter up the individual legal guides with all this, these insights are distilled and collected in Chapter 7.

First, though, there is an obvious underlying question: why worry about a bunch of odd things that seem so unlikely? One reason is that they let us think more generally about interesting constitutional issues, like immunity, pardons, disability, succession, impeachment, and term limits. The rest of this introduction will offer a more direct reason—that cliffhangers do happen—and will consider what causes these constitutional gaps to arise and persist.

It'll Never Happen (Until It Does)

None of the six scenarios in this book has ever happened. That is why they are in the book—they are unprecedented, so they present legal uncertainty. But constitutional cliffhangers arise all the time; these are just six that have not arisen yet. Indeed, Scenarios 1 and 2 have "happened" recently in one sense of the word: prosecutors have considered prosecuting presidents and have had to analyze presidential immunity, and at least one president considered pardoning himself and had his lawyers look into it. Scenarios 5 and 6 have happened in another sense of the word: officials other than the president have been impeached after leaving office, and leaders other than the president have used loopholes to subvert term limits. Moreover, all six of the scenarios have been recognized and seriously discussed at the highest levels of power. This book is not about idle chatter.

As Nassim Nicholas Taleb has memorably explained, humans tend to underestimate the likelihood of rare but momentous events, which he calls "Black Swans." When Black Swans occur, we may write them off as flukes, or we may abuse hindsight and say that the risk was obvious. Either way, we keep underestimating the chances of new Black Swans.[1]

American constitutional history is full of such unexpected debacles and near misses; to say otherwise "require[s] a quite remarkable exercise of historical amnesia." Some of these incidents arose out of ambiguous constitutional provisions—what I call cliffhangers. In other cases, the constitutional rules were crystal clear but not very good, and led to chaos.* In all cases, some people warned about the problems in advance, but the rest of the country was content to ignore them. As an example, consider our most contentious presidential election.[2]

The whole election turned on a few hundred disputed votes in Florida. There had been ultra-close presidential elections before, and there had been ambiguous results in individual states before; it was only a matter of time before both happened at the same time. Unfortunately, no steps had been taken to prevent it.

The problem was that there were no rules for resolving a dispute like this. The quintessential American mixture of politics and litigation filled the void. The Republicans fought to defend their initial lead; the Democrats fought to open things back up and recount the votes. The Republicans controlled key posts in the state government; the Democrats won key victories in Florida state court. The Republicans took their case to Washington, D.C., where Republican-appointed Supreme Court justices declared that there was no time for recounts, handing the election to the Republicans. And so, in 1877, Rutherford B. Hayes became our nineteenth president.[3]

You might recall some similar things that happened in 2000. The underlying quandary—an electoral system in which it is easy for the margin of error to greatly exceed the margin of victory—was no secret before 1876, let alone in 2000. And yet it dangled out there unsolved, waiting to snag both elections. For the most part, it dangles still.

The all-time weightiest (albeit non-presidential) cliffhanger should have been even less surprising. Before 1861, it was unclear whether states could secede from the Union. Different Americans interpreted the Constitution

---

* The term "constitutional crisis" is often overused to refer to political crises, or to heated disagreements about the Constitution, that are resolved through our normal constitutional processes. *See generally* Sanford Levinson & Jack Balkin, *Constitutional Crises*, 157 U. Pa. L. Rev. 707 (2009); Keith E. Whittington, *Yet Another Constitutional Crisis?*, 43 Wm. & Mary L. Rev. 2093 (2002). I agree with the Levinson-Balkin definition of a constitutional crisis as one that represents a threat to civil order. *See* Levinson & Balkin, *supra*, at 742. Levinson and Balkin distinguish among three types of crises in which the Constitution is (1) baldly ignored, (2) followed assiduously in a way that is disastrous, or (3) the subject of a disagreement that escalates into potential violence or force. The situations described in my Chapters 3 and 4 would represent Type 3 crises; those in Chapters 1 and 6 might be Type 1 or 2, depending on which side you're on. *Cf. id.* at 729 n.88 (saying that *lack* of controversy over term limits could cause a Type 2 crisis).

differently, but people mainly just watched as tensions rose. After one side put its theory into practice, the country divided into armed camps and settled this legal dispute on the battlefield. The Civil War killed hundreds of thousands of people, largely because of an ambiguity in the Constitution that we couldn't find another way to resolve.

Returning to the presidency, here are some highlights from the list of predicaments and close calls:

- In 1800, the original clunky system for electing presidents produced a tie between Thomas Jefferson and his running mate, Aaron Burr, throwing the election into the House of Representatives. The House deadlocked as some mischievous members—anti-Jeffersonian lame ducks—flirted with selecting Burr until, after seven days and thirty-six ballots, enough of them relented.
- In 1841, President William Henry Harrison died. Vice President Tyler declared himself president; others strongly insisted Tyler was only acting president. The Constitution was ambiguous on the point, but Tyler's view eventually prevailed. This established a precedent that, as a side effect, made it constitutionally awkward for vice presidents to take power *temporarily* when presidents were disabled. This left the country without a functioning presidency on multiple occasions, including several months in 1881 (while the mortally wounded President Garfield lingered) and 1919 (when President Wilson was completely incapacitated by a stroke).
- In 1872, presidential candidate Horace Greeley died between Election Day and the meeting of the electoral college. Some electoral-college members voted for the dead Greeley, while others scattered their votes among four alternative Democrats. Luckily, Greeley had lost to Ulysses Grant on Election Day. Had he won, the presidency could have been left up in the air.
- In 1881, when President Garfield died and President Arthur took office, there was nobody in the line of succession for weeks. Four years later, it happened again, when Vice President Hendricks died and left President Cleveland with no backup. Had either Arthur or Cleveland died, there would have been no president for a while.

- In 1933, an assassin shot at President-Elect Franklin Roosevelt. He missed and instead killed Chicago mayor Anton Cermak, who was standing next to Roosevelt. While logic suggests that Vice President Elect Garner would have been inaugurated as president if Roosevelt had been killed, the original Constitution was unclear; the Republicans could have seized upon this ambiguity and called for a new election. But there was double luck. Not only had the assassin missed Roosevelt, but the Twentieth Amendment had been ratified three weeks earlier. It filled the constitutional gap and specified that Garner would have been inaugurated.

- Finally, a more recent example. In 2008, controversy swirled over the circumstances of the births of both presidential candidates, and whether they were "natural born citizens" as required by the Constitution. Republican nominee John McCain's birth in the Panama Canal Zone presented a thorny enough legal question that the Senate felt the need to pass a resolution on the matter. Meanwhile, Democratic nominee Barack Obama faced conspiracy theories about the circumstances and documents surrounding his birth. Had the situations been different—had the cases against McCain or Obama been stronger, or had the election been close— things quickly could have gotten messy.[4]

There are *many more* potential cliffhangers out there than just the six in this book. Viewed individually, each one may seem unlikely to flare up. Viewed collectively, though, the odds are good that something will happen, just as it has (or almost has) so many times before. This is worth worrying about.[5]

How Does This Happen?

Writing constitutions is hard. To write a perfect one, drafters would have to imagine every contingency that could arise over the next few centuries, agree on the best way to handle each one, draft airtight legal language, end up with a document that is not too complex to be ratified, and ensure that future generations understand both exactly what it says and exactly what it means. Each step in that process provides an opportunity for imperfection, and thus for constitutional cliffhangers.

Most people think of the Constitution—and battles over it—in the context of governmental powers and individual rights. In these areas, the Constitution is "short and vague," as Talleyrand reputedly said constitutions should be, using indefinite terms like "executive power," "due process," and "unreasonable search and seizure." But the Constitution is not just a flexible framework of powers and rights; it also sets out the nuts and bolts of constitutional structures and procedures. Here, brevity and vagueness (as well as sloppiness and miscalculation) can be dangerous weaknesses. It is no coincidence that the Constitution's original provisions for electing the president were longer than its provisions defining presidential power, nor is it a coincidence that after the election of 1800 mentioned previously, the original election provisions had to be scrapped and replaced with an even longer version.[6]

For the most part, the Constitution's structural and procedural provisions are clear and precise. To be elected president, for instance, a candidate must receive an electoral-college "majority," not just a "reasonable number" of electoral votes. But there is pressure for these provisions to have other, contradictory characteristics. For instance, these provisions ideally cover as many foreseeable situations as possible—witness the super-long election provisions in the last paragraph—which can cause confusing complexity, and which increases the number of places where problems can creep in. Another example is that while certainty is helpful, some situations—take presidential disability, for instance—call for case-by-case flexibility, and thus for "short and vague" formulations. On top of everything else, these provisions must be politically feasible. Thus, constitutional drafters cannot be perfect. The Constitution does not and cannot provide conciseness and completeness, certainty and flexibility, perfection and popularity, all at the same time.[7]

The Twenty-Second Amendment offers a good example of how these conflicting goals can produce a potential cliffhanger. The amendment's drafters wanted to send presidents home after two terms. As they debated how to count partial terms toward the limit, Senator Warren Magnuson persuaded them to sweep all complications aside and instead use simple, straightforward language. Unfortunately, as detailed in Chapter 6, his simple, straightforward language created a loophole that a determined president and a sympathetic electorate could exploit to evade term limits. Adding insult to injury, Congress proceeded to re-clutter up Magnuson's language anyway.

It's like telling a child in the backseat to stop touching his brother, a simple and straightforward command. Everyone knows what comes next, though: the motivated boy will stick his finger as close to his brother's face as he can without touching it. Modifying the command ("Don't annoy your brother!") seems to address that loophole, but it sacrifices clarity—it's too subjective to be effective if, as is likely, the child is still motivated enough. Now consider the considerably more powerful enticement that is the White House. During a conflict over control of the presidency, you can imagine how strong the incentives are to zero in on any potentially useful weak spot in the rules. And weak spots are inevitable whenever one drafts legal language, let alone language for a constitution that is supposed to be concise and accessible.[8]

Another problem is that when a constitution is still in effect hundreds of years after its drafting, some of the drafters' underlying assumptions and common understandings will have faded away. Chapter 2, for example, deals with the Constitution's failure to specify whether presidents can pardon themselves. There is a strong argument that the Constitution's Framers thought that it literally went without saying that presidents cannot pardon themselves. Similarly, Chapter 5 deals with impeaching ex-presidents; there is a strong argument that the Framers thought that "late" impeachment was too obviously acceptable to bother saying so. But without any specifications in the text, and with the hazy distance of two centuries, the Framers' unwritten assumptions have been transformed from things that everyone understood into fodder for argument and disagreement.

More modern and immediate problems abound as well. Chapters 3 and 6 deal with language drafted in the twentieth century, not the eighteenth. Both chapters show how the contemporary amending process is painfully slow in some parts while rushed and utterly blithe in others. The process is good at constructing a consensus for a particular goal, but it is not as good at drafting airtight legal language to achieve that goal. Chapter 3 describes how it took years of discussion among legislators and legal experts to reach agreement on how the Constitution should handle presidential disability. Once all the hard-fought compromises had been struck, the amendment's proponents lumped persnickety grammarians together with those who opposed the amendment altogether. Both groups were obstacles to the main goal of just enacting the darn thing.

The proponents had already guided the amendment through the Senate successfully on previous occasions; knowing precisely what the amendment was supposed to do, they were comfortable that their text did those things well enough. They were intimately acquainted with every letter and punctuation mark. They wanted to move on, not debate word choices. Legislative initiatives are like great white sharks—they die if they don't keep moving forward—and reopening a text for micro-editing by hundreds of members of Congress is a pretty effective way to stop that forward progress. Some late changes got through, because their proponents were sufficiently persuasive, politic, or lucky. But more were quashed, including some that would have been helpful, because it was better to maintain momentum with a good draft than to maximize legal precision with a perfect draft. This fact is embodied in the typographical error that found its way into the final version of the amendment, now enshrined forever in the Constitution.[9]

A similar reason explains why potential cliffhangers, once discovered, typically are not addressed until something actually goes wrong. Chapter 3 mentions some fixes to the Twenty-Fifth Amendment that were rejected by the Senate because it was too late in the day to pick such nits. If it was too late in the day even before the Senate voted, it was certainly too late once the amendment passed and was ratified by the states. Cranking up the machinery needed to amend the Constitution is no small task, and Congress generally only puts that effort forth when there is a political payoff for doing so. That means solving big problems, not fussing around with little details. If the little details ever produce a big problem, we worry about it then.

As discussed more in Chapter 7, the Constitution itself promotes this sort of cost-benefit analysis. Because the Constitution sets up a robust structure for our political institutions, it simply is not worth the effort to find and repair every conceivable glitch. If something goes awry, we depend on that structure and those institutions to work things out. As a more general matter, the Framers of the Constitution made the same choice when they left some tricky questions unanswered (for instance, who is qualified to be a Supreme Court justice) and chose instead to simply designate an answerer (for instance, the president and Senate, via the nomination and confirmation processes).

This approach reflects faith in our politics, or perhaps a certain fatalism; if we can't count on the people running our institutions to resolve a dispute over, say, a presidential self-pardon, then the self-pardon is probably the least of our worries. More than faith, though, it reflects a sensible humility. We leave vague or shoddy procedures in the Constitution, but not because we know that Congress and the courts will get everything right in the end. Rather, we know that we lack the perfect foresight needed to solve every constitutional conundrum in advance. Congress and the courts are reasonably good backstops, so we stop striving for perfection once the effort of closing loopholes and addressing pitfalls in advance becomes more trouble than it's worth—which it quickly does.

Recall the election of 1800 mentioned previously. The defects in the electoral system were obvious before the crisis, but the political process in the House of Representatives eventually reached the right result. Jefferson won and Burr lost. Afterward, it seemed clear that there should be separate balloting for president and vice president, and the Twelfth Amendment swiftly accomplished that. It should have been clear beforehand too, and a foresighted legislator in 1797 could have sponsored a constitutional amendment that would have prevented the electoral crisis from even happening. But who would have listened? Surely it was easier to motivate Congress and the states to redesign the system in the wake of a real debacle. The most effective way for a curious young child to learn to avoid hot stoves is to touch one; so too with a young republic. This doesn't mean that we *want* children to get burned, but sometimes it means that there is no use trying to explain physics and physiology to a two-year-old who isn't really listening, especially if the stove is not hot enough to do permanent damage. Similarly, if one trusts the constitutional backstop (the House, in Jefferson's case) and the amendment process, then it is good enough to address problems as they crop up, instead of trying to theorize, predict, and fix them in advance.

To be sure, the constitutional stove may have been hotter for the election of 1800 than it needed to be; the House's failure to elect Jefferson until the thirty-sixth ballot showed dangerous weakness. In the following chapters, we will see that in some cases, our political institutions would not resolve constitutional cliffhangers very well at all. Nevertheless, it would be a mistake here to characterize the flexibility of the constitutional system as a defect rather than a feature.

These themes—the risks and stakes of constitutional cliffhangers, the reasons that they arise, and the fact that they are not always worth worrying about—have only had their surfaces scratched here. In the next six chapters, they will remain in the background as the focus shifts to providing specific legal guidance for each cliffhanger. Then, in Chapter 7, these themes will reemerge, and I will dig deeper to offer some further thoughts on how cliffhangers get settled, and how and when to prevent them from arising in the first place.

Prosecuting a President

For two years, federal special prosecutor Jack Flaherty has been investigating a sordid White House scandal involving bribery, extortion, and a sprinkling of sex and drugs. Recently, Flaherty turned the investigation toward President David Hobson after concluding that Hobson had been aware of some of the crimes and covered them up.

Before, President Hobson had been cooperating fully with Flaherty's investigators. This bolstered his claims that he was uninvolved in any crimes, and kept him afloat politically. Now that Hobson is a target, though, he decides that Flaherty is an overzealous bully intoxicated with the idea of bringing down a president. He contemplates asking his attorney general to fire Flaherty but figures that the political cost would be too high—it would make Hobson look like he has something to hide and would drag down his party in the upcoming midterm elections.

Things heat up when Flaherty announces a deal with Jon Kupitsky, a target of the investigation whom President Hobson recently fired as his chief of staff. Kupitsky pleads guilty to some charges and testifies that Hobson ordered a cover-up. In exchange, Flaherty drops other charges against Kupitsky and recommends a lighter sentence for the remaining ones. Hobson forcefully denies Kupitsky's accusation. His media team highlights Kupitsky's own indisputably spectacular corruption and suggests that Kupitsky fabricated his allegations (and several documents) right after he was fired.

The House of Representatives begins an impeachment inquiry, but President Hobson's defense is believable enough, and he has kept enough public and partisan support to stall things in committee. Flaherty soldiers on, though, presenting more evidence against Hobson to the grand jury. The president's lawyers negotiate to try *to delay the proceedings for two-and-a-half years, until Hobson's second term expires. But Flaherty refuses to extend any special treatment to the president. He hopes that the impeachment effort will be revived when Hobson is indicted or, failing that, when damning testimony comes out at trial. At Flaherty's urging, the grand jury indicts the president.*

Hobson's political support is affected, but not much—most people had made up their minds about him already—and he resists the suggestion that he temporarily cede power to the vice president. "I'm innocent," he says, "and we cannot let one person's baseless slander determine who occupies the White House. I owe it to my fellow Americans to continue working hard for them."

Politically, Hobson still cannot fire Flaherty, but he can challenge the indictment in court. So he does, claiming that it is unconstitutional to prosecute a sitting president. His supporters take to the airwaves and enthusiastically endorse and amplify his constitutional arguments; his enemies line up behind Flaherty and Flaherty's constitutional arguments against presidential immunity. The country, which was already transfixed by the scandal, turns its attention to this legal technicality.

FOR AS LONG AS THERE HAS BEEN A PRESIDENCY, Americans have debated whether sitting presidents can be prosecuted. There are good arguments on both sides, and nobody has tried to prosecute a president yet, so reasonable minds have differed and the issue remains unresolved. But if a prosecutor ever brings criminal charges against a sitting president, the question will no longer be avoidable. This chapter discusses how such a case might arise, what the two sides would argue, and how such a controversy might be prevented.[1]

Practicalities

As they were designing the presidency, the delegates at the Constitutional Convention in 1787 discussed hypothetical criminal presidents. In recent decades—the era of the independent counsel—things have gotten less hypothetical, with serious investigations affecting Presidents Nixon, Reagan, Bush, Clinton, and Bush.

Nixon and Clinton came closest to being prosecuted in office, and their cases reveal some important practical points. First, prosecutors are reluctant to prosecute presidents, especially if it means getting ahead of the impeachment process. Nixon certainly appeared to be a crook, but special prosecutor Leon Jaworski asked the grand jury only to declare him an "unindicted co-conspirator." Jaworski had no reason to stick his neck out, because Congress was investigating Nixon and eventually began impeachment proceedings. When Nixon resigned, the immunity issue became moot. President Clinton's pursuers let Congress go first too. After Clinton was acquitted by the Senate, criminal prosecution still loomed. On January 19, 2001, one day before any presidential immunity he had would have expired, Clinton settled with prosecutor Robert Ray, admitting wrongdoing and accepting some non-criminal sanctions. Jaworski and Ray proceeded as though they *could* prosecute sitting presidents, but decided that they would not.[2]

Prosecutors have plenty of incentive to wait. Any person politically formidable enough to become president and avoid impeachment would have a good chance of finding at least one sympathetic juror. Moreover, a sitting president could complain that the prosecutor was trying to overturn an election and was bypassing Congress (the appropriate forum for accusing presidents). As a constitutional matter, the president's arguments would have some obvious holes,* but as a political matter they could have some power. Any sensible prosecutor would avoid these added burdens if possible.

Most likely, then, a presidential prosecution would go forward only if the president had enough time left in his term (unlike Clinton) but Congress was off the case (unlike Nixon). The prosecutor might move forward if the Senate had acquitted the president (like Clinton) or if the House was not pushing impeachment at all (like our hypothetical President Hobson). If a

---

* As discussed later in this chapter, prosecuting a president does not necessarily amount to removing him from office, even if he is convicted. Moreover, removing a president does not overturn an election as such, since the president's running mate would just take over. Under the Constitution's original system, though, the vice president was the runner-up in the presidential election, so removing a president really would have reversed the election. *See* Jay S. Bybee, *Who Executes the Executioner?*, 2 Nexus 53, 64–65 (1997) (noting this problem with prosecuting presidents before addition of the Twelfth Amendment).

president survives or avoids impeachment, it does not necessarily mean that the criminal case against him is weak. Some in Congress might believe that the president is guilty, but that his offense is not an impeachable one; others might consider removal from office too harsh a penalty. By contrast, prosecutors and jurors would not care whether the president's offense was a "high crime or misdemeanor," and it would not be their job to select a punishment.[3]

Certain cases are good candidates for prosecution but not impeachment, or vice versa. Some factors are tricky. For instance, if the president's crime is horrendous and his guilt is obvious, prosecutors will want to go after him, but so will Congress. The crime would have to hit a small target: heinous enough to motivate the prosecutor, non-heinous enough for Congress to let it go. Similarly, the preliminary evidence of the president's guilt would need to be compelling, but not too compelling.

Other factors are easier. The more "private" the crime is—like drugs, assault, or tax evasion, as opposed to bribery—the more likely it is to warrant criminal prosecution but not impeachment. Other one-way factors are the president's level of political support (crucial in Congress, less relevant in court) and the temperament of the prosecutor (a key factor for the criminal case, but not in Congress).

That last point is significant. Prosecutors are trained to make deals with low-level offenders in order to bring down the big boss, as in this chapter's opening scenario. But prosecutors also balance their punitive impulses with considerations of efficiency, proportion, and fairness, and independent counsels can be insulated from these considerations. They often have no other cases. Immersed in the details of their main target's imperfections, it is easier for them to lose perspective and cross the line from "sensible" to "obsessive." (If the prosecution is instead in state court, the D.A. might be more accountable, but only to local voters or state officials.)[4]

.None of this—a president accused of a crime early in his term, Congress unwilling to take up the case, an aggressive prosecutor—is hard to picture. It might not be likely that these factors will come together, but surely it is imaginable.

For its part, the public probably would not care much about the finer legal points in which the lawyers and judges would traffic. For an average citizen, the best reason to allow a sitting president to be prosecuted would be "I think he's guilty" or "I never liked that guy." The main argument *for* immunity would be the opposite. That this completely ignores the legal principles (and the reason for having a trial at all) is beside the point; a president who lacks sufficient popular support and who is credibly accused of a serious crime would be impeached or would resign. If the president is in a position to tough it out, though, public opinion would be less important as the more legalistic and less political courts take center stage.[5]

The Legal Case for Immunity: Federal Prosecution

> The Constitution vests all federal executive power in one man: the president. The voters twice sent President Hobson to that office, and he is working hard for them every day. The Constitution doesn't allow a loose cannon like Jack Flaherty to take President Hobson off the job. I'm not saying that the president is above the law, I'm saying that this case has to wait until he is just David Hobson, not President Hobson. Constitutionally, only Congress can hasten that day.
> —PRO-HOBSON PUNDIT[6]

Past presidential lawyers and their opponents have already written detailed legal arguments on both sides of this issue; the only thing missing is an actual court decision that chooses a winner. This section will explore the president's legal case for temporary federal immunity. (State immunity is covered later, separately.)

The president's claims are relatively subtle. Acknowledging that the text of the Constitution says nothing explicit about his immunity, the president would argue that the *structure* of the Constitution protects the presidency from being impeded or obstructed. Structuralism is a common technique for interpreting constitutional provisions. Rather than just reading individual provisions in isolation, structuralism tries to fit them into the overall framework of government that the Constitution creates. Here, the president's arguments would center on two aspects of that framework: the president's unique constitutional position and Congress's preeminent role in pursuing the president.[7]

The President Is Special

> Prosecute anyone else in the government and life goes on.
> Prosecute the president and things—life-and-death things—
> don't get done.
> —PRESIDENT HOBSON'S SPOKESWOMAN

The president's argument begins with the notion that he is constitution-ally unique. This is crucial for his case because federal judges, cabinet secre-taries, and two vice presidents have been prosecuted while in office, ahead of or instead of any impeachment. Members of Congress (who are subject to expulsion, not impeachment) have been prosecuted while in office too. If none of these officials is totally immune from prosecution while in office, why would the president be?[8]

The answer is that the president really is uniquely indispensable. Vice pres-idents are legally inessential, day to day. Cabinet secretaries have narrow port-folios and a seemingly unlimited supply of deputies ready to fill in for them. The federal judiciary can constitutionally be whittled down to almost nothing, and it contains hundreds of interchangeable judges. Congress was designed to be in recess much of the time, and when it is in session, it can operate with nearly half of its 535 members absent. Moreover, judging and legislating are deliberative, even leisurely processes. In sum, prosecuting one of these other sorts of officials does not prevent the government from functioning.[9]

By comparison, the president is head of state, head of government, and head of the executive branch, and he is just one person. The president is on call all day, every day, and must be ready to make snap decisions. If an emer-gency occurs during a congressional recess, the Constitution relies on a watchful president to reconvene Congress. The nature of the president's job—commanding the military, engaging in diplomacy, protecting the country, and generally taking care that the laws are executed—requires this level of vigilance.* The Constitution has several detailed provisions for

---

* Presidents also differ from state governors, some of whom have been prosecuted in office. In almost every state, governors are not unitary executives—they work alongside, not above, attorneys general, secretaries of state, and treasurers, who are elected in their own right. Even in the few states where governors are unitary executives, they do not have the weighty responsibilities of defending the entire country. Indeed, when disaster strikes, one of a governor's key tasks is often to call on the president for federal assistance.

ensuring that if the president is gone he immediately has a substitute. But if the president is merely impeded, as he would be if he is prosecuted, then essential functions of government may be impeded too.[10]

The president's special role requires special protection. In other contexts, courts have recognized that the Constitution can block actions that "unduly trammel" presidential authority or "interfere impermissibly" with presidential duties. Courts must consider this before they exercise jurisdiction over the president. Even if they have a good reason to drag the president into court, they still "must balance the constitutional weight of the interest to be served against the dangers of intrusion on the authority and functions of the executive branch." The Supreme Court has used a similar balancing test to make presidents permanently immune from civil liability for official acts, to reject temporary immunity for sitting presidents from civil liability for private acts, and to find a limited "executive privilege" to withhold documents. Clearly, this is the test that would be used in this case. The core of the president's argument is that prosecuting a president before he leaves office is more disruptive to the president, and thus to the country, than any punitive interest can justify.[11]

To be sure, courts have ample power to check the executive branch; they can issue injunctions against the president for official action, for instance. More to the point, as Jonathan Turley has argued, when the doctrine of separation of powers protects presidents from courts, it is in just that context: the president's official *powers*. Private conduct is another matter altogether. On the civil side, the Supreme Court has ruled that sitting presidents can be subjected to *private* lawsuits. Turley questions whether a criminal court really "would gain control" or "would interfere with" the presidency, since the prosecution "would be brought against a citizen who happens to be President, not the presidency itself."[12]

But the president can argue that he is the only person in the government for whom the personal and the official are linked so inextricably. The Constitution vests federal legislative power in a House and Senate, and judicial power in a set of courts, but it gives executive power—the task of steering the ship of state—to just one person. As Alex Bickel put it, "In the presidency is embodied the continuity and indestructibility of the state." Even if there are dozens of people running the executive branch, their authority is supposed to flow from the president's. If the president is arrested, prosecuted, or jailed, the presidency and the executive branch of the government are too, in a way that just isn't so with an injunction or a private civil suit.[13]

Another approach is to ask *whom* the Constitution empowers to disrupt the presidency. Here again the president's uniqueness comes into play. The president is the country's only nationally elected official (other than his understudy, the vice president). Members of Congress represent a district or, at most, a state. Federal judges are appointed for life and insulated from representing anybody, so that they can focus on being true to the law. Members of the cabinet and other federal officers are unelected and serve at the pleasure of the president. While these other officials surely see themselves as working for the nation as a whole, they do not have the same electoral connection as the president to all three hundred million Americans. Therefore, unlike everyone else, it is inappropriate for the president—the nation's tribune—to be displaced from his duties by just anyone.

The Constitution puts Congress (which collectively is responsible to roughly the same electorate as the president) in charge of dealing with allegedly criminal presidents, through the impeachment process. Contrast that with the president's civil liability for off-the-job conduct, for which impeachment is not available, and from which sitting presidents are not immune.* Even impeachment was controversial to the Framers. When they drafted the Constitution's impeachment and removal provisions, they hotly debated whether to make sitting presidents subject to them. There was a strong presumption that presidents would serve out their terms, in other words, and it took some effort to give Congress the power to impeach and remove a criminal president. It would be odd if the Framers, who were so hesitant to allow criminal presidents to be pursued by Congress, had been willing to let

---

* Some people define impeachable offenses—high crimes and misdemeanors—as excluding private conduct. If private crimes are not impeachable, and if a president commits such a crime, it becomes easier to argue that the Constitution allows prosecutors to get ahead of Congress. Politically, though, it would be hard for a president who committed a serious but private crime to avoid impeachment, so this may be a moot point.

them be pursued by anyone else. Similarly, it would be odd if a president who survived impeachment—the constitutionally specified removal process, designed to be hard to do—could then be displaced by a single prosecutor, judge, and jury.[14]

Who's in Charge Here?

According to the Constitution, the president is the boss. Not "the president plus any special prosecutors who decide to disagree with him." If the president says someone shouldn't be prosecuted in federal court, then that person doesn't get prosecuted. If they get prosecuted anyway, that's unconstitutional.

—PRO-HOBSON PUNDIT

The president's opponents would note that the prosecutor, not the court, is imposing on the president here. Because the president sits atop the federal prosecutorial hierarchy, this eliminates the separation-of-powers problem; no other branch is "unduly trammeling" the presidency if the president is, in essence, prosecuting himself. Indeed, if a sitting president consents to being prosecuted by his subordinates, there is no constitutional cliffhanger to worry about. But this chapter presumes the opposite: our President Hobson is pursued by an independent counsel who, while technically subordinate to the president, is politically insulated. A president who is unwilling to fire an independent counsel may not necessarily consent to everything the counsel does in court.[15]

Thus, the president could focus on this other constitutional snag: if an independent counsel pursues a federal prosecution over the president's objections, it violates the structural notion of the "unitary executive." The Constitution succinctly states that "[t]he executive Power shall be vested in a President of the United States of America," not in a president and assorted independent counsels. Prosecution is a core executive function, and removing it from the president's control is unconstitutional.

The Supreme Court ruled on this issue in 1988 in *Morrison v. Olson* and seemingly rejected the unitary-executive theory. The Court upheld an independent-counsel statute (which has since expired), even though the statute restricted the president's power to fire the independent counsel.

President Reagan's control over Morrison's prosecution of Olson was not, the Court said, "central to the functioning of the executive branch." But Olson was a mere assistant attorney general. If Morrison had been pursuing *Reagan*, it would be easy to imagine the Court declaring that Reagan's lack of control over the prosecutor *would* affect the functioning of the executive branch. The president could thus argue that under *Morrison*'s central-functioning test, it is unconstitutional for an independent counsel to prosecute an unwilling president. Of course, this might just mean that the president would have to be able to fire the independent counsel; our President Hobson's only problem would be his lack of political will to do so. But even if *Morrison* doesn't give the president formal power to micromanage individual prosecutorial decisions, its central-functioning test makes it seem constitutionally incongruous for a federal prosecutor to pursue his unwilling boss.[16]

Another structural argument is that sitting presidents must be immune from federal prosecution because they can always just pardon themselves. A president in truly dire straits would have little reason not to take this exceptional step. But we cannot assume that such a president would *necessarily* pardon himself, just as we cannot assume that he would necessarily fire the independent counsel. Again, though, the mere possibility of a self-pardon is more evidence that it is constitutionally awkward to let a federal independent counsel prosecute an unwilling president. (As discussed in Chapter 2, the president might *not* have the power to pardon himself. But if that's the case, prosecuting the president would still be structurally awkward. Anyone else in the country would be able to avoid federal prosecution with a presidential pardon; only the president would not.)[17]

In contrast to all this structural weirdness, impeachment beckons as a constitutionally proper path. The inherently politicized trial of a sitting president would be handled by Congress—the nation's chief political body, and its most politically accountable one. The president can argue that he embodies the continuity of government, and that the Constitution gives Congress alone the grave task of short-circuiting that continuity when necessary—not the courts, and certainly not independent counsels. Prosecution can wait.[18]

Prosecution Is Disruptive

Hey Flaherty, can't this wait?
—PRO-HOBSON BUMPER STICKER

So far, the president's argument has turned on the notion that it would be unacceptably disruptive to the nation for him to be prosecuted, and that a conviction and possible imprisonment would amount to removing him from office. But these assumptions are disputable, and they merit a closer look.

The prosecutor might contend that criminal prosecution is no more disruptive to presidents than impeachment is. But that's not right. Impeachment allows for more flexible, casual, and stripped-down procedures than a criminal trial and is necessarily conducted just down the street from the president's home office. Moreover, if a president is impeached and convicted, it's final; he is immediately replaced and a new presidency speeds ahead. With serious criminal prosecution, by contrast, a conviction is just a midpoint in the disruption; who would sit in the Oval Office during a lengthy, defiant appeal process? Even if impeachment is disruptive, it comes only after serious deliberation by the politically accountable House of Representatives, not a relatively unaccountable prosecutor and jury.[19]

Impeachment aside, the prosecutor could argue that presidential prosecution just isn't that disruptive. In Scott Howe's words, the probability that some disability-by-prosecution "would occur without spurring impeachment seems remote, and surely it would not happen recurringly. The probability is too speculative to read Article II, Section 1, as requiring that the President remain unaccountable while in office." Presidents commonly face crises and scandals that divert their attention. Assuming that the president would waive his right to a speedy trial, it could take months or years for his case to go forward. Even if the president is dragged into court, and even if this interferes with his job, the modern administrative state is big and self-powered. Things hum along quite nicely without the president's direct involvement.[20]

But this misses a crucial point. If a war, natural disaster, or political campaign requires the president's attention, we expect him to give it, because these so-called distractions are part of his job. The presidency can juggle a multitude of demands, but *public* ones. The point of immunity is to allow the president to focus on those public demands. Responding to criminal charges would present a uniquely difficult proposition, distinct not only from the president's official duties, but also from the more minor disruption of a civil suit. The president would have to deal with many intrusive things personally, especially if he is subject to arrest or bond before trial, or imprisonment afterward. The trial itself would be uniquely disruptive too; a criminal trial, unlike a civil trial or impeachment, would typically require the president's physical presence. Dealing with the investigation and trial would be no "mere blip on the president's calendar." It is one thing for the president to let the government hum along by itself; it is quite another for someone else to force him to.[21]

Immunity can coexist with any level of disruption. If the crime and accompanying disruption really are minor, the president might just waive his immunity. It might be *less* disruptive to deal with the case (perhaps pleading guilty and accepting light punishment) than to hide behind immunity and have the case hanging over his head for the rest of his term.* But that would be a political decision, and the president would be making it for himself. At the other extreme, if the crime is significant, or if the swirling accusations undermine the president's ability to do his job despite his immunity, Congress can always step in—either to remove him or to absolve him—and help clear the air. The president could also voluntarily hand over temporary power to the (undistracted) vice president, again despite his immunity.[22]

As a separate matter, the prosecutor might disagree that convicting the president, or even imprisoning him, is tantamount to removing him from office. It isn't automatically or literally so. But if a criminal conviction prodded the president to resign (perhaps as part of a plea bargain), an otherwise unwilling Congress to impeach and remove him, or the cabinet to declare him disabled, it would be fitting to say that the prosecutor drove the non-immune president from office. It would be better for the prosecutor to

---

* In 2006, Kentucky governor Ernie Fletcher settled criminal charges brought against him, even after the state supreme court ruled that he was immune from prosecution while in office.

let first things be done first, presenting his evidence against the president to Congress rather than seeking a grand-jury indictment. This is precisely what Kenneth Starr did with President Clinton. If the Senate had removed Clinton in 1999, it would have been because the Senate thought it was best for the country, not because Starr and some jurors did.[23]

On the other hand, if the prosecutor does press on and get a conviction, there is no guarantee that Congress will remove the president, or that he will resign. Most felons are not sentenced to prison, and the judge could impose a delayed or flexible sentence to minimize disruption to the presidency. Even if he was sent to prison, moreover, a brazen president theoretically could run the country from his cell.* The prosecutor might cite this as evidence that prosecuting a president is not tantamount to removing or unduly interfering with him, but it also seems like an argument against allowing prosecution at all. As to the flexible sentence, why not just wait until the president has left office and give him the full punishment he deserves? As to running the presidency from prison, that is unacceptable. The president's duties include meeting with his cabinet, staff, and members of Congress. His status as leader of the "free" world makes international travel important. To be sure, the text of the Constitution mentions none of this (other than the president's duty to receive foreign ambassadors), but as a structural matter the Constitution arguably precludes others from

---

* A president who tried to run his administration from prison might need new legislation to provide the necessary technological and legal support to do so. If Congress were unwilling to pass such legislation, it might spur the vice president and cabinet to invoke the Twenty-Fifth Amendment to declare the president "unable to discharge the powers and duties of his office." The president could contest this, in which case two-thirds of both the House and Senate would need to agree before he could be displaced from office. If Congress could do that, though, it might just impeach the president (with a simple House majority) and remove him (with a two-thirds Senate majority). That said, impeaching and removing a president for "high crimes and misdemeanors" might still be a harder sell than declaring a jailed president to be temporarily disabled. See Adam R. F. Gustafson, Note, *Presidential Inability and Subjective Meaning*, 27 Yale L. & Pol'y Rev. 459, 467–68 (2009) (distinguishing disability from impeachability); see also Eric M. Freedman, *The Law as King and the King as Law: Is a President Immune from Criminal Prosecution Before Impeachment?*, 20 Hastings Const. L.Q. 7, 54–57 (1992) (discussing Twenty-Fifth Amendment implications of presidential prosecution).

interfering with these core interpersonal duties. There is a limit to modern teleconferencing technology, and there is a limit to the amount of contact a prisoner can have with the outside world while still being considered a prisoner. In sum, a president cannot really be an inmate.[24]

This sort of disruption to the presidency—inflicted by unaccountable prosecutors and unrepresentative juries instead of Congress—is problematic. It might not rise to the level of a constitutional violation, but the president would certainly argue that it does.[25]

Summing It Up

Any president in this situation would surely wish that the Constitution had a simple clause protecting him from federal prosecution while in office. Nevertheless, as set out here, the president can still argue that the Constitution sets up a *system* that requires such immunity. If a president is unable to go on politically—turned out of office by the voters, thrown out of office by Congress, or hounded out of office by dire political reality—or if his term simply expires, then he loses his vital responsibility, and with it his immunity. But as long as he is carrying the weight of the country on his shoulders, no prosecutor can try to trip him up. That would be his argument, anyway.

The Legal Case Against Immunity: Federal Prosecution

Nobody is above the law. Does President Hobson think he can obstruct justice without being prosecuted, just as long as he's president? If someone is president, it's more important to stop his crime spree, not less. He says that the prosecution can wait two-and-a-half years, until his term is over. Can you imagine the damage he can do during that time? How much evidence might "vanish"? How many witnesses he could lean on?

President Hobson thinks that it is unconstitutional for this case to go forward now, but he can't point to a single constitutional provision that even hints at such a rule. "I don't like what you're doing to me, and I'm president, so it must be unconstitutional"? Please. The courts have ruled that sitting presidents can be sued and subpoenaed. They have made it clear that the rule of law trumps the president's personal comfort.

If he's not guilty, let's clear the air. If he is guilty, he should answer for his crimes just like anyone else.
—INDEPENDENT COUNSEL FLAHERTY'S SPOKESMAN

Constitutional law is complicated. There are gaps and flaws in virtually any constitutional-law argument, and in unsettled issues like presidential prosecutability, there are big gaps and big flaws. But this is true on both sides, so the fact that the president's arguments for immunity might seem thin and self-serving does not guarantee a win for the prosecutor. The prosecutor must proffer his own arguments against immunity.

The Constitution Says Nothing About It

I've got a copy of the Constitution right here. If you can show me the page where it says the president can't be prosecuted while he's in office, I'll pay you $10,000.
—ANTI-HOBSON CABLE NEWS COMMENTATOR

The prosecutor's simplest argument is that the Constitution says nothing about sitting presidents being immune from prosecution. For those who focus on the Constitution's text—who worry just about what the Constitution *says*, and not about what else it might *mean*—the prosecutor's argument is strong. Its simplicity is compelling.[26]

Article I of the Constitution specifies that *senators and representatives*, "in all Cases, except Treason, Felony, and Breach of the Peace, [are] privileged from Arrest during their Attendance at the Session of their Respective Houses, and in going to and from the same." It also specifies that "they shall not be questioned" for anything they say in "Speech or Debate." If the Framers had wanted *presidential* immunity, they could have said something similar. But Article II, which covers the presidency, is silent about immunity.[27]

Note that congressional immunity is limited: members of Congress are privileged from arrest only for minor crimes, and shielded from civil and criminal liability only for their speech and debate (that is, their official acts). It would be odd if the president had some unwritten immunity that was more powerful than Congress's explicit one. The president might claim that broader notions of immunity are implicit in the Constitution's structure—not just for presidents, but also for members of Congress—and that Article I's Immunity Clause is there to *limit* that inherent privilege. To be sure, the congressional clause is clearly phrased as a grant of a privilege, not the restriction of one. But the Supreme Court has found other sorts of implicit immunity for presidents and other officials; it has not read Congress's explicit immunity as the only kind under the Constitution. There is fodder for both sides' arguments on this point.[28]

The prosecutor can easily defeat another textual argument that, despite its weakness, is raised quite often. After the Constitution describes the punishments available in impeachment cases, it states that "the Party convicted shall nevertheless be liable and subject to Indictment, Trial, Judgment and Punishment, according to Law." Interpreting this as a time line, some have argued that impeachment and removal from office must precede criminal prosecution. But this argument is specious. The clause simply provides that impeachment does not preempt criminal prosecution or present double-jeopardy problems; unlike English impeachment, American impeachment is a supplement, not a substitute, for the criminal law. The clause says that someone can *still* be prosecuted after being convicted by the Senate, not that he can be prosecuted *only if* he is convicted by the Senate. Indeed, many federal officials have been prosecuted without being impeached first. Some have been prosecuted while in office, and *then* impeached. Because the clause does not distinguish between presidential and non-presidential impeachments, these precedents destroy this "sequentialist" argument for immunity.[29]

Looking just at constitutional text (or, more precisely, looking at the lack of constitutional text) the prosecutor's case against immunity looks strong. Even though courts have recognized various presidential immunities and privileges that are not stated in the Constitution, it helps to have the text on your side, and the prosecutor does.[30]

Moving beyond pure text, the prosecutor has some "structural" arguments too. Some appeared in the last section, as counterarguments to the president's structural arguments, but the prosecutor need not fight this battle only on the president's turf. Looking at the Constitution's structure, the president would see separation of powers and a unitary executive, but the prosecutor would see the rule of law.

Respecting the Rule of Law

> If we were supposed to have royal privileges in this country, we
> never would have fought the revolution. David Hobson is not a
> king. He's a person. A regular citizen. If he commits a crime,
> he should answer for it, not declare himself immune.
> —ANTI-HOBSON PUNDIT

By "respecting the rule of law," I mean rejecting the notion that might makes right, in favor of a system in which law constrains might. The classic formulation is that ours is a government of laws, not men, and a corollary is that the law applies equally to all members of society. Our prosecutor would assert that the president is a fallible person, like everyone else—and everyone else can be prosecuted. This is a direct assault on the president's argument that his constitutional uniqueness makes him immune while in office.[31]

The rule of law has a subtle role here. The law can bestow privileges on people. Because the president would be arguing that the Constitution grants him immunity, he could also argue that he has the rule of law on his side. Respecting the rule of law means respecting the Constitution, after all. Moreover, because his immunity would only be temporary, and because impeachment looms, immunity would not put the president completely "above the law." But the prosecutor would deploy an opposite rule-of-law argument: because no statute and nothing in the Constitution gives presidents immunity, conjuring up such an imperial privilege out of thin air subverts the rule of law. All this just begs the question of whose constitutional arguments are right. But if we refrain from assuming the conclusion, the rule of law has some *independent* force, and it favors the prosecutor. Put simply, the notion at the core of the rule of law—that no person is above the law—seems to cut against presidential immunity, and to weigh down any interpretive flights of fancy that the president might like to take.[32]

Immunity Is Disruptive Too

The prosecutor can counter the president's "disruption" argument with some practical considerations that run the other way. In particular, the president's argument that his immunity is just temporary—really just a matter of scheduling—is vulnerable. The president might claim that the delay would be no more than four years, but it could be four years longer if he is reelected. If the crime was committed before the president's term began, moreover, then it could take longer still between crime and prosecution. Such delays could effectively make the president immune permanently if the statute of limitations runs out, or if the evidence degrades.[33]

The president could concede these points and argue that they are outweighed by the nation's interest in an unimpeded presidency. But he need not concede them. For instance, he can say that his immunity would necessarily stop the statute-of-limitations clock. Alternatively, he could say that the prosecutor can indict him (stopping the clock) and would just have to wait to hold the trial. But these arguments take the president further and further away from the Constitution. It is one thing to argue that the Constitution implicitly provides temporary presidential immunity. It is quite another to say that the Constitution implicitly provides for tolling the statute of limitations, or for allowing an indictment but not a trial. The more intricate the Constitution's unspoken "requirements" are, the harder it is to argue that the Constitution actually requires them. In the meantime—as the Supreme Court noted in *Clinton v. Jones* when it declared that sitting presidents are not immune from civil lawsuits—judges can use discretion, being flexible and proceeding in ways that minimize disruption to the presidency and the country. A court might thus use its discretion to give a particular president temporary immunity in a particular case, while tolling the statute of limitations, without having to say that the Constitution *requires* that result.[34]

Summing It Up

The prosecutor has good, simple arguments: immunity is not mentioned in the Constitution, it would place the president above the law, and it would upset justice. These arguments are powerful enough to make it difficult to assume that sitting presidents are immune from federal prosecution. Still, the president's arguments are resilient enough that one cannot simply assume the opposite either.

State Prosecution

In a tearful prime-time interview, Noreen Caverty tells how she was raped in a hotel room by Tad Bruce, a man she had dated a few times. A record audience tunes in to watch, because Tad Bruce is the president of the United States. Nonstop media coverage ensues.

President Bruce admits having sex with Caverty that night but claims (in his own prime-time interview) that it was consensual. A widower, Bruce makes no apologies for maintaining a "social life," and he long ago lost the support of those voters who look askance at such things. Bruce's partisans hint that Caverty is emotionally unbalanced, and they argue that the whole story is being pushed by the president's opportunistic political opponents.

Caverty doesn't back down. She explains that she reported the rape promptly to local authorities, but they refused to pursue her case. Now that Caverty's claims have gotten such prominent public attention, the district attorney begins a state criminal investigation and finds enough evidence to justify convening a grand jury. The grand jury indicts the president.

Many politicians and pundits call for President Bruce's impeachment, but many others believe that Bruce's guilt has not been established. (The party identification of most of the members of these two groups is unsurprising.) Some believe that rape is not an impeachable offense in any case. Bruce rejects calls to resign or to cede power to the vice president until the trial is over. "I'm innocent," he says, "and we cannot let one person's baseless slander determine who occupies the White House. I owe it to my fellow Americans to continue working hard for them."

President Bruce's lawyers challenge the indictment, arguing that it is unconstitutional for a state to prosecute a sitting president. The district attorney and most of the people who believe Caverty take a different view of the Constitution. While the main question on everyone's mind is still whether or not their president is a rapist, the nation turns its attention to this legal technicality.

The Law

Under our Constitution, the federal government is supreme over the states, and all federal executive power is vested in the president. Tad Bruce is the president of the United States— all of them. One official from one part of one state can't do this to our president. I'm not saying he's above the law, I'm saying that this case has to wait until he is just Tad Bruce,

not President Bruce. Constitutionally, only Congress can
hasten that day.

—PRO-BRUCE PUNDIT

Does Tad Bruce really think he's too busy and important to be
bothered with this case? Well, he should have thought of that
before he raped Noreen Caverty.

—SPOKESMAN FOR NOREEN CAVERTY

If a sitting president is prosecuted in state court rather than federal
court, the immunity arguments shift a bit. The textual part stays the same:
the Constitution still does not explicitly give the president immunity. Much
of the structural argument still turns on the president's status as the
embodiment of the executive branch, always on duty.

But another structural point—who can knock him off that perch—plays
out differently. First, we no longer worry about whether the federal executive
branch can pursue a case against its own unwilling head, because the
president has no authority over state prosecutors. Second, instead of
separation of powers, the issue is federal supremacy. Rather than asking
whether the judiciary can supplant Congress by dislodging a criminal
president, we ask whether state authority can supplant federal authority
by dislodging a criminal president. The president's federalism argument
begins with the venerable case of *McCulloch v. Maryland.* In *McCulloch,*
Maryland used targeted, punitive taxation to attack a branch of the
federally chartered national bank. The Supreme Court struck down
the Maryland tax, ruling that one state cannot overpower the federal
government: "The difference is that which always exists, and always must
exist, between the action of the whole on a part, and the action of a part on
the whole."[35]

This principle is not absolute, of course; the Constitution does not endow
federal officials with the right to become a lawless marauding horde.
McCulloch provides a helpful dividing line: "If we apply the principle for
which the State of Maryland contends, to the constitution generally, we shall
find it capable of changing totally the character of that instrument. We shall
find it capable of *arresting all the measures of the government, and of prostrating
it at the foot of the States.*" Ordinarily, states can enforce their laws and prosecute federal officials without thwarting the normal functions of the federal

government. But, the president would argue, prosecuting the president would cross that line. Under *McCulloch*, no county D.A. is allowed to "arrest" all the executive powers of the government and "prostrate" them at the foot of the states. The point is not to protect the president's personal interests (though immunity has that temporary effect). Rather, it is to protect the public interest of the American people—all three hundred million of them—to have a functioning government. In whose name can a president be held to answer for a crime? Not in the name of one outlier county, but only in the name of all Americans, through their chosen representatives, via impeachment.[36]

The arguments on the other side, against state immunity, track the ones against federal immunity: Federalism, like separation of powers, is all well and good, but it does not change the fact that the Constitution nowhere mentions presidential immunity, or that no other federal official is immune from state prosecution. Federalism does not warrant giving presidents the ability to evade punishment for their crimes. However disruptive a state prosecution might be, it would not amount to putting the federal government under the control of a single county or state, or to removing the president from office. At worst, state prosecution of a president would be bad policy, not a constitutional violation.[37]

Practicalities

On the whole, state crimes would be less likely to result in impeachment. Recall that impeachment is reserved for "high" crimes and misdemeanors, which arguably includes "public" offenses (like bribery), but not "private" ones (like rape). A president's public conduct would be more likely to implicate federal law, while his private conduct would more likely be a matter of state law. Because a prosecutor is more apt to pursue a president if impeachment is off the table, a state case would thus be more likely to come to a head.[38]

Some perspective is important. If there is strong evidence that the president is a rapist, temporary immunity wouldn't matter, because the president would be hounded into resigning. As a practical, political matter, if he did not resign he would probably be impeached, technical definitions of "high" crimes be damned. Still, if the evidence in the case is not so clear, things can get complicated.

Another practical point is that local prosecutors might be more likely than federal independent counsels to throw restraint to the wind. For one thing, local prosecutors are typically chosen in partisan elections or appointed by partisan officials, as opposed to independent counsels, who are (ideally) selected solely with an eye toward their integrity and neutrality. Local prosecutors also have a shorter time horizon. Independent counsels typically stay with a case until they have wrapped it up to their satisfaction, so they might not mind as much if they have to wait a couple of years for the president to leave office so that the case can proceed. Local prosecutors, by contrast, need to look to the next election, which gives them a powerful incentive not to leave a high-profile case gathering dust.

For these reasons, then, a presidential prosecution is more likely to go forward in state court than in federal court. Still, it is just as hard to predict what the courts would say about immunity.

History Weighs In, on Both Sides

Some Framers and later experts were sure that sitting presidents cannot be prosecuted. Others were sure that they can be. Ideally, this would mean that neither side would use historical arguments, but in real life it means that both sides do. Because the historical evidence is inconclusive, it is covered separately here, instead of further tangling up the back-and-forth legal arguments set out in this chapter.

The Founders

In 1787, the Constitutional Convention discussed presidential privileges and immunities, but there was no consensus, and nothing in the final draft of the Constitution about it. This left two possibilities: either presidents have no immunity, because the Constitution does not explicitly give them any, or presidents have immunity that literally goes without saying.

Delegate Charles Pinckney, for instance, declared that the decision not to mention presidential privileges reflected an understanding that there were no such privileges. James Wilson agreed, saying that "not a *single privilege* [was] annexed to [the president's] character," and that the president was "amenable to [the laws] in his private character as a citizen."[39]

On the other side were those who accepted immunity, if more subtly. When delegates discussed whether the president should be impeachable, some clearly assumed that the president was otherwise unanswerable for any crimes while in office. Later, Alexander Hamilton wrote in *The Federalist* that criminal presidents can be impeached and removed and "would *afterwards* be liable to prosecution." These men probably did not envision federal independent counsels and just assumed that no president would prosecute himself. But their locutions reflect a certain preferred timing that would preclude a state prosecutor from pursuing a sitting president too.[40]

One colorful data point from the early days of the Republic came as two senators chatted with Vice President John Adams about presidential prerogatives. Senator Maclay asserted that the president is not above the law, but Adams and Senator (later Chief Justice) Ellsworth disagreed, saying that "you could only impeach him and no other process whatever lay against him" while in office. Maclay protested: "Suppose the President committed murder in the street. Impeach him? But you can only remove him from office on impeachment. Why, when he is no longer President you can indict him. But in the mean time he runs away. But I will put up another case. Suppose he continues his murders daily, and neither House is sitting to impeach him. Oh, the people would rise and restrain him. Very well, you will allow the mob to do what legal justice must abstain from." This did not faze Ellsworth or Adams, who dismissed Maclay's scenario as too improbable to worry about. Senator Schuyler walked up at that point and, when asked what he thought, endorsed the Adams-Ellsworth view, saying, "I think the President a kind of sacred person" (a rather jarring sentiment to modern ears). Many others took sides on this question; the only thing that was clear about presidential prosecutability was that it was unclear.[41]

Later Commentary

A generation later, Supreme Court justice Joseph Story, a seminal thinker on American constitutional law, considered presidential immunity. He wrote that among the "incidental powers[] belonging to the executive department" is "the power to perform [its functions] without any obstruction or impediment whatsoever." Story reasoned that "[t]he President cannot, therefore, be liable to arrest, imprisonment, or detention, while he is in the discharge of the duties of his office." This puts Story seemingly in the pro-immunity camp. But Story might not have been referring to criminal punishment; his very next line concludes that the president "must be deemed, in civil cases at least, to possess an official inviolability" (a proposition that, in any case, the Supreme Court rejected when it held in *Clinton v. Jones* that presidents can be sued while in office for their personal conduct). Moreover, as Jonathan Turley has noted, Story seems to be talking about protecting the president's official use of his powers—which Congress can only encroach through impeachment—and not about protecting the president from the consequences of his "private" criminal acts. As discussed already, it is such "private" crimes that would most likely lead to our constitutional cliffhanger.[42]

More recent authority is similarly muddled. In 1973, President Nixon's Department of Justice and some members of Congress concluded that presidents are immune from criminal prosecution; other members of Congress and the independent counsel pursuing Nixon disagreed. This stalemate reemerged in 2000, between President Clinton's Justice Department and the independent counsel pursuing him.[43]

Both academic debaters and lengthy congressional hearings have been similarly divided. As with the legal arguments on immunity, history gives us no answer; it just underlines how tough the question is.[44]

So What Can We Do?

Unfortunately, this entire discussion brings us no closer to a solution. Short of a constitutional amendment, the only way to answer the immunity question would be to prosecute a president, have the president assert immunity, and have the courts rule definitively on what the Constitution requires.* But if it came to that, the country would be badly distracted and divided by the political fallout from the case. With the legal issues wrapped up in a political package, it would be harder for justice to be done and be publicly accepted. Luckily, Congress can head all this off through simple legislation.

Admittedly, Congress might not care enough to act preemptively; it tends to wait for things to happen before it addresses them. On the other hand, this issue affects congressional prerogative—immunity would protect the preeminent role of Congress and its impeachment process—so Congress might have enough extra motivation to be proactive. Regardless, though, things *have* happened already. The last several administrations have been pursued by independent counsels, and Presidents Nixon and Clinton came close to being prosecuted. Their potential immunity was an issue for prosecutors. Although Nixon and Clinton left office before any prosecution would have begun anyway, these near misses take the immunity issue well inside the realm of possibility. Recognizing this, Congress held hearings on presidential immunity in 1998, but no legislation emerged. Meanwhile, the specter of presidential prosecution still lurks.

It would be best to consider immunity legislation in the shadow of a recent presidential criminal investigation, rather than in the midst of an ongoing one. If Congress had passed a presidential immunity law in 1999, it would have been seen as a sop to President Clinton. Similarly, if it had tried to limit immunity in 1999, it would have been seen as an attack on Clinton. A couple of years later, though, the issue could be discussed—not

---

* Scott Howe has argued that the Constitution does not require immunity, but that the Court could grant it as a matter of federal common law. Because Congress would have the power to supersede such a holding, this intriguing possibility is compatible with the legislative suggestions in this section. *See* Scott W. Howe, *The Prospect of a President Incarcerated*, 2 Nexus 86 (1997); *see also* Daniel A. Farber et al., Cases and Materials on Constitutional Law 1118 (4th ed. 2009) (noting courts' creation of other immunities "essentially as constitutional common law—inspired by constitutional values but possibly subject to congressional override"). *But see* Nixon v. Fitzgerald, 457 U.S. 731, 753 (1982) (defining presidential privileges as constitutionally mandated, not just as common-law prudence).

too abstractly ("Remember how close we came?") but also not too personally ("Clinton is gone; let's talk about how we want the *next* accused president to be treated").

Whenever Congress does act, the debate could get entangled in partisan preferences. In normal partisan times, it would be impolitic for a majority party to deliver immunity to its own president, and improbable for it to deliver such a plum to a president of the other party. If Congress really were interested in legislating immunity, though, it could sidestep this problem simply by making the legislation effective after the next presidential election. Without any way to know which party the immune president would belong to, politics could be filtered out.

Assuming that Congress can be motivated to act, what could it do? There are several options. Amending the Constitution is not one of them. Amendments require too strong a consensus. It is doubtful that two-thirds of Congress and three-fourths of the states could agree on the need to act here, let alone on which side to take.

Regular legislation is thus more likely (if still not exactly probable). For instance, there might be sufficient support to legislate immunity for sitting presidents. Nobody argues that the Constitution *forbids* such statutory immunity, so such a law could be passed regardless of who is right about whether the Constitution *requires* immunity. For federal prosecutions, this law would be within Congress's authority to structure the Department of Justice and define federal criminal law. For state prosecutions, it arguably could fit under Congress's power under the Necessary and Proper Clause to safeguard federal governmental functions, and thereby to preempt state law.[45]

By passing such a law, Congress could also smooth over some problems. For example, the legislation could definitively toll the statute of limitations while the president is in office, to prevent him from escaping punishment by running out the clock. Even with tolling, delayed prosecutions are more likely to fail, but Congress can address this too. Ideally, Congress would give less protection to presidents who are guilty than to presidents who are innocent. The person who knows best whether the president is guilty is the president himself, and creative legislation could influence the president's calculations. Perhaps, for instance, the statute could enhance the criminal penalties that a president faces if he invokes his immunity but is convicted after leaving office. A guilty president might calculate that stalling would not be worthwhile if the penalty upon conviction were so heightened. He could waive immunity and proceed with the case immediately or, seeing the handwriting on the wall, he could resign; either way, he would avoid the enhanced penalty. Or he could keep his immunity and take his chances. Whatever his decision, though, the statute would make immunity less of an incentive for improper behavior.[46]

Congress could also pinpoint when immunity kicks in: before indictment, before trial, or before sentencing. If Congress chooses to allow indictments, the president might still be able to argue that the Constitution protects him, but if the new law reduces the disruptiveness of the criminal proceedings by delaying the trial, it would weaken the president's argument.

A final advantage of granting the president immunity legislatively is that it would define everyone's roles more clearly. Special prosecutors would know that the president is off limits while in office; members of Congress would know that it is their responsibility to decide what to do with the alleged criminal sleeping in the White House.[47]

On the other side, it would be hard for Congress to legislate *against* immunity. First, the president would be able to veto any such legislation, requiring the House and Senate to muster two-thirds majorities. Second, if the president was prosecuted, he could still argue that the Constitution makes him immune, and that the anti-immunity statute is thus unconstitutional. We would be back to square one: the court would still have to decide whether the Constitution provides immunity, and the president's lawyers could make all the same constitutional arguments they would have made in the absence of any statute. Congress could take actions short of stripping immunity, though. For instance, it could legislate the extended statutes of limitations and heightened incentives discussed previously. The president might not veto them if they were part of a package deal that included temporary immunity. Another possibility is for Congress, if it ever revives the independent-counsel law, to give such counsels exclusive authority to prosecute presidents for federal *or state* crimes; if the courts reject immunity, this would at least circumvent the federalism problems associated with state prosecutions.[48]

Congress can signal its opposition to immunity in other ways. The House and Senate could pass procedural rules (which are not subject to presidential veto) on impeachments and impeachment trials that favorably recognize prior criminal indictments and convictions. For instance, the House could fast-track impeachment for indicted presidents—say, requiring a committee vote on impeachment within fifteen days of an indictment, and automatically incorporating the files from the criminal case into the House committee's record. The Senate could make similar provisions for trials. The legal significance of these rule changes would go beyond the technical changes themselves; they would represent an expression of Congress's opinion that sitting presidents can be prosecuted. Of course, a court considering immunity could hold that Congress misinterpreted the Constitution, but a strong statement from Congress would carry some weight in court, especially to the extent that Congress would be conceding limits to its own impeachment powers.

Notwithstanding these possibilities, Congress seems more likely to legislate in favor of immunity than against it. Many immunity opponents freely concede that prosecuting a sitting president would be a bad thing, and would say that while the Constitution does not require immunity, Congress ought to grant it. Using some of the ideas described here (like tolling the statute of limitations and enhancing penalties), the legislation could also satisfy the complaints of those who have policy arguments against immunity.

As long as presidents continue to expose themselves to prosecution, the goal should be twofold: to make sure that presidents are not above the law, and to punish criminal presidents as completely as possible while punishing the nation as little as possible. Presidents should be properly accountable for their actions, but for the good of the nation, so too should their pursuers. Whether or not the Constitution requires that presidents be out of office before they can be prosecuted, Congress should consider requiring it. Smart immunity legislation would simultaneously reinforce impeachment's preeminent role, protect the presidency, and protect any criminal victims. It might also head off an interesting constitutional cliffhanger, but that's definitely a price worth paying.

2

The Presidential Self-Pardon Controversy

The last year of President Bob Erwin's second term has been dominated by scandal and the accompanying media frenzy. The scandal centers on allegations that Erwin and his operatives abused the power of the presidency for political purposes. It has all been quite confusing; there is a good argument that the president and his team violated certain vague federal laws, and a good argument that they didn't. The attorney general refuses to appoint an independent counsel.

Erwin has paid a price for the scandal, but the complexity of the case and the backdrop in Washington—intense partisan politics—let him fight back. He strenuously maintains his innocence and attributes the scandal to the political opportunism, dishonesty, and malice of his opponents. Indeed, his most vocal critics have been so shrill and hypocritical that Erwin's approval ratings have never dropped too low.

The turmoil came to a head in last month's presidential election, which Erwin's vice president, Marian Strickland, narrowly lost to Governor Tina Sanchez. Sanchez promised during the campaign that she would order a criminal investigation against Erwin and his associates. Her rumored choice to manage the case, Gerald Kensington, is a tough prosecutor and a prominent public critic of Erwin's conduct.

With a few weeks left in office, Erwin considers resigning and asking for a pardon from Vice President Strickland (who was not personally implicated in the scandal). But Erwin can't be sure that Strickland would pardon him, and he fears that resigning would make him look guilty. So Erwin makes a fateful decision. He pardons his aides embroiled in the scandal "for any crimes they may have committed in the course of their employment" during his two terms and then pardons himself using similar language. Announcing his decision on television, he states that he and his aides are innocent and that the country should be spared the expense and distraction of investigations led by his vindictive enemies. "For ten months these scurrilous accusations have paralyzed the country. We've been unable to work on the real problems Americans face," he says. "That problem was about to get worse. Enough is enough. With this pardon, I'm ending this expensive distraction."

Erwin's opponents are enraged. They claim that the self-pardon is constitutionally invalid and they call for the investigation to continue. Erwin's supporters—publicly defensive, privately gleeful—assert that presidents can pardon themselves and that Sanchez and Kensington should drop the case. Nobody seriously doubts that if the parties were reversed, everybody would be making the exact opposite legal arguments, and just as loudly.

It seems that the expensive distraction is not over just yet. President Sanchez takes office and Kensington gets a grand jury to indict ex-president Erwin. Citing his pardon, Erwin moves to dismiss the indictment. This case is going to the Supreme Court.

CAN A PRESIDENT COMMIT A CRIME AND then pardon himself for it, avoiding prosecution and punishment? As in the last chapter, nobody knows, and America can probably only find out the hard way: after a politically charged prosecution, a constitutional brouhaha, and a controversial Supreme Court decision.[1]

A self-pardon would only happen in an extreme situation, but such situations are no less imaginable for being extreme. Shortly before President Nixon resigned, his lawyer advised him that he could pardon himself, and Nixon considered doing it. More recently, the legal travails of Presidents Reagan, Bush, Clinton, and Bush have led some commentators, congressmen, and citizens to broach the subject. The political environment has never been quite right for a self-pardon, but the question never quite goes away, and political winds have a way of shifting quickly.[2]

Article II of the Constitution gives presidents "Power to grant Reprieves and Pardons for Offences against the United States, except in Cases of Impeachment." Pardons are thus limited to federal crimes; they cannot affect civil lawsuits, state criminal matters, or congressional impeachments.* But other than those explicit limitations, the president's power is flexible and seems unrestricted.[3]

Presidents can pardon people at any point after they commit an offense: before charges are brought, during a prosecution, during a sentence, or long afterward.† The president can give amnesty to a vast group, as President Carter did with Vietnam War draft evaders. He can cover a broad, unspecified range of crimes, as President Ford did when he pardoned ex-president Nixon "for all offenses . . . which he . . . has committed or may have committed or taken part in." He can grant reprieves, free prisoners, and commute sentences. He can attach conditions. As long as the crime is federal and has already been committed, a presidential pardon can reach it.[4]

Courts cannot overturn—or even review—an ill-advised pardon, but they can reject an invalid one. Self-pardons are on the margin. There is a good, simple argument that self-pardons are valid, and a worthy, more complicated argument that they are not. There is no consensus among lawyers or scholars sufficient to stop a president from pardoning himself, or to deter a prosecutor from challenging such a pardon. So the prosecutor would prosecute, the president (or ex-president by that point) would resist, and the courts would decide the issue.[5]

The rest of this chapter examines the dueling legal arguments that the courts would confront, and some practical considerations that would arise

---

* Some commentators suggest that people cannot be pardoned for a crime if they have been impeached for it. *See, e.g.*, Richard M. Pious, *The Constitutional and Popular Law of Presidential Impeachment*, 28 Presidential Stud. Q. 806, 811 (1998). This is false. The pardon cannot stop or undo the impeachment itself, but it can stop or undo the criminal prosecution in court. *See* Mark J. Rozell, *President Ford's Pardon of Richard M. Nixon: Constitutional and Political Considerations*, 24 Presidential Stud. Q. 121, 125, 131 (1994) (discussing and rejecting this misinterpretation).

† Theoretically, a president could pardon himself for a federal conviction obtained before he became president. It's hard to imagine a serious convict getting elected, though. George W. Bush was the first convicted criminal ever elected president. His crime was a twenty-four-year-old state misdemeanor, and even that almost cost him the presidency when the press revealed it a couple of days before the 2000 election. This chapter thus focuses on presidents pardoning themselves preemptively, before any conviction. Most of the same analysis nevertheless applies with equal force to post-conviction pardons.

in a self-pardon case. It does not conclude with any suggestions for reform, because no realistic ones exist.

The (Ex-)President's Lead Argument

> Gerald Kensington would love it if the Constitution kept Bob Erwin from ending Kensington's vindictive campaign against him. But Mr. Kensington's fervent hopes can't cause new words to magically appear in the Constitution. A president can pardon himself if he decides it's the right thing to do. The Constitution doesn't say a single word to the contrary. That means a lot, because the Constitution is very specific when it talks about pardons. I'm confident that the Supreme Court will read what the Constitution says, will notice what it doesn't say, and will see things as clearly as former president Erwin does.
>
> —EX-PRESIDENT ERWIN'S SPOKESPERSON

The president's main advantage (and by "the president," I mean the ex-president who pardoned himself, not the successor who is prosecuting him) is the simplicity of his lead argument: the Pardon Clause in the Constitution does not purport to bar self-pardons. The clause explicitly limits other pardons—they cannot reach impeachment cases or civil liability or state crimes—and that implies that there aren't any other limits. This interpretation follows the legal canon of *expressio unius est exclusio alterius*: the expression of one thing excludes others. If the Constitution says that you cannot do *W*, *X*, or *Y*, it implies that you are allowed to do *Z*. The president would argue that this reading of the Pardon Clause is consistent with the Supreme Court's most recent major pardon case, *Schick v. Reed*, which said that any limits on the pardon power "must be found in the Constitution itself."[6]

In the public debate, the president's team would stick with the straightforward implications of the last paragraph and avoid talking much about *Schick*, *expressio unius*, or anything else in italics. But in court, even as the president's lawyers get more technical, their underlying argument ("It doesn't say he can't!") would still be pretty simple—at least until they had to reply to the prosecutor's relatively complex legal claims.

The Prosecutor's Arguments and the President's Replies

Anyone trying to prosecute a self-pardoning president could try plenty of arguments. Even if they are more complicated than the prosecutor might like, they would not defy simplification: "By definition, a pardon is something you give someone else," "presidents aren't kings," "no one can be the judge in his own case," and "we must respect the rule of law." In court, and in more erudite public debates, the president's pursuers could add a fifth statement: "The Founding Fathers didn't want self-pardons."[7]

There is real legal content behind these slogans, and it shows that, at the very least, self-pardons are incongruous. The prosecutor would want to go further and establish that self-pardons are unconstitutional outright, but his constitutional arguments are far from irrefutable. They might be good enough to win in court, but they might not.

Text

> What ex-president Erwin tried to do wasn't even a "pardon." By definition, a pardon is something you give someone else. Legally and historically, it has never been understood any other way.
>
> Erwin's lawyers keep saying that the Pardon Clause doesn't explicitly mention self-pardons, which is true. But looking at one clause in isolation is no way to read the Constitution. They're missing the forest for the trees. Heck, they're missing most of the trees too.
> —ANTI-ERWIN PUNDIT

> You can bark up all the trees and forests you want, but the Constitution still doesn't say anything against self-pardons.
> —PRO-ERWIN PUNDIT

The prosecutor's first task is responding to the president's powerful textual argument that self-pardons are not mentioned, let alone forbidden, in the Constitution. The prosecutor can begin with a different sort of textual argument. He can say that by definition, a "pardon" is given to someone else. Presidents lack the power to pardon themselves because a self-pardon isn't really a pardon.[8]

Here's an analogy. As discussed earlier, a pardon can only forgive past actions. A president cannot use the pardon power to preapprove an offense, because that is a suspension of the law and not a pardon. This is just inherent in the word "pardon," and it limits the president even though the Pardon Clause says nothing more explicit about it. The prosecutor would argue that self-pardons are inherently invalid in the same way.[9]

The *Oxford English Dictionary* seems helpful to the prosecutor. It defines a pardon as "[A]n act of grace on the part of the proper authority in a state, releasing an individual from the punishment imposed by sentence or that is due according to law." It further defines "grace" as "favour, favourable or benignant regard or its manifestation (now only on the part of a superior)." Thus, a pardon is an "act of grace" visited on an inferior by his superior. Though one could argue that a president can be a superior (in his official capacity) and inferior (in his personal capacity) at the same time, a more natural reading is that an act of grace requires two people in the equation. The *OED* also traces the verb "pardon" to the Latin *perdōnāre*, whose root, *dōnāre*, is the root of two other verbs, both of which are also inherently bilateral: "condone" and "donate." Linguistically, just as you cannot condone your own actions, and you cannot donate to yourself, you cannot pardon yourself.[10]

But dictionary arguments are tricky. The editors of the *OED* have no legal power to set the meaning of constitutional terms. The Supreme Court defined a pardon as an "act of grace" in its first major pardon case, but it subsequently suggested that pardons are policy judgments, not acts of grace. Policy judgments can affect their makers—when the president signs a law lowering taxes, for instance, his taxes go down too—so the modern view of pardons is less inherently bilateral.[11]

Moreover, the picture is less clear in the dictionaries commonly relied on by the Supreme Court. Roughly tracking the *OED*, *Webster's Third New International Dictionary* uses "act of grace" language and defines a pardon as "a release by a sovereign or an officer having jurisdiction from the legal penalties or consequences of an offense or of a conviction." But *Black's Law Dictionary* calls a pardon "[t]he act or an instance of officially nullifying punishment or other legal consequences of a crime." Nothing inherently bilateral there. For those seeking a Founding-era definition, Dr. Johnson's dictionary defines a pardon as "Forgiveness of an offender" and "Remission of penalty," among other things. "Forgiveness" might imply something bilateral, but Johnson's definition of forgiveness just refers back to "pardon." To be sure, the prosecutor has some fodder for his definitional argument, just not as much certainty as that argument would seem to require.[12]

Alternatively, the prosecutor could offer some historical context. The roots of the pardon power—and thus of the meaning of the word "pardon"— involve English sovereigns forgiving their subjects. Legally, the English king "could do no wrong" and never needed forgiveness. A prosecutor could thus assert that centuries of royal usage, in which pardons were given always to the subject and never to the sovereign, established a "pardon" as something inherently bilateral. But presidents aren't absolute monarchs; they are subjects as well as sovereigns. Presidents are term limited and legally fallible, which is what raises the possibility of self-pardons in the first place. The question is, what happened when we translated the pardon power from English to American? (As discussed in a few pages, though, the prosecutor has a good argument there too.)[13]

When someone says that a word "means X by definition," he is saying that when he thinks about the word, he thinks only of X. But an opponent or a judge might retort that the word makes *her* think of Y. A prosecutor is just assuming his conclusion if he argues that the definition of pardons excludes self-pardons. To be sure, he can reinforce his argument with all the others that follow in this chapter. The bottom line, though, is that the dictionary does not clearly settle the question.

The prosecutor has another textual line of attack: contesting the president's expressio unius argument. Recall the president's contention that, because the text of the Pardon Clause specifies an explicit limit on pardons (for impeachments), this implies that no other limits exist. The prosecutor can retort that the president's expressio unius reading ignores the universe of *implicit* constitutional limits.

Consider this analogy from elsewhere in the Constitution. The Elections Clause states that Congress can regulate the "Times, Places, and Manner" of electing senators and representatives, "except as to the Place of chusing Senators." As with the Pardon Clause, there is a grant of power with one specific exception. The expressio unius reading would say that the specific restriction (against regulating the place of choosing senators) makes

Congress's remaining election power unlimited. But could Congress really do anything? Could it restrict the "place" of all House elections to Nome, Alaska? Or the "manner" of House elections to voting in person (in Nome), with absentee voting allowed only for members of the House and their staffs? It is unimaginable that the courts would declare such laws to be constitutional. Indeed, courts *have* rejected the expressio unius reading of the Elections Clause and have detected implicit limits on Congress's power there. If you cannot accept that Congress could use the Elections Clause to pass the Nome Voting Law, you must think twice before reading the president's power under the Pardon Clause just as expansively.[14]

Unfortunately for our prosecutor, this proves only that the pardon power might have other limits. It tells us nothing about what those other limits are. If the prosecutor's definitional argument is not enough—if he cannot establish that, inherently, a pardon is something a president gives to another person—then he needs to show that self-pardons offend *something else* in the Constitution. Otherwise, the president's continued refrain would be right: he can pardon himself because the Constitution doesn't stop him, either explicitly or implicitly.[15]

Structure

> Ex-president Erwin's act was a brazen affront to our most basic principles: Presidents are not kings. No one can judge his own case. No one is above the law. It's sad that President Erwin doesn't see the rule of law when he looks at our system of government, but it's there.
>
> Look, I don't have a problem with presidential pardons. But this wasn't pardoning, it was pillaging. Mr. Erwin thinks that he's untouchable, a law unto himself. That's just not what the presidency is all about, and it's not what this country is all about.
>
> —PROSECUTOR GERALD KENSINGTON

> I give Gerald Kensington credit: he's a dogged prosecutor. Wrong, but dogged. He doesn't like what the Constitution says here, so he talks about what he'd like it to mean.
>
> Presidents make policy decisions, and that's just what this was. When ex-president Erwin issued these pardons, he was

doing what was best for the country. I'm sorry, Gerald Kensington, if you think it's better for America to waste even more time, money, and energy on this witch hunt, but Mr. Erwin didn't think so. As president, the Constitution gave him power to do something about it, so he used that power.

—LAWYER FOR EX-PRESIDENT ERWIN

Looking for implicit limits on the pardon power reminds us to examine the entire constitutional framework. As mentioned earlier, the Supreme Court said in *Schick v. Reed* that the limits of the pardon power "must be found in the *Constitution* itself," not just in the Pardon Clause.[16]

In part, the argument over the meaning of the pardon power would be an argument over the meaning of the presidency. One battleground is the president's role as the nation's chief prosecutor. Through such (admittedly blunt) instruments as his ability to pardon people, and to fire the attorney general and U.S. attorneys, the president could point out—correctly—that he has ultimate authority over federal prosecutions. Next, he could argue that he can use his position to avoid federal prosecution even without using a pardon. First, he can refrain from prosecuting himself; the Constitution never requires that an independent counsel be appointed. The statute of limitations could run out before the president leaves office, keeping his successor from reviving the case. Alternatively, a president could *ensure* his own prosecution and make a favorable deal—perhaps pleading no contest to a minor charge and getting a slap on the wrist—that would preclude any further charges. A self-pardon, the president would argue, fits the same mold as these other maneuvers, which are clearly within his power. But, as the prosecutor would no doubt reply, self-pardoning is different, because it would be more powerful. Applying the statute of limitations or approving a plea deal would require independent judicial approval; a self-pardon would be a completely unilateral act. The president's successor might revive a neglected prosecution in some cases, at least, but she could never undo a pardon.[17]

The prosecutor might continue with his own structural argument. If a federal criminal defendant feels unjustly accused, he must convince one of the following to back him: the U.S. attorney (who can drop the prosecution), a majority of the grand jury (which can refuse to indict), the judge (who can dismiss the case), a member of the trial jury (which can fail to unanimously convict), or the president (who can pardon). But people cannot prosecute, judge, or sit on juries in their own cases. A president who could get a pardon from himself (rather than from his successor) would be the only person in America who could directly head off his own conviction.

The president could distinguish himself, though. Prosecutors, judges, and jurors can be kept off of their own cases because they have plenty of potential substitutes available. Not so the president; nobody else can pardon him while he is president, so the prosecutor's argument would make the president the only person in America ineligible for a federal pardon. Moreover, the president is elected, while federal judges, jurors, and prosecutors are not. This is one reason why the president has the pardon power in the first place: he is uniquely accountable to the public for his decisions. Therefore, as a structural matter, he has more trust reposed in him, with impeachment as a check. This necessarily includes the power to deal himself things in a way that judges, jurors, and prosecutors cannot.[18]

That said, a self-pardon would most likely be considered by a president with nothing to lose. When the prospect of a self-pardon arose for the elder President Bush, he had already been defeated for reelection; when President Nixon considered pardoning himself, he was disgraced and about to resign. By contrast, a president who still has some political capital—enough to avoid impeachment, fend off special prosecutors, and get reelected—would have no *need* to pardon himself and probably would not want to pay the high political price of doing so. In other words, the only likely candidate for a self-pardon is an utterly unaccountable president. As a structural matter, self-pardons are hard to justify.

The prosecutor could also offer structural arguments based on the Constitution's creation of a limited presidency. As already discussed, the presidential pardon power has roots in the English royal pardon power. But kings could not self-pardon, and it is unlikely that the Constitution would have made the president's power broader than the king's. To be sure, kings never pardoned themselves because they never needed to. Presidents, by contrast, are vulnerable to prosecution, impeachment, and political defeat. The power to self-pardon would not give presidents more power than kings; it would just mitigate the extent to which presidents are *less* powerful than kings. But self-pardons still seem incongruous. The king's immunity from prosecution was backed up by his continued power as monarch. A sitting president might be immune from prosecution (see Chapter 1), but when he is not the president anymore—and some day he will not be—he is vulnerable. A self-pardon would be presidential plunder. Because self-pardons would allow presidents—even thoroughly discredited, impeached ones—to project their temporarily kingly power so far beyond their tenure in office, they clash with the idea of limited terms at the constitutional heart of the presidency.[19]

This argument is not airtight, though. If self-pardons offend the notion of limited terms, then so do regular pardons. Any time the president pardons anyone, the pardon cannot be undone, and the effects linger forever after the president has left office. The situation might be *worse* in the case of a self-pardon, but this still makes it harder for the prosecutor to say that self-pardons are *so* different or *so* much worse that they are unconstitutional.

A better structural argument—one that explains why the prosecutor's last two arguments, about the "politically accountable prosecutor" and the "limited executive," resonate—is that the Constitution frowns on people being the judges in their own cases.

The prosecutor could point to a list of constitutional provisions that address financial self-dealing: A member of Congress cannot simultaneously hold any "office under the United States," and cannot resign to take such a job if it was created or had its pay raised during the current congressional term. Congress cannot legislate a pay raise for itself that takes effect before the next congressional election, and presidential salary increases must wait for an intervening presidential election. The president cannot receive any other "emolument" from the United States besides his salary. In other words, the Constitution precludes Congress and the president from feathering their nests, at least until after the voters can weigh in.[20]

If self-pardons can be likened to stealing from the till, though, it is only metaphorically. It is hard to draw a convincing logical chain from (1) very specific written provisions about pay to (2) a general principle about self-dealing to (3) a very specific *unwritten* provision about self-pardons. Consider also that the limit on congressional pay raises took 215 years and a constitutional amendment to create; if it could not just be inferred from the other self-dealing provisions, how could a ban on self-pardons?[21]

Self-judging is an important subset of self-dealing and it gives the prosecutor more direct structural evidence against self-pardons. Vice-presidential impeachments are one example. The Constitution says that the vice president presides over the Senate, except when an impeached president is on trial there, in which case the chief justice presides. But what about when the *vice* president is on trial? If the vice president cannot be trusted to preside over the president's trial (more evidence of the Constitution's distaste for self-dealing, by the way) how can he be trusted to preside over his own? It would be quite odd if the Constitution's drafters meant to require this result. But if you think that self-pardons are valid, you would be hard pressed to deny that vice presidents can preside over their own impeachment trials.[22]

Another self-judging issue arises with the Expulsion Clause, which provides that a chamber of Congress can expel a member by a two-thirds vote. Nothing in the clause explicitly prevents someone from voting on his own expulsion (nor do congressional rules against self-interested voting), but members of Congress never do so. Perhaps this is just self-restraint rather than a constitutional requirement, but congressmen are not noted for their self-restraint (especially not the no-goodniks who get expelled). The strength of this custom suggests that something deeper is binding them.[23]

Compared to these two restrictions on self-judging, the case against self-pardons is even stronger. In a vice-presidential impeachment, the senators could override any questionable rulings by the vice president or maybe even remove him from presiding, with a simple majority vote. By contrast, a self-pardoning president would get the last word. Nor does it matter much if congressmen vote in their own expulsion cases; single votes rarely matter. Pardons, by contrast, have one solitary "voter," whose decision is all that matters. Also, the effect of an expulsion only lasts until the next election, while pardons stand forever.

Whatever their power as analogies, though, these anti-self-judging examples still do not amount to a clear constitutional prohibition of self-pardons. Structural arguments provide plenty of raw material for a discussion of what the Constitution is all about, and whether self-pardons are consistent with that. They might even prove persuasive to a court. But structure cannot provide a definitive rule. Self-pardonability is still up in the air.

History

The Founding Fathers didn't think that the Constitution lets presidents pardon themselves. If you look at their debates, that's obvious.

——ANTI-ERWIN COMMENTATOR

Obvious to whom? The Founding Fathers didn't say one word about self-pardons. Nothing. Not in their debates, and—more importantly—not in the Constitution they wrote.

——PRO-ERWIN COMMENTATOR

Arguing from history—asking what the English, the colonists, and the Framers thought about pardons centuries ago—is controversial. Some people discount historical evidence, while others seemingly discount everything *but* historical evidence. Historical evidence is also usually vague and malleable, and the evidence on self-pardons is no exception. All that said, history boosts the prosecutor's argument. Some judges could be swayed by it, and the prosecutor would surely press this possible advantage.

As mentioned already, the American pardon power is derived from its English royal counterpart. English monarchs had the power to pardon well before the Norman Invasion in 1066. By the mid-1500s, the royal pardon power was absolute and reached any offense against the Crown. Self-pardons were never an issue in England. Legally, the king could do no wrong, so he never needed a pardon. Parliament occasionally deposed kings, but self-pardons were obviously irrelevant then too.[24]

Germane to the self-pardon issue, Parliament limited pardons in response to the case of the Earl of Danby. Danby, a lord high treasurer under King Charles II, faced impeachment for conspiring with France. The French had been bribing Charles, and Danby was just following his orders, but the king was legally impervious, so impeaching the hapless treasurer was the best that Parliament could do. To end the impeachment and cover up the embarrassing truth about himself, Charles pardoned Danby in 1679. Charles won the battle but the monarchy lost the war: in the 1701 Act of Settlement, Parliament forbade pardons from ever again preempting an impeachment inquiry.[25]

In America, most colonial proprietors and governors had broad pardon powers delegated by the Crown. After independence, having just fought a revolutionary war against overweening monarchy, several states restricted or eliminated pardons, and early drafts of the federal constitution omitted the pardon power altogether. But the Framers did add a royal-looking broad pardon power. Tracking the Act of Settlement, the president was kept from using pardons against impeachments.[26]

The debate on pardons at the Constitutional Convention was limited, but one part did relate to self-pardons. Using a Danby-like hypothetical, Edmund Randolph argued that presidents should not be entrusted with the pardon power in cases of treason: "The President may himself be guilty," worried Randolph. "The Traytors may be his own instruments." Some suggested that this danger was best handled by transferring the pardon power to Congress. James Wilson responded that the power to pardon—including in cases of treason—should stay with the president, despite the potential for abuse. Highlighting the distinction between Randolph's hypothetical and King Charles's Danby episode, Wilson noted that "[i]f [the president] be himself a party to the guilt he can be impeached and prosecuted." Wilson's view carried the day; Randolph's motion failed. The message seemed clear: presidents are not above the law, and they cannot use pardons to save themselves.[27]

Admittedly, this evidence is indirect; the Framers never discussed self-pardons as such. When Randolph raised the specter of a treasonous president using pardons, his proposed solution was only to eliminate pardons for treason, not to prohibit self-pardons too. Perhaps the possibility of self-pardons didn't occur to anyone. Randolph's scenario was similar to the Danby case, so maybe his image of the pardon power was rooted in seventeenth-century England. Perhaps the self-pardon was lost in the translation from king to president.

But Wilson's response took the difference between kings and presidents seriously. A president, Wilson reminded Randolph, can be impeached and prosecuted. How could a president be prosecuted if he could pardon himself, as a perfidious president in that situation surely would before the slow impeachment process concluded? No one asked, which suggests that the illegality of self-pardons literally went without saying. Wilson likely assumed that self-pardons were impossible and thus (as he argued later, in another forum) that presidents could not avoid prosecution. Like King Charles II, the president could free his treasonous cohorts, but unlike King Charles II, the president could not shield himself.[28]

Perhaps the Framers thought that presidents could pardon themselves and just did not mind, but this is implausible. True, the Framers determined that it was worth unifying the pardon power under the president's control, even with the risk of abuse. But the debate presupposed that the president himself could be prosecuted and did not endorse anything like a self-pardon. Randolph's scenario was not one of mere political differences but one of outright insurrection; treason was narrowly defined in the Constitution as "levying war" against the United States or "adhering" to its foes. If the power to pardon his co-conspirators was "too great a trust" for Randolph to repose in the president, the possibility of the president pardoning himself would have been much worse. Wilson successfully assuaged the Convention's fears not by saying that it was a chance worth taking, but by noting that a treasonous president could be prosecuted. If the delegates had assumed that self-pardons were valid, Wilson would have been asking them to rely on a traitor's self-restraint, repentance, and willingness to suffer the penalty for his treason, even though he had the power to avoid it. If this was what Wilson meant, it seems doubtful that his argument would have passed unrefuted, let alone that it would have carried the day.[29]

Ultimately, one can only speculate on what the Framers thought about self-pardons. Given the course of their debate, however, it is reasonable to conclude that they believed the power to be invalid, or at the very least, that they did not think about it. Either way, when the Framers gave the president an abusable pardon power with few explicit limits, they would not have thought that they were potentially placing him above the law.

The prosecutor in our case might press these arguments, and while they would not provide a slam dunk for his case, they would add something that the previous section, on structure, would not. To any judge who thinks that she must consider the Framers' understandings when she interprets a constitutional clause, the argument from history provides an actual basis for outlawing self-pardons—a slender reed, perhaps, but a reed nonetheless.

Case Law and Common Law

> Our courts have long enforced the maxim that nobody can set
> the law at defiance with impunity. A president giving himself a
> get-out-of-jail-free card? That's something that the courts do
> not countenance.
>
> —ANTI-ERWIN BLOGGER

> Except for when they do.
>
> —PRO-ERWIN BLOG COMMENTER

While the prosecutor can undermine the president's simplistic textual reading, he still needs to build up his own argument *against* self-pardons. We have seen the prosecutor use text ("by definition, a pardon is given to another person"), structure ("our general constitutional framework is incompatible with self-pardons"), and originalism ("the Framers did not believe in self-pardons"). But the textual argument is contestable, the structural argument is thin, and the originalist argument is irrelevant to non-originalist judges. The prosecutor has one last sort of argument: judicial decisions.

The prosecutor must confront the sweeping language the Supreme Court has used to discuss the pardon power. Cases like *United States v. Klein* ("[T]he power of pardon . . . is granted *without limit.*") and Ex parte *Garland* ("The [pardon] power thus conferred is *unlimited.*") would provide the president with impressive-sounding precedents to support his position. But those cases were not describing the president's power in a vacuum; they were talking about the president's power vis-à-vis Congress. In both cases, the Court rejected legislative attempts to reinstate punishments that the president had pardoned away. Read in context, the quotations reflect that quite clearly and their usefulness to the president fades away.[30]

The prosecutor's most potent claim is that no one can be the judge in his own case. This concept already appeared as a structural argument, but it was not decisive there. Here, the prosecutor gets another chance, arguing that there is *judicial* precedent against self-judging.

Justice Chase's opinion in *Calder v. Bull*, one of the Republic's earliest cases, speaks to the fundamental disfavor for self-judging in Anglo-American law: "[Regarding] a law that makes a man *a Judge in his own cause* . . . [i]t is against all reason and justice, for a people to entrust a Legislature with SUCH powers; and, therefore, it cannot be presumed that they have done it."[31]

While Chase's natural-law approach has lost favor over the centuries, judges still draw lines like this and strike down actions that cross those lines. In one relatively recent case, the Supreme Court carefully interpreted a statute to avoid a self-judging problem. It traced the origins of the self-judging principle from philosophy through jurisprudence and into the case law, labeling it a "mainstay of our system of government." In another recent case, the Court cited "the maxim that '[n]o man is allowed to be a judge in his own cause'" as the basis for a *constitutional* requirement that judges recuse themselves from cases in which they have substantial, direct pecuniary interests.* When the courts consider a contestable constitutional provision like the Pardon Clause, a constitutional "mainstay" like the anti-self-judging principle could tip the interpretive balance against the president. Perhaps these statements against self-judging are just rhetorical flourishes, adorning decisions based on other principles. But they are compelling flourishes.[32]

The other relevant principle the prosecutor would draw from precedent is the rule of law, which arises much like it did in Chapter 1. The core principle that ours is "a government of laws, and not of men," was explicated more thoroughly in *United States v. Lee*: "No man in this country is so high that he is above the law. No officer of the law may set that law at defiance with impunity. All the officers of the government, from the highest to the lowest, are creatures of the law and are bound to obey it. It is the only supreme power in our system of government, and every man who by accepting office participates in its functions is only the more strongly bound to submit to that supremacy, and to observe the limitations which it imposes upon the exercise of the authority which it gives."[33]

---

* Unfortunately for opponents of self-pardons, it would be hard to use this case to argue that the president must recuse himself from his own case. When a judge fails to recuse himself in his own case, the party on the other side can claim that its due-process rights have been violated. In the case of a pardon, however, there is no party on the other side (unless, perhaps, the president uses the pardon to evade an otherwise mandatory requirement that he pay restitution to his victims).

The president could argue that this begs the question: perhaps "the authority" that the law "gives" him includes a very broad pardon power. But the prosecutor could argue forcefully that it would violate the spirit of *Lee* for a president to single-handedly and permanently exempt himself from the criminal law. If the president truly deserved to go free, he could do what any other citizen must do and appeal to the rightful authorities. That is the message of *Lee*: leveling and equality under law.

Lee is cited in cases at the constitutional margins, like those that consider personal immunity for senators, representatives, executive officials, and judges. When the Court limits immunity, it cites *Lee*. When the Court expands immunity, the dissent cites *Lee*. In *Nixon v. Fitzgerald*, for instance, a 5–4 Court granted civil immunity to presidents for their official actions; a strong dissent reminded the Court of the "unanswerable argument that no man, not even the president of the United States, is absolutely and fully above the law." The president would note that this lofty language was in dissent—*Lee* is not "unanswerable," as it turns out. But when our prosecutor argues that self-pardons put the president above the law, he can rely on *Lee* to heighten the court's discomfort with the president's action.[34]

Following Justice Chase's thoughts in *Calder*, one can imagine a court invalidating a self-pardon because it so grossly violates these fundamental principles. But it is unreasonable to assume that any particular judge would do this; there are other principles at stake in the case, and the president still has his powerful textual argument on his side. Once again, it is impossible to predict how judges would use these concepts in a real case.

Functional Self-Pardons and Some Practical Considerations

There is one other set of arguments that would arise in a self-pardon case, drawing on functional considerations. Presidents can use pardons to protect themselves without resorting to self-pardons. But if these other abusive pardons are valid, and if they are the functional equivalent of self-pardons, then it becomes harder to argue that self-pardons could not be valid too.[35]

The elder President Bush's case presents one example. Bush pardoned all the significant targets in the Iran-Contra investigation besides himself, arguing that the investigation represented "the criminalization of policy differences," which should be dealt with in the voting booth rather than in court. His mandate slashed, Independent Counsel Lawrence Walsh gave up the case. Nobody questioned that the pardons were legally valid, but some said that by issuing them, Bush had effectively pardoned himself. That argument missed an important point, though: Bush was still vulnerable after his pardons. By clearing the field, he had left himself as the only Iran-Contra figure left to prosecute. Furthermore, Bush's pardons meant that his associates could be forced to testify against him. Because they couldn't be prosecuted, they couldn't incriminate themselves with their testimony, so they could no longer plead the Fifth Amendment and clam up. Perhaps the pardoned witnesses would have been unhelpful to the prosecution, either out of gratitude to Bush or because they no longer had any reason to cooperate in exchange for a plea deal, but even so, Bush was going out on a limb. A self-pardon would have protected him much more. In the end, Bush's gamble paid off and Walsh dropped the case, but Walsh dropped it for tactical, practical reasons, not constitutional ones. While it might be problematic when a president pardons his associates, it is not the functional equivalent of a self-pardon.[36]

The same conclusion emerges from President Nixon's case. Nixon decided against pardoning himself, then resigned and got pardoned by President Ford. But Nixon had no leverage and made no deal with Ford to pardon him. Ford had no personal stake in the matter. Moreover, the pardon probably cost Ford the election two years later. Ford's action was thus a considered policy judgment by an accountable president—the ideal pardon—and not a go-for-broke, corrupt self-pardon. Ford later wrote: "Although I respected the tenet that no man should be above the law, public policy demanded that I put Nixon—and Watergate—behind us as quickly as possible." Consider how hollow Ford's words would have sounded if Nixon had written them. Though a president might resign and his successor might pardon him, this too is not the functional equivalent of a self-pardon.[37]

Even if the Bush and Ford pardons had worse facts, they still would not necessarily undermine the case against self-pardons. The main reason is that they would have been easier to punish than self-pardons. If Bush had pardoned his associates in exchange for their silence, then he could have been prosecuted for conspiracy or obstruction of justice. (The pardons probably would still have stood, but Bush could have been prosecuted for the underlying corruption.) Similarly, if Nixon had made a deal with Ford to resign in exchange for a pardon, Ford's pardon probably would have been valid, but Ford and Nixon could have been prosecuted for conspiracy or bribery. If Nixon had handed over power to Ford only temporarily under the Twenty-Fifth Amendment, had Ford pardon him, and then retaken power and pardoned Ford, *those* pardons probably would have been valid too, but they again would have been part of a bribery conspiracy, and Nixon and Ford could have been prosecuted for them.[38]

By contrast, corrupt self-pardons would be very hard to prosecute. In the earlier hypothetical, if Bush had just pardoned himself, he would not have been obstructing justice; if he were, then every preemptive pardon would be an obstruction of justice. If Nixon had told Ford that he would pardon himself and then resign, it would not be part of a conspiracy or a bribe, because the pardon would be an inherently unilateral act, with Ford not really involved.

To be sure, a self-pardon might be a criminal act.* For instance, Nixon could have agreed with Ford that Nixon would pardon himself, in order to spare Ford the political cost of doing so, and Ford could have agreed to pay Nixon cash for his trouble. That self-pardon would be part of a bribery conspiracy. *Some* self-pardons could be criminal. But *all* the corrupt schemes discussed previously, with presidents protecting themselves by pardoning others, would be criminal. Corrupt presidents can pardon others to protect themselves, but they can be prosecuted for it. Only with a self-pardon could a president ever truly place himself above the law.[39]

Even if a self-pardon is not prosecutable, it might still be quite costly for the president. Presidential pardons do not protect against public infamy, civil liability, state criminal liability, or—perhaps most important—the impeachment proceedings that a self-pardon could inspire. Given all these potential

---

* If a pardon was a criminal act, the president could try to pardon himself for *it*. A pardon can only reach past acts, though, so the president would need a separate, second pardon to forgive the crime of the first one. But the second pardon could be a crime too. He might keep pardoning himself, but eventually he would leave office and his last pardon could expose him to prosecution.

obstacles and penalties, what harm is there in allowing self-pardons? Why accept the prosecutor's complicated and indirect constitutional arguments to achieve such minimal gains?[40]

One response is that none of these additional punishments and penalties necessarily applies. The president's crime might be one that doesn't expose him to civil liability or state prosecution. The underlying crime might be too minor to justify impeachment, especially if (as discussed in Chapter 5) the president has already left office. A president might even avoid "infamy": he could pardon himself secretly, bringing the document out of his files only if he is indicted, and sparing himself the public shame of a self-pardon if he is not.[41]

More importantly, even if the president did face all these other consequences, he could face them whether or not he pardoned himself. There is no reason to give him a bonus. To reuse an earlier analogy, would we let a vice president preside over his own impeachment trial just because he was also susceptible to public infamy? Even if a president deserves a pardon on the grounds that he has already "suffered enough," his successor is the one who should make that call.[42]

In any case, these practical considerations do not really speak to the constitutional issue. If the Constitution allows self-pardons, it allows self-pardons, and the other penalties that the president might face are neither here nor there. And if the Constitution bars self-pardons, it bars them regardless of what else might happen to the president.

Conclusions

The discussion ends as it began: indecisively. Only a desperate president would pardon himself, but the law is unclear enough that, given his desperation, it might be worth a try. The prosecutor might as well fight the pardon, given that he thought it was worth prosecuting the president in the first place.

The courts would have to decide, and they would have plenty of basis to come out either way. Depending on whom you ask, judges either set their personal preferences aside in favor of neutral legal principles or follow their hearts and only pay lip service to principles. The truth is likely somewhere in between. But this case—in which there are enough principles to support either result, in which the case would be inextricably linked with the character and politics of the president and his pursuers, and in which the decision could easily be characterized as a one-off that would not affect any other areas of the law—is a good candidate for poisoning by personal preferences.[43]

What to Do?

So what can be done to prevent this constitutional cliffhanger? Not much. Congress has no power to restrict—let alone define—the pardon power. An upright president might influence the debate by forswearing self-pardons, but he could not legally bind his less scrupulous successors.[44]

If the Constitution allows self-pardons, changing that would require an amendment. Realistically, only a real scandal could motivate constitutional change; if a president successfully pardoned himself (or otherwise abused the pardon power), and if the public was outraged enough, then there *might* be enough support for an amendment to tweak the pardon power. Given how hard it is to amend the Constitution, an angry public might be satisfied with an alternative: impeaching that president, and holding up his bloodied reputation as a warning to his successors.[45]

Without a real event to galvanize the public, though, nothing will happen. If a member of Congress or a well-meaning law professor were to warn that presidents might be able to pardon themselves, some people would disagree, and some people would agree but not mind, but most people just would not care. That doesn't leave nearly enough people to pass a constitutional amendment. There really is nothing to do but sit and wait and hope for the best.[46]

3

Removing a "Disabled" President

Frances Philips is halfway through her second term as president. Her management style, which was always "hands off," has become downright lax. She skips meetings, neglects decisions that need to be made, and shows little interest in being president. Some members of her cabinet and staff worry that she is clinically depressed, but—swayed by the increased power that comes with having a figurehead for a boss—none of them does anything about it.

Then President Philips starts alternating her periods of utter inertness with bursts of aggressive and arbitrary micromanagement. At a cabinet meeting, she rants for ten minutes about the use of blue pens instead of black ones. Next, without explanation, she announces that she is killing a carefully developed policy initiative in which she had previously taken no interest.

Several cabinet secretaries become convinced that the president is unable to perform her job. They start to discuss Section 4 of the Twenty-Fifth Amendment, which allows the vice president and a majority of the cabinet to declare the president "unable to discharge the powers and duties of [her] office," and transfer power to the vice president. Crucially, though, Vice President Merrick opposes the effort. Although he worries that President Philips's mental condition is deteriorating, he is reluctant to lead what could be perceived as a coup.

Things come to a head when war unexpectedly breaks out in the Middle East. After hearing the initial reports, President Philips paces in the Oval Office, muttering to herself but issuing no orders and taking no action. After several excruciating hours pass like this, Vice President Merrick has had enough, and he gathers the cabinet to file a Section 4 declaration. He is joined by a solid majority: eleven out of fifteen cabinet members.

President Philips is blindsided, but her chief of staff Tom Cooper (who Merrick erroneously thought would support the Section 4 declaration) is not. When Philips asks what her options are, Cooper reads to her from Section 4: if the president sends a counter-declaration to Congress that "no inability exists," she can "resume the powers and duties of [her] office." Cooper notes, however, that Section 4 allows the vice president and cabinet to reassert the president's unfitness within four days, sending the matter to Congress for a final decision, and giving power to the vice president in the meantime.

With renewed focus, Philips executes Cooper's plan. First, she signs a letter declaring herself fit and transmits it to Congress. Next, she summons the cabinet and addresses the eleven mutinous members: "If you don't think I can discharge the powers and duties of my office, watch this. You're fired." Finally, she replaces them, naming eleven of her most trusted subordinates as acting cabinet secretaries.

In response, Vice President Merrick rallies the old cabinet, and he and the original eleven challengers sign a second declaration of Philips's disability. Merrick claims that Philips has misread Section 4: Philips never retook power, her firings are invalid, the second disability declaration is valid, Merrick is the acting president, and Congress must now step in. Unfortunately, as advised by Chief of Staff Cooper, Philips refuses to back down. She says that she is in control, with the unanimous support of the "legitimate" cabinet, and that Congress has no basis to act.

The nation is in crisis. There are two presidents and two cabinets. The situation in the Middle East is spinning out of control, and nobody knows for sure who the rightful commander in chief, secretary of state, and secretary of defense are. Congress assembles while dueling sheaves of legal pleadings and memoranda flood the federal courts.[1]

UNLIKE THE OTHER THREE SECTIONS OF THE Twenty-Fifth Amendment, Section 4 has never been used. Still, as numerous books, movies, and television programs have recognized since the amendment was ratified in 1967, Section 4 offers a lot of potential drama. It would be spectacle enough to have a disabled president like our fictional Frances Philips (whose story is based on instances of similar behavior by real presidents). A full-blown power struggle might be more excitement than we can handle.[2]

Presidential disability and succession rules should be certain and swift, because it is obviously important to know exactly who is president at any given moment. The Twenty-Fifth Amendment was intended to provide this kind of certainty and swiftness, and it successfully covers most of the bases. A conflict like the one suggested here would only arise in an unusual and extreme situation. But extreme situations are when clear rules are *most* important, and like it or not, the text of Section 4 of the amendment is unclear. Luckily, as discussed at the end of this chapter, there are plausible, simple, and effective ways to fix the problem.[3]

Presidential Disabilities and Section 4

Section 4 reads:

Whenever the Vice President and a majority of either the principal officers of the executive departments or of such other body as Congress may by law provide, transmit to the President pro tempore of the Senate and the Speaker of the House of Representatives their written declaration that the President is unable to discharge the powers and duties of his office, the Vice President shall immediately assume the powers and duties of the office as Acting President.

Thereafter, when the President transmits to the President pro tempore of the Senate and the Speaker of the House of Representatives his written declaration that no inability exists, he shall resume the powers and duties of his office unless the Vice President and a majority of either the principal officers of the executive department or of such other body as Congress may by law provide, transmit within four days to the President pro tempore of the Senate and the Speaker of the House of Representatives their written declaration that the President is unable to discharge the powers and duties of his office. Thereupon Congress shall decide the issue, assembling within forty eight hours for that purpose if not in session. If the Congress, within twenty one days after receipt of the latter written declaration, or, if Congress is not in session, within twenty one days after Congress is required to assemble, determines by two thirds vote of both Houses that the President is unable to discharge the powers and duties of his office, the Vice President shall continue to discharge the same as Acting President; otherwise, the President shall resume the powers and duties of his office.

To sum up: (1) the vice president takes over if he and the cabinet declare the president disabled; (2) the president can respond that she is not disabled, but the vice president and cabinet can object within four days; (3) if they don't object, the president gets her powers back; (4) if they do object, the vice president stays in control while Congress deliberates; and (5) the vice president keeps power indefinitely only if Congress votes—within twenty-one days, and by two-thirds majorities in both houses—that the president is disabled. Congress can substitute a different group for the cabinet, but it has never done so.[4]

A "constitutional cliffhanger" would require more than just an argument over whether the president is disabled. That would be a question of fact— the president would disagree with the vice president and cabinet, and Congress would decide. Dramatic, but not really a constitutional dilemma, because the Constitution provides a clear path.

This chapter is about where the path gets muddy: the second of the five steps, in which the vice president and cabinet have four days to re-challenge the president. It is indisputable that Section 4's creators intended for the vice president to remain in charge during this waiting period, and there is ample evidence that Section 4 so provides. Unfortunately, the text of Section 4 is unclear, so it has occasionally been misread as placing the president in charge during the waiting period. As seen in this chapter's hypothetical scenario, if push ever comes to shove, things could go very badly.

When Push Comes to Shove

Section 4 treads on inherently dangerous ground. When it was being debated, Senator Robert Kennedy worried about a situation in which "[t]here would be two Presidents and two Cabinets." Representative Henry Gonzalez has criticized Section 4 as "a threat to the stability of elected government in this country." This skittishness might explain why Section 4 has never been used.[5]

It is not as though presidents are never disabled; they get sick, physically and mentally, sometimes very seriously. It is just that their disabilities are traditionally downplayed, or even covered up.[6]

Before the Twenty-Fifth Amendment, disabled presidents typically clung to power—sometimes completely disabled, sometimes for months. Presidential disability was covered by Article II of the Constitution, which provides that the vice president takes over "[i]n Case of the . . . [president's]

Inability to discharge the Powers and Duties of [her] Office." This implicitly allowed a president to declare herself disabled or for the vice president to do so if the president could not (say, if she was in a coma). It also implicitly allowed Congress to legislate some standards and procedures, using its power under the Necessary and Proper Clause. But Congress never used that power. Moreover, Article II seemed to preclude the vice president from handing power back to a disabled president who later recovered.* This made it politically difficult to declare presidents disabled, even when they clearly were. The Twenty-Fifth Amendment was designed to rectify all this.[7]

Like Article II, the Twenty-Fifth Amendment does not define "inability," but this was a conscious choice. Rather than try to predict every possible situation, the amendment—just like many parts of the original Constitution—gives a general standard ("unable to discharge the powers and duties") and assigns decision makers (the president, the vice president, the cabinet, and Congress) to apply it. It counts on these decision makers to use their best practical and political judgment. It also assumes that they will proceed in good faith; if they don't, fine shades of constitutional meaning won't matter much anyway.[8]

It is significant that the dispute in this chapter could arise even if both sides were using their best judgment and proceeding in good faith. The vice

---

* Article II is unclear on whether a vice president permanently takes over a dead or disabled president's "office," or only temporarily takes over her "powers and duties." When President Harrison died, Vice President Tyler declared that he had assumed the office and was not just acting as president. The eventual acceptance of this precedent made it logical to assume—or at least worry—that vice presidents took over the office from *disabled* presidents as well, and that they would not hand power back if the disabled president recovered. In contrast, Article II makes clear that people further down the line of succession must hand power back when the disability ends. *See* S. Rep. No. 89-66, at 5–7 (1965) (discussing this problem with Article II, and resulting trouble during Garfield and Wilson administrations); John D. Feerick, From Failing Hands 50–51 (1965) (describing origin and nature of the problem); Ruth Silva, Presidential Succession 69–81 (1951) (discussing intense debates over the question); Robert E. Gilbert, *The Genius of the Twenty-Fifth Amendment, in* Managing Crisis: Presidential Disability and the Twenty-Fifth Amendment 25, 29 (Robert E. Gilbert ed., 2000) (noting powerful incentive this gave presidents not to admit their disabilities); *cf.* Joel K. Goldstein, *The Vice Presidency and the Twenty-Fifth Amendment, in* Managing Crisis, *supra*, at 165, 169–71 (rejecting this interpretation of Article II).

president could reluctantly but sincerely decide that the president is unfit for office. The president could reasonably want to guard her power and honestly feel capable of exercising it. The vice president could conclude, correctly, that Section 4's creators meant for him to be in charge during the four-day waiting period. The president, feeling besieged, and emboldened by a superficially plausible textual reading of Section 4, might be unwilling to hand over power to mutineers just because they cite some decades-old legislative history.

The stakes would almost certainly be high. Unless the president has an undeniable and extreme disability like being missing or in a coma, Section 4 would probably only get invoked if the country was in the midst of an external crisis. There are several factors that discourage the use of Section 4 in calmer times (if such times are possible anymore). One is that the president exercises most of her power through her subordinates, who can still exercise much of their authority even if the president is largely incapacitated. Relatedly, their personal power and status may depend on the president remaining in office. Another factor is that public confidence might be shaken if the president's poor condition is widely advertised, or if control of the White House seems wobbly. Finally, vice presidents have been reluctant to assert themselves, generally for fear of looking power hungry.[9]

Therefore, as a practical matter in close cases, Section 4 requires not just that the president be disabled, but that her disability have serious consequences. If times are quiet, it is much easier to leave the president in nominal control while her cabinet and staff maintain actual control, as with President Wilson after his stroke, or Presidents Reagan and Garfield after they were shot, or our fictional President Philips before war broke out. But times aren't always quiet. Unfortunately, that means that Section 4 is most likely to be used—and this constitutional cliffhanger is most likely to occur—at the worst possible time.[10]

Who's in Charge?

Section 4 of the Twenty-Fifth Amendment was well intentioned. It reflected years of high-level debate. It was designed specifically to eliminate the problems caused by the inartful drafting of Article II. It covered the extremely sensitive subject of presidential continuity. The drafters were mindful of who would have control while the Section 4 process played out. But even with all these reasons to be careful, Section 4's drafters were not perfect. Some problems with Section 4 are minor,* but the poor drafting of the four-day rule is serious.[11]

First Legal Arguments

President Philips: What can I do?

Chief of Staff Cooper: You just need to send a letter to the Hill saying that you aren't disabled. Merrick and the cabinet have four days to say that you are disabled—if and when they do, Merrick would take over again until Congress decides. A majority of the cabinet needs to come out against you the second time, though, so you should fire the [expletive] who voted against you. As I read Section 4, as soon as you declare you aren't disabled, you are president unless they send that second letter, and if you are president you can fire them before they do that.

Philips: If I fire them, wouldn't their deputies just vote the same way?

Cooper: It doesn't matter, because you have the power to appoint different people as acting secretaries. I've got some reliable folks lined up for that. All the papers are right here.

* As an example, Section 4 has a typo. The first paragraph calls the cabinet "the principal officers of the executive *departments*," but the second paragraph says "department," singular. This error was surely inadvertent, and probably harmless, but such carelessness is unnerving. *See* John D. Feerick, The Twenty-Fifth Amendment 202 n.‡ (2d ed. 1992) (explaining error). Even properly pluralized, there are problems with the phrase "the principal officers of the executive departments." "Principal officer" is a term of art for someone who must be appointed by the president and confirmed by the Senate. Section 4 can thus be read as requiring participation by every executive principal officer (of which there are many dozens), not just the fifteen cabinet secretaries. Article II, drafted more clearly, refers to the cabinet as "the principal Officer in each of the executive Departments." Saying the principal *officer* in *each* of the departments clearly refers to the department heads alone. As with the typo, the legislative intent is perfectly clear here; the common understanding of Section 4 is that it refers to the cabinet. Still, a mischievous textualist could make a case otherwise. *See* Birch Bayh, One Heartbeat Away 232–33 (1968) (endorsing desire for "precise language so that there is no ambiguity whatsoever" in this clause).

Philips: Are you sure about all this, Tom?

Cooper: The Constitution isn't totally clear, but that's how I read it. Anyway, you have nothing to lose. Who knows what Congress will do if they get a hold of this? Why take a chance? Besides, Madame President, taking these official actions is good evidence that you aren't disabled.

Philips: Bring me a pen and I'll sign them. A blue pen.

President Philips's opening argument would be simple. Section 4 explains how she can "resume the powers" of the presidency. When she declares that she is not disabled she retakes power immediately, and when she retakes it, she retakes it. That means she can fire people—who just tried to depose her, after all.[12]

The key is the meaning of "unless" in Section 4: "[W]hen the President transmits . . . [her] written declaration that no inability exists, [she] shall resume the powers and duties of [her] office *unless* the Vice President and a majority of [the cabinet] transmit within four days . . . their written declaration that the President is unable to discharge the powers and duties of [her] office."

The president is interpreting "unless" in the sense of "unless and until." It is like saying, "I will be the driver unless it starts to rain," meaning that I will start out driving, and you will take over if and when it rains. Something happens, and it continues *unless* the condition is satisfied. The vice president's reading of "unless" is like saying, "I shall repossess your car unless you pay your bill within four days." Nothing happens *unless* the condition is satisfied. The vice president's reading seems more natural, but both readings are possible. As detailed in the following pages, smart people have read it the president's way before.

The president could also note that the key clause refers to the "vice president" joining the cabinet to make the second disability declaration. If the vice president were in charge during the waiting period, the drafters should have referred to him instead as the acting president—every other time that the Twenty-Fifth Amendment assigns the powers of the presidency to the vice president, it calls him the acting president.

The vice president could make a similar sort of argument: Section 4 says that after the first declaration of disability, the vice president "immediately" takes over as acting president. By contrast, Section 4 does *not* say that when the president declares her fitness, she "immediately" takes her powers back. This lack of immediacy suggests that the "unless" is purely conditional—if there is a second disability declaration, the president does not give up power; she instead fails to "resume" it.

Although the vice president's textual arguments are stronger, it is undeniable that Section 4 could have been drafted better. In fact, a previous version of Section 4 clearly put the vice president in charge during the waiting period (which was seven days in that version): "Whenever the President makes public announcement in writing that his inability has terminated, he shall resume the discharge of the powers and duties of his office *on the seventh day after* making such announcement, or at such earlier time after such announcement as he and the Vice President may determine." That, the president can say, is what Section 4 would have sounded like if the vice president were meant to stay in charge during the waiting period. The final version of Section 4 could have said it like that, but it didn't, and that's meaningful.[13]

The very next sentence in that earlier draft also would have stopped the president from stacking the cabinet as our President Philips tried to do: "But if the Vice President, with the written approval of a majority of the heads of executive departments *in office at the time of such announcement* [i.e., the president's announcement of her recovery], transmits to the Congress his written declaration that in his opinion the President's inability has not terminated, the Congress shall thereupon consider the issue." Once again, the president can say that there is a way to ensure that the old cabinet votes, and that while this earlier version did it, the drafters consciously chose to get rid of that language in the final version.[14]

As seen in the next section, though, the president probably would not want to trumpet the drafting history of Section 4 too loudly. That history is at the core of the vice president's case, because it makes it abundantly clear that Section 4's creators thought that they were keeping the president out of power during the waiting period. Even as the phrasing changed between drafts, that intention did not.

Legislative Intent

*White House Counsel Keith: Madame President, the legislative history of
Section 4 is clear as a bell. You do not get to come back until this goes through
Congress, unless the cabinet went four days without re-challenging you. But the
cabinet did re-challenge you. I'm sorry, ma'am, but Vice President Merrick is in
charge and you cannot fire anybody.*

*President Philips: [Expletive] the legislative [expletive] history, [expletive]
Merrick, and [expletive] you, you [expletive] traitor [expletive]!*

As the Twenty-Fifth Amendment moved through the Senate, the
language of Section 4 shifted from the construction quoted in the previous
section (the president retakes power if and when the waiting period expires
without a second declaration) to the final version (the president retakes
power "unless" there is a second declaration during the waiting period). But
this edit was meant to make the amendment more concise, not to change its
meaning. The following exchange on the Senate floor, shortly before the
Senate unanimously approved the new language, makes this clear:

Mr. ALLOTT. The President would then send to Congress his written
declaration. Who would be President during the 7 days?

Mr. BAYH. The Vice President, the Acting President. I thank the
Senator from Nebraska for his suggestion. It makes a considerable
difference. . . . Such a provision would cut down the number of times
the power of the Presidency would change. We desire to keep it to a
minimum. . . .

Mr. ALLOTT. To get to the question in another way, so the issue will
be clear, if a Vice President had assumed the duties of acting President,
and the elected President then decided that he wished to state that there
is no inability any longer, it would be 7 days before he could possibly
resume the office of President.

Mr. BAYH. That is correct.

Mr. ALLOTT. There is no question about that. That is the intent.

Mr. BAYH. That is the intent.

The exchange—among several others in both houses—shows that Section
4's intended meaning was completely clear to Senator Bayh (the father of the
Twenty-Fifth Amendment), to Senator Allott, and to the rest of Congress.[15]

After the Senate approved this language, the House of Representatives took up the draft and changed the waiting period to two days, but it too understood that the vice president would retain control during that time. One representative proposed changing the language to restore the president during the waiting period. The proposal failed after a serious debate, in part because of objections that if presidents could regain power immediately, they would be able to fire their cabinets and prevent a second declaration. Sound familiar?[16]

The House and Senate understood completely that Section 4 puts the vice president in charge during the waiting period, and the House consciously rejected specific language that would have changed that. As evidence of legislative intent goes, this is as clear and definitive as it gets. Our hypothetical President Philips is getting Section 4 wrong.

The legislative history also provides some structural evidence, from the juxtaposition of Sections 3 and 4. In Section 3, the president can declare herself disabled and then retake power immediately by declaring that she has recovered. The drafters consciously contrasted Section 4, in which (they thought) a challenged president would have to wait at least four days to retake power. By structuring it this way, the drafters gave the president an incentive to admit that she is disabled and thereby avoid the complicated and unnerving Section 4.[17]

So what could the president argue in the face of such definitive evidence against her reading of Section 4? Indeed, given this legislative history, would a president ever really attempt to take immediate power and fire her cabinet opponents?

She might. In any Section 4 dispute, tensions would be high and time would be of the essence. In quieter times, the administration probably would have prepared Twenty-Fifth Amendment contingency plans, but in an internal struggle like this any such plans could go out the window. The plan would likely focus on direct issues (like assessing medical evidence) anyway and provide little guidance on the arcane constitutional wrinkles at the heart of this chapter. For the unschooled players at the heart of the controversy, the text of Section 4 would be the easy and obvious place to look for answers. The legislative history would not be.

As an example of how limited knowledge can be, and how hard it can be for law to be followed in a crisis, consider the immediate aftermath of the shooting of President Reagan in 1981. The administration was unprepared to discuss transferring power, and "the men gathered in the Situation Room [did not] know what action they were authorized to take or expected to take." Away from the White House (and to no effect), lawyers in the Justice Department studied the legislative history of the Twenty-Fifth Amendment as President Reagan was in surgery. Reagan's White House counsel subsequently prepared a formal disability plan—something all administrations since then have done as well—but nothing is guaranteed. In our case, even though lawyers somewhere in the administration might study Section 4's legislative history, the president's inner circle might not rely on (or even trust) those lawyers any more than they did in 1981.[18]

The text of Section 4 could easily be interpreted the president's way, even by someone who lacks her strong incentives. For example, two legal experts, criticizing the way Section 4 was portrayed inaccurately on the television drama 24, ironically seemed to misread it President Philips's way. One, Professor Peter Shane, wrote that the president "can reclaim his office by providing an immediate certification to Congress of 'no disability,'" and that after this the vice president and his supporters could "re-oust the President" with the second declaration. The other, Gregory Jacob, wrote about how "the President could nullify the Cabinet's decision and reinstate himself simply by declaring himself fit to resume his duties." And Senator Allott (among others) was unsure who would be in charge until Senator Bayh straightened him out.[19]

The president would have responses to the straightening out too. The use of legislative history to interpret texts is controversial, and the president would have some support for discounting it. Some judges, most notably Supreme Court justice Antonin Scalia, argue that the only intent of the drafters that matters is that which they manage to express in the final text; if they meant something else, then they should have said it. Scalia and his ilk have succeeded in reducing judges' use of legislative-history evidence, focusing arguments more on the actual text.[20]

Coming as it did before Scalia's "new textualism," the debate over the Twenty-Fifth Amendment in the 1960s is a stark example of how much legislators relied on legislative-history evidence (which is not to say that they have since stopped). Senator Bayh fully expected that Section 4 would be interpreted according to his stated intent.[21]

In some instances, as in our case, Bayh stated the drafters' intent for the record, as a reply to people confused by ambiguous language. In other cases, though, Bayh used the legislative record to go further and establish intentions that were not drawn from the text at all. For instance, in the prior draft of Section 4 quoted earlier, the vice president could agree with the president to waive the waiting period and let the president return to power immediately. When Section 4 was redrafted, this waiver provision was taken out. Nevertheless, Senator Bayh and others indicated that the vice president could still hand back power early. But this is not supported by the text—nothing there empowers the president and vice president to shorten the waiting period—and it seems inconsistent with the whole idea of the mandatory waiting period.* Senator Bayh's contention to the contrary—in essence saying, "We completely removed that clause, but you should act like it is still there"—is disputable and somewhat frustrating. Even if in practice no one challenged such a waiver, and even if the waiver were legally defensible, this sort of drafting is just asking for trouble.[22]

Admittedly, it is unfair to take Bayh's excessive reliance on legislative history in one place (in which he summoned meaning from beyond the text) and equate it to our less problematic one (in which he used it to resolve an ambiguity in the text). Still, as a senator strongly cautioned Bayh at a key hearing, one should be wary of blithely treating legislative intent—even if it is unequivocal—as though it were actually part of the text.[23]

Later, Senator Albert Gore Sr. tangled with Senator Bayh over another (unrelated) divergence in Section 4 between intent and text. Gore noted that "uncertainty cannot be eliminated by a statement of legislative intent." He argued persuasively for a particular interpretation of the text at odds with Bayh's intent and delayed passage of the amendment to urge a simple fix to

---

* Though it is not what Bayh had in mind, there is a way to abort Section 4's waiting period. The vice president and cabinet can immediately challenge the president's declaration of fitness and send the matter to Congress. Then, they can ask Congress to quickly vote in the *president's* favor, which would restore her to power immediately. In another example of imperfect drafting, Section 4 arguably gives Congress three weeks to reconsider its vote, but the better reading is that a positive vote for the president ends the matter. *See* H.R. Rep. No. 89-554, at 4 (1965) (Conf. Rep.) (expressing this understanding).

the language. Senator Bayh replied that Gore's proposed language ably expressed the intent of the drafters, prompting Gore to harrumph, "If that is what is intended, why could not the conferees write it into the amendment?" An exasperated Senator Bayh (fresh from the weeks-long struggle to get the amendment through a conference committee) argued persuasively that it would be impossible to draft the amendment perfectly, let alone to do it so late in the process. After lots of debate, Bayh won the argument, thus carving the problematic language unchanged into constitutional stone. Gore was right, though: uncertainty is the real enemy here, and overreliance on legislative intent promotes it.[24]

Sort-of-Structural Arguments

White House Counsel Keith: Madame President, you can't retake power for at least four days, and so you can't fire these people to stop them from making a second declaration that you are disabled. If Section 4 let you do that, it would make the whole process pointless.

President Philips: It is pointless. I'm not disabled. I'm the [expletive] president of the United [expletive] States. You can't [expletive] do this to me!

Besides the text (which more or less favors the vice president) and legislative intent (which conclusively favors the vice president), our contenders could also argue about constitutional structure. On balance, the structural arguments favor the vice president's position too.

The vice president has the first, best structural argument, which we already saw discussed in the legislative history: if the president could retake power during the waiting period, she could fire and replace everybody who voted against her and always prevent Congress from considering a dispute.* Since

---

* Nobody knows for sure, and Section 4's text is no help, but Congress probably intended that if a cabinet member is fired and replaced with an acting secretary, the acting secretary gets to vote on the president's disability. *See* H.R. Rep. No. 89-203, at 3 (1965); John D. Feerick, The Twenty-Fifth Amendment 203 (2d ed. 1992) (summarizing legislative intent). *But see* 111 Cong. Rec. 3284 (1965) (statements of Sens. Hart and Bayh) (offering contrary legislative intent); Antonin Scalia, *The Twenty-Fifth Amendment Needs Clarification in Regard to Presidential Succession, in* Amendment

Section 4 is specifically designed to empower Congress to resolve disputes over presidential disability, it would be strange if Section 4 provided a way (and a very destructive one, at that) for one side in the dispute to short-circuit the whole congressional process. Admittedly, the president has the undisputed power to thwart the process by firing her cabinet before—or even during—the vote on the *first* declaration. But the president would not necessarily be "in the loop" enough to do this. With the second declaration, by contrast, she would *always* control the timing and always be able to subvert the process, if her interpretation of Section 4 were correct.[25]

The president can respond that this overstates things, because Section 4 lets Congress designate a group other than the cabinet to declare the president's disability. Congress could choose the "old" cabinet, an independent group, or anyone, really. If Congress waited until the middle of a crisis to do this, the embattled president could veto it, but Congress could override that veto with the same two-thirds majorities it would need to declare the president disabled. Thus, the president could claim that she is not untouchable under her interpretation of Section 4. Nevertheless, under the president's interpretation, Congress would *have* to jump through all these complicated hoops; under the vice president's reading of Section 4, none of this would be necessary.

The vice president's second argument (which also appeared in the legislative history) is that under the president's interpretation, control of the White House would change hands three or four times in a dispute. First the vice president would take over (first declaration), then the president would come back (presidential response), then the vice president would retake power (second declaration), and then, if she won in Congress, the president would be restored. By contrast, under the vice president's reading of Section 4, there would just be one or two transfers of power in a dispute. The vice president would take over (from the first declaration onward), and the president

XXV: Presidential Disability and Succession 109, 113 (Sylvia Engdahl ed., 2010) (noting text's ambiguity). If Congress is not in session, however, the president could fill the cabinet vacancy with a recess appointment, and that person would have a stronger claim to a vote than a mere acting secretary would. *See* 111 Cong. Rec. 15,382 (1965) (statement of Sen. Kennedy of New York) (mentioning recess-appointment possibility).

would retake power if and when Congress failed to back the vice president. The point of Section 4 is to provide for smooth transfers of power, and one or two transfers is smoother than three or four.[26]

The president can offer a different sort of structural argument. She can say that, as president, she deserves a strong presumption of fitness, especially if she has the wherewithal to declare herself able to return. It should be hard, not easy, for the vice president and cabinet to cast aside a duly elected president against her will. This presumption of presidential fitness is reflected in Section 4's requirement of two-thirds majorities in both houses to declare the president disabled. Nevertheless, Section 4 says what it says. The drafters preferred leaving the vice president in charge during any dispute, because the president's fitness would be in doubt but the vice president's (presumably) would not. While it should be hard to depose a president, it shouldn't be any harder than Section 4 makes it.[27]

Another argument supporting the president would be that, during the four-day waiting period, the country has more to fear from a usurping vice president than from a disabled president. A doddering or unstable president—of which we have had several—would be dangerous, but she would be limited by her subordinates' unwillingness to follow her orders, or by her need to keep firing and replacing them. By contrast, a power-mad vice president could do a lot of damage during the crucial hours and days before Congress could end the struggle. But if palace coups are more dangerous, they are also much less likely (the disloyal vice president needs the cabinet to be disloyal too, for one thing), which diminishes their risk significantly. Section 4's drafters considered this and, even if they used imprecise language, consciously decided that disabled presidents clinging to power were a greater hazard than usurping vice presidents. Besides, even under the president's view, a bad vice president would have plenty of time as acting president, both before the president's declaration of fitness and (if there is a second declaration) while Congress deliberates. People are perfectly entitled to prefer having the president in charge during the waiting period, but that hardly means that Section 4 requires it.[28]

The president has little to gain from moving beyond the text of Section 4. The legislative history severely weakens her case, and these structural arguments (some of which are really just dressed-up policy preferences) undermine it even more. One would hope that the president would realize this and not bring the country into this mess in the first place. But there is one overarching practical consideration that could egg her on: "I am the president, and people are trying to depose me." In a fast-paced, high-pressure situation, that notion would mean more to her than any sort of legal argument ever would.

Who Decides?

Vice President Merrick: Let's do this. We'll go to Congress and argue that President Philips isn't in power, and that our second declaration is valid. Hopefully they'll agree with us quickly and then agree that she's disabled.

Attorney General: Those congressional [expletives] don't do anything quickly. Let's get an injunction. I trust the courts to get it right—and we are right—more than I trust Congress. And even if Congress would get it right, a court would do it faster. With a court order behind us, Congress will follow along. Everyone will see that we're following the law, and that the old lady isn't.

An important side question is, who decides who is in charge during the waiting period—Congress, the courts, or both? The answer turns on the complicated "political-question doctrine."

Before the Twenty-Fifth Amendment, both the courts and Congress could have claimed to be the proper forum to sort out a dispute over presidential disability. If a vice president had tried to take over, claiming that the president was disabled, and the president had claimed that she was just fine, either one of them could have taken the matter to court for a quick resolution, via a quo warranto action. But if one of the claimants had presented some official act to Congress (like a veto, or an appointment that required Senate confirmation), one or both houses would have had a chance to weigh in on the legitimacy of the putative president. Whichever body decided first, courts or Congress, the other forum likely would have deferred to its decision.[29]

Section 4 of the Twenty-Fifth Amendment seemed to change this by designating the House and Senate as the only deciders. But even as Section 4 simplified the settlement of disagreements about presidential disability, it opened up potential complications like the one in this chapter. In our fictional President Philips's case, the House and Senate would have to make a "jurisdictional" determination. If the president's interpretation of Section 4 were correct, she would be in charge, there would be no second declaration of disability, and there would be nothing for Congress to decide. If the vice president's interpretation were correct, *he* would be in charge and the matter would be properly before Congress. Congress would need to decide this preliminary issue.

To win on the jurisdictional question, the vice president would need simple majorities in both houses; he'd lose if either house rejected his claim at this stage. (This should not be too daunting, given that he would eventually need two-thirds majorities in both houses to win on the merits.) Unfortunately, under the terms of Section 4, this preliminary debate could take a while. When a second declaration is sent to Congress, Congress must assemble within two days, but it can take up to twenty-one days to rule on the president's disability (if it holds a vote at all; Section 4 does not require one). Congress would first need to hear arguments from both sides and debate the jurisdictional issue. To be sure, Congress would have every incentive to be quick, but it would not be a simple question, and Congress is not known for holding efficient debates.[30]

All this would give the two contenders—and especially the vice president—a big incentive to turn to the judiciary. While Section 4 takes the ultimate issue (is the president disabled?) away from the courts, the preliminary issue (is the president in charge during the waiting period?) might be fair game for them.*

Even so, the court still might declare this to be a "political question" and refuse to take the case. A case presents a political question if the Constitution assigns it exclusively to Congress or the president (the "political" branches) to decide instead of the courts. The simplest way for this to happen is by "textual commission": the Constitution can assign a matter to the political

---

* With different facts, the waiting-period question might not get to Congress *or* the courts. Imagine that the vice president and cabinet invoke Section 4. The president later announces that she is not disabled and retakes power immediately, but nobody challenges her. In such a case, the president would have taken power back too soon, and the precedent would further muddy the waters.

branches explicitly, in its text. Examples include the provisions that each house is "the Judge of the Elections, Returns and Qualifications of its own Members," and that "[t]he Senate shall have the sole Power to try all Impeachments." Section 4 commits the final determination of the president's disability to Congress this way; the problem is that it doesn't expressly commit disputes over Section 4's *initial procedures* to Congress. The former power might imply the latter one, but who knows?[31]

Political questions are also found when a case is purely a matter of policy, as opposed to a legal question, or when it is important to respect the decisions of the political branches for the sake of the separation of powers, finality, or uniformity. But the question of who is in charge during the waiting period is a matter of interpreting Section 4—a bona fide legal issue, not merely a matter of policy. As for the separation of powers, the court would be doing something squarely within its job description—interpreting the Constitution—and not intruding on Congress's or the president's authority here (unless, as mentioned in the last paragraph, one interprets the Twenty-Fifth Amendment as committing the resolution of disputes about its procedures to Congress). Finally, if the courts act quickly, before Congress does, it is the *courts* that would represent finality and uniformity. A definitive court decision would also avoid the possibility of an ambiguous "split decision" in Congress, in which one house agrees with the president's reading of Section 4, but the other one doesn't, and the president wins by default without really settling the issue. Indeed, members of Congress might be happy to leave this to the courts.[32]

The courts still might declare this to be a political question. If the courts were confident that Congress could act swiftly and decisively, and especially if Congress had begun to do so, the courts might want to avoid interfering. Then again, recent experience (including *Bush v. Gore*) shows that the Supreme Court feels confident in its role as the ultimate constitutional arbiter, and as a provider of stability. Other than "textual commissions," political questions seem rooted more in the courts' self-restraint than in definitive constitutional requirements, and it is unclear how much of that self-restraint is left.[33]

If they did take the case, the courts would almost certainly rule in favor of the vice president, for all the reasons argued previously. Then the process would move forward and Congress would decide whether the president is disabled or not. If, for some reason, the courts instead ruled in the president's favor, Congress might be prevented from getting the case, but at least the reason would be that the president had effectively rebutted the notion that she could not exercise her powers. Alternatively, Congress could try to overrule the court, but that's a chapter for a whole other book; if Congress really believed that the president was out of line, it would be easier at that point just to impeach and remove her.[34]

What to Do?

In some ways, the Twenty-Fifth Amendment refutes the notion, expressed elsewhere in this book, that it is pointless to call for a constitutional amendment to fix some structural imperfection in the Constitution. The amendment represents an impressive effort at doing just that. Still, Section 4 is not perfect, as even the main sponsor of the amendment, Birch Bayh, has written. It just isn't plausible to imagine Congress willingly charging back into the amendment process here. As several commentators have opined, any such attempt would likely create more problems than it solved. This section will thus resist the temptation to draft a new constitutional amendment and concentrate instead on more realistic suggestions for patching up Section 4.[35]

The following suggestions would clarify and reinforce the vice president's control during the waiting period. The reason is not that vice-presidential control is the best solution—that point is debatable. Rather, it is because Section 4 is *supposed* to establish vice-presidential control. The goal here is to achieve that purpose more effectively.

One way is for Congress to use its Section 4 legislative power to designate a group other than the cabinet to vote on the president's disability. Lots of discussion, during the amendment's drafting and since then, has focused on finding groups that would identify presidential disabilities more effectively than cabinet members, whom some commentators criticize as skittish and medically ignorant. More to the point of this chapter, Congress could choose decision makers who would reduce the risk of a constitutional crisis. One good way comes from an earlier draft of Section 4; Congress can simply designate the cabinet in place when the president declares her fitness. That way, Congress could stop the president from using her firing power to keep the case out of Congress, even if she somehow managed to retake power during the four-day waiting period. To be safer still, and to also prevent the *vice* president from firing people to stack the second vote, Congress could require that the participants in the second vote just be the same ones from the first vote (perhaps with an exception if much time has passed).[36]

Congress can use more subtle means to bolster the proper reading of Section 4. For instance, it could legislate that during the waiting period, the deciding group is one that is convened or certified in some way by the "acting president." This would communicate that, as far as Congress is concerned, the vice president remains acting president throughout the waiting period. To be sure, a president who tried to take control during the waiting period could challenge this law as unconstitutional. But such a law would add weight to the other side of the scale—especially if the president signed the law, assuming that it was being legislated during calmer times—and it would foster awareness of the correct interpretation of Section 4.[37]

By far the best solution is for the president to act to bury the "bad" interpretation. Every president since Reagan has promulgated a detailed plan for when and how to follow the Twenty-Fifth Amendment, should the need arise. These plans are kept classified, but some parts of them could be made public. One good part to publicize would be a declaration that Section 4 puts the vice president in charge during the waiting period. This would not *legally* bind the president (let alone bind her successors), but it would *inform* everyone. As such, it would make it less likely that a future president or her staff, in the heat of the moment, would pick up the Constitution and read Section 4 the way that our President Philips did. Similarly, the Office of Legal Counsel in the Department of Justice could help settle matters with a loud and clear public opinion affirming the proper reading of Section 4. Such declarations would foster consensus and understanding and greatly reduce the chances of this constitutional cliffhanger. By removing the possibility of a meltdown like the one in this chapter, it could also make vice presidents less reluctant to wade into Section 4's waters in cases where they should act.[38]

The legal arguments in this chapter are one sided. Danger looms anyway. If the Twenty-Fifth Amendment were drafted more clearly, so that its intentions were better reflected by its text, this wouldn't be an issue. But it isn't, and they aren't, so it is—at least until a president steps in to provide the simple fix outlined here.

4

The Line of Succession Controversy

The United States is deeply divided over the war. Everyone agreed that we needed to fight back when Ruritania attacked our bases, but after two years of intensive combat, things are not going well. Addressing the nation, President Joanna Lewis announces her intention to seek a negotiated settlement. The half of the country that agrees with her breathes a sigh of relief.

The other half boils with rage. Responding to the president, Speaker of the House Peg Wilton says, "We are losing this war—not because our cause is hopeless, but because we have a cowardly commander in chief. We should never surrender to fascist aggression." "Coward" is a mild epithet compared to what other hawks call President Lewis.

Complicating matters is that a few weeks ago, the vice president suffered a fatal heart attack. President Lewis nominated a candidate to fill the vacancy, but the hawks in Congress have stalled the vote. They are motivated by their distaste for the nominee's unsurprisingly dovish position on the war, but everyone notices that while the vice presidency is vacant, Speaker Wilton is next in line for the presidency (followed by the president pro tempore of the Senate, and then members of the cabinet, starting with the secretary of state).

As President Lewis arrives at a public event one morning, an assassin detonates a huge bomb, killing the president and dozens of others. In a homemade video produced before the assassination, the bomber decries "the coward Lewis" and announces his intention to kill Lewis so that the stalwart Wilton will become president and continue the war. Within two hours of the assassination, the video has saturated television and the Internet.

The assassin seemingly gets his wish. Wilton condemns the assassination in the most strident terms, obviously, but she takes an oath of office that morning as acting *president. Her political position is tenuous. Supporters of the martyred President Lewis blame Speaker Wilton for fueling the rhetoric that led to Lewis's assassination, and for her role in stalling to keep the vice presidency vacant. In other words, they feel as though the country has just suffered a coup d'état. They latch onto a legal argument that, just hours earlier, had been an academic one: that it is unconstitutional for the succession law to include members of Congress. Wilton's opponents argue—with the support of several prominent legal experts—that the dovish secretary of state, John Allen, is the legitimate acting president.*

Secretary Allen decides to contest Wilton's claim to the presidency. He too takes an oath of office as acting president and, without using force, he assumes physical control of the White House. "The struggle over our war policy has been ugly, but it's a political struggle," he says in a national address from the Oval Office. "In America, we don't settle political questions by mass murder."

It has only been ten hours since the assassination—a shocking and surreal day. No violence has broken out yet, but it feels like only a matter of time before it does. No one is in the mood to compromise, and control of the government and the military hangs in the balance as Allen and Wilton vie for control.

EVERY AMERICAN SCHOOLCHILD LEARNS THAT the Speaker of the House and the president pro tempore of the Senate (PPT) follow the vice president in the line of succession. Fictional portrayals of presidential disasters often draw on this rule too. But these versions of presidential succession typically ignore a crucial issue that has been worrying important politicians and legal scholars for over two hundred years: it's constitution-ally problematic for the Speaker and PPT to be in the line of succession. Not all legal experts agree on this point, but most of them do, and their criti-cism is harsh. They call the succession law "the single most dangerous statute in the United States Code," "intolerable," "disastrous," and "an acci-dent waiting to happen." Even if one thinks that these experts are wrong, their arguments cast a dark shadow of uncertainty over presidential succession.[1]

Uncertainty and presidential succession are a frightening combination, especially in an era marked by terrorist attacks. One congressional report worried that if a Speaker or PPT ever assumed the presidency, it would "lead to [a] contest over it that would disquiet the nation, unsettle business, and disturb the peace of the country." Even if this theoretical legal disagreement did not necessarily spark a full-blown constitutional crisis, the potential to "disquiet the nation" would be there, and for no good reason. Congress could remove this threat very easily, if only it were so inclined.[2]

Succession Law History

The Constitution puts the vice president first in line for the presidency but leaves it to Congress to legislate the line of succession after that: "Congress may by Law provide for the Case of Removal, Death, Resignation or Inability, both of the President and Vice President, declaring what Officer shall then act as President, and such Officer shall act accordingly, until the Disability be removed, or a President shall be elected."[3]

The first time Congress passed a succession law, in the 1790s, it became entangled in the constitutional thicket featured in this chapter. These problems are avoidable; between 1886 and 1947, the succession law excluded congressional leaders. But in 1947, Congress knowingly revived the controversy.

The 1792 Law

In the 1790s, Congress's attempt to legislate a line of succession foundered over politics. An early choice to follow the vice president was the secretary of state. But the secretary of state was Thomas Jefferson, who was a bitter rival of another possible choice, treasury secretary Alexander Hamilton. Primarily to keep Jefferson (and then Hamilton) out of the line of succession, the 1792 statute compromised and put the PPT of the Senate next in line, followed by the Speaker of the House.[4]

Most of the members of the House of Representatives who had been delegates to the Constitutional Convention objected to this version of the succession law after it passed the Senate. One significant part of their objection seems to have been that the Constitution limits the line of succession to "officers," and that, as James Madison later put it, "[i]t may be questioned whether [the PPT and Speaker] are *officers*, in the constitutional sense." The

House voted instead to designate the secretary of state as the next in line. But the Senate stood firm and rejected these constitutional concerns. Its precise reasoning is unknown, because the Senate's debates and votes were secret; by contrast, the political desire to slight Thomas Jefferson is clear from other sources. Back in the House, most of the former convention delegates objected again, but enough of their colleagues relented that the Senate version carried the day.[5]

The 1886 Law

The 1792 act was never used during its ninety-four-year run, but the vice presidency was vacant for a quarter of that period, and some practical problems with the succession law emerged alongside the constitutional ones. One arose when Vice President Johnson became president after President Lincoln was assassinated. When President Johnson was impeached in 1868, avoiding conviction by only one vote in the Senate, PPT Benjamin Wade had a tremendous conflict of interest—he was a leader in the effort to oust Johnson, and he would have become acting president had it succeeded.[6]

In September 1881, Vice President Arthur became president upon the assassination of President Garfield. (As echoed in this chapter's opening, Garfield's assassin declared his intent to make Arthur president, because he preferred Arthur's "Stalwart" political faction to Garfield's.) When Garfield died, Congress was in a long recess and, as was often the case, had not selected a PPT or Speaker. For three weeks, President Arthur had no backup—if he had died, there would have been no president for a while. In 1885, after President Cleveland succeeded Arthur, Vice President Thomas Hendricks died at a time when there was no PPT or Speaker, leaving Cleveland with no backup.[7]

With the Johnson, Arthur, and Cleveland precedents in mind, and still very concerned about the constitutional problems with the 1792 act, Congress passed a new succession statute in 1886. The new law took the PPT and Speaker out and replaced them with the members of the cabinet, in order of the establishment of their departments, starting with the secretary of state.[8]

The 1947 Law and the Current Situation

When Vice President Truman took over after President Roosevelt's death in 1945, he was uncomfortable with the 1886 act. Cabinet succession meant that Truman could potentially appoint his own successor, and he felt strongly that this was undemocratic. In 1947, Truman spurred Congress to pass the current succession law. It places the elected Speaker and PPT at the front of the line, this time with the Speaker first. The secretary of state and the rest of the cabinet are next in line but can be "bumped" once a Speaker or PPT qualifies.[9]

The bill sped through the House in 1945. In the little time they had, the bill's opponents noted the constitutional problems with Speaker succession, but there was no serious engagement of the issue. After "perfunctory consideration," the Speaker-first bill passed the House "amid cheers for [Speaker] Sam Rayburn." After a more serious constitutional debate, the Senate killed the House bill. But in 1947, the Republicans had won control of Congress and discovered an upside to having congressional leaders next in line for the presidency. After a debate that "ignored or dismissed" the important constitutional questions that had stopped the bill in the previous session, the Senate passed an essentially identical version, by a strong party-line vote. The House passed it easily, as it had two years earlier.[10]

The 1947 act thus reintroduced the constitutional problems of the 1792 act (and added some serious practical ones). These problems did not pass unnoticed, but just as the partisan Congress brushed off the constitutional arguments in 1792, the identical objections were rebuffed in 1947, to the extent that they were engaged at all.[11]

Like its two predecessor statutes, the 1947 act has never been invoked.* The Twenty-Fifth Amendment, ratified in 1967, allows presidents to fill vice-presidential vacancies, making a double vacancy much less likely (and superseding President Truman's objection to presidents appointing their unelected successors). It passed just in time; in 1973–74, when Vice President Agnew and President Nixon both resigned, the amendment elevated Gerald Ford to the vice presidency and presidency. Without the

---

* The law has, however, been updated to include new cabinet positions. *See* 3 U.S.C.A. § 19 (West, Westlaw through 2006 amendments) (listing amendments).

Twenty-Fifth Amendment, the presidency would have passed to Speaker of the House Carl Albert.[12]

Nevertheless, potential problems remained. The president and vice president could still suffer some combination of death, resignation, removal, and disability in rapid succession. If they ever did, the practical and constitutional concerns about the 1947 act might split the country in two. Indeed, some members of Congress still worry about the constitutional and practical problems with the succession law, just as their predecessors did in 1792 and 1947. Recent congressional hearings demonstrated a rough—if not unanimous—consensus among legal experts that the current law is unconstitutional. Even if the consensus is wrong, it could foment a crisis if the law is ever invoked, and so Congress should fix the law to eliminate the danger. But it hasn't.[13]

The Legal Arguments

Members of Congress and leading legal scholars have known literally for centuries that it is unconstitutional to put the Speaker in the line of succession. The Constitution clearly states that only "officers" (like me) can be in line, and the Constitution makes it just as clear that members of Congress and their leaders aren't "officers."

Under cover of this illegitimate law, because of her opposition to President Lewis's peace plan, Peg Wilton has effectively staged a coup today—keeping the vice presidency vacant, fueling the murderous rage that killed our president, and now claiming the presidency herself so that she can stop the peace talks.

Even if this weren't unconstitutional, it would violate the democratic traditions on which this country is based. But it is unconstitutional, and we can—we must—resist and reject this illegal takeover. I am the constitutionally legitimate successor to President Lewis. I am the acting president of the United States.

—SECRETARY ALLEN

Some people have raised theoretical objections to the succession law today. These arguments were considered and rejected in our Founding Fathers' generation, and they were considered and rejected again by President Truman and

Congress in 1947. As Speaker, I was an officer of the House of Representatives, and like every Speaker since 1947, I served with the knowledge that I might have to step in as president.
—SPEAKER WILTON

Article II, Section 1 of the Constitution authorizes Congress to declare what "officer" acts as president when both the president and vice president are unable to serve. The current succession statute places the Speaker of the House and the PPT of the Senate up front, followed by the secretary of state and the rest of the cabinet. The crux of the secretary of state's constitutional argument is that, unlike cabinet members, the Speaker and PPT are not "officers," and therefore the Constitution forbids them from being in the line of succession. That would logically make the secretary of state the acting president. It is a good argument with a long and distinguished pedigree. The Speaker has a decent counterargument, but her main strengths in this struggle lie elsewhere.[14]

Who Are "Officers"?

For the secretary of state, the argument begins with the Constitution's Incompatibility Clause, which provides that "no Person holding any Office under the United States, shall be a Member of either House during his Continuance in Office." In other words, you cannot be a member of Congress and hold a federal "office" at the same time. Members of Congress thus are not "officers." This is a core principle of the separation-of-powers doctrine in the Constitution, and a distinct rejection of the English parliamentary system.[15]

The Constitution distinguishes members of Congress from officers "of" and "under" the United States in other places as well. For instance, a member of the electoral college cannot be a "Senator or Representative, *or* Person holding an Office of Trust or Profit under the United States." Similarly, the Fourteenth Amendment refers to people who have "taken an oath, as a member of Congress, *or* as an officer of the United States." There are several more such examples.[16]

In other areas, the Constitution is less direct but is still helpful to the secretary of state. The Appointments Clause explains that the president appoints

"Officers of the United States," with Senate confirmation. "Inferior" officers can be appointed by the president without Senate confirmation, by heads of departments, or by courts. But members of Congress are not appointed in any of these ways; they are elected as provided in Article I and the Seventeenth Amendment. Relatedly, the president commissions "all the Officers of the United States." She does not commission members of Congress. Finally, the president, vice president, and "all civil Officers of the United States" are subject to the impeachment process. Members of Congress are not.[17]

There are some other constitutional references to officers and offices that shed no light on the question, but that, by the same token, do not undermine the impression set by the examples mentioned here.[18]

The Speaker has two main counterarguments to all this. The first, which was very effective in both 1792 and 1947, is "officers shmofficers"—many people simply do not care whether the Speaker and PPT are officers of the United States or not.* When opponents pointed to the constitutional evidence, cited here, distinguishing members of Congress from officers of the United States, some proponents simply brushed them off. One sponsor of the 1947 act, recognizing the serious constitutional dispute here, said that if Congress simply stated that the Speaker and PPT were officers of the United States, this would solve the problem. In a justiciable constitutional dispute, though, no court would ignore the Constitution and simply accept "Congress said so" as a winning argument.[19]

More serious, but still not adequate, is the argument that Speaker/PPT succession is constitutional because of its venerable pedigree—it was invented by an early Congress and signed by George Washington—and its subsequent approval. This sort of deference to history is understandable, but it would be more defensible if it were based on true premises. Sponsors of the

---

* In the case of the Twentieth Amendment, this view is justified. Ratified in 1933, that amendment gives Congress the power to decide who acts as president if something happens to both the president-elect and vice president elect before Inauguration Day. It specifically lets Congress choose which "person" would be in charge instead of which "officer." U.S. Const. amend. XX, § 3; H.R. Rep. No. 77-61, at 3 (1941) (noting "person" language). Earlier drafts of the amendment said "officer," though, and there is no indication that the amendment's drafters realized that they were enacting such a distinction when they changed it to "person."

1947 act noted that the 1792 act featured PPT and Speaker succession, and they argued that if an early Congress thought it was constitutional, it probably is. But this neglects the partisan reasons for the 1792 act, and the strong constitutional objections voiced at the time. (Bizarrely, one prominent representative in 1947 denied there had been *any* constitutional objections to the 1792 act.) Similarly, advocates in 1947 ignored the prominent role these constitutional concerns played in the genesis of the 1886 act. Others misused a Supreme Court decision that they wrongly said established that members of Congress are "officers of the United States" under the Constitution. Moreover, even without all these misrepresentations, the fact is that Speaker succession has never actually been tested in court, let alone approved there.[20]

The best argument for the Speaker, first made in 1792 by Elbridge Gerry, points out that the Speaker and PPT are officers of *Congress*. There is something to this. The constitutional clauses cited in this chapter, in which officers are distinguished from members of Congress, always refer to offices and officers as "of the United States" or "under the United States." But the Succession Clause opens the succession to all "officers," not just "officers of the United States." Arguing that all members of Congress are "officers" would take things too far, but the Speaker and the PPT *are* constitutionally created officers of their respective legislative chambers, and that is good enough.[21]

The text of the Constitution provides some support. Its very first use of the word "officer" is when it provides that "the House of Representatives shall chuse their Speaker and other Officers." The Speaker clearly is an officer of the House. A similar clause, following the designation of the vice president of the United States as the president of the Senate, directs the Senate to "chuse their other Officers, and also a President pro tempore." The PPT might not be an officer of the Senate—the clause says "other officers, and *also* a PPT," not "other officers *including* a PPT"—but in parallel to the Speaker, the PPT might count as an officer of the Senate, and the Senate has treated him as such.[22]

Gerry's reading has some flaws, though. First, there is evidence that "officers" in the Succession Clause means "officers of the United States." An earlier draft of the Constitution referred to "officers of the United States" in the Succession Clause, not just "officers." That language was sent to the Committee of Style, which changed it to just "officers." But the Committee of Style was just that—a committee of style. Its changes to the text were not meant to be substantive and, in this case, were apparently not even discussed by the Convention. Second, the Framers specifically rejected legislative succession when they created the vice presidency. Initially, the design was for Congress to elect the president, and for his backup to be the leader of the Senate; but the Framers rejected this model in favor of having the independent electoral college select both the president and his understudy.[23]

Even if the Committee of Style had made a substantive change, it seems unlikely that lopping "of the United States" from "officers" was meant to bring in congressional leaders in particular (as opposed to, say, state officers). From the start, congressional "officers" have included the Speaker and the PPT, but the "other officers"—the House clerk and Senate secretary, the sergeants-at-arms, chaplains, doorkeepers, and so on—have been nonmembers. Gerry's reading thus produces the odd hypothesis that the Committee of Style made a momentous but stealthy alteration that opened up the line of presidential succession to the Senate doorkeeper, but not to the Senate majority leader.[24]

Resignation, Incompatibility, and the Separation of Powers

If the president and vice president are either gone or disabled, and the Speaker meets the Constitution's presidential age, citizenship, and residency requirements, the succession law provides that the Speaker "shall, upon [her] resignation as Speaker and as Representative in Congress, act as President." Similarly, if things get past the Speaker, the PPT "shall, upon his resignation as President pro tempore and as Senator, act as President."

This resignation requirement is awkward. The Succession Clause (*"such Officer shall act accordingly*, until the Disability be removed, or a President shall be elected"*) seems to suggest that the acting president is a current officer on temporary assignment, not a former officer. This was the common understanding—by both sides—before the 1947 act, and it still suggests itself. Picture a Speaker who becomes acting president. She resigns from the speakership and the House and takes the presidential oath. The next week a foreign reporter asks her, "How did you come to be acting president?" The former Speaker answers, "Because the Speaker of the House acts as president when the president and vice president are disabled." Then the reporter asks, "So why are you acting president? Isn't Veeblefester the Speaker now?"[25]

Admittedly, the Succession Clause can be read more liberally; perhaps it means to say, "Such [ex-]Officer shall act accordingly." Even if the Constitution permits it, though, resignation is very clumsy. If the real president only has a temporary disability, the ex-Speaker would serve briefly and then not get her old congressional seat or her speakership back. But—here's the point—Congress didn't require the Speaker to resign because it's a good idea, it required the Speaker to resign because the *Constitution* apparently requires it. If the Speaker did not resign and attempted to serve as president and Speaker at the same time, this could violate the Incompatibility Clause mentioned a few pages ago: "no Person holding any Office under the United States, shall be a Member of either House during his Continuance in Office." Even putting the Incompatibility Clause aside—the Speaker might quibble about whether an acting president "holds" the office*—it is hard to imagine a more stunning violation of the separation of powers than for the nation's chief executive and legislative leaders to be the same person.[26]

These very same considerations arose when Congress included the PPT and Speaker in the first succession law in 1792. Soon after the law passed, James Madison noted a Catch-22 argument: if the Speaker/PPT stayed in office while acting as president, the two "incompatible functions" would be combined, but if he left office to act as president, he would no longer be an

---

* Seth Tillman has argued that the presidency is not an "office under the United States." If Tillman is right, then there is no Incompatibility Clause problem with the Speaker or PPT simultaneously serving as president. *See* Seth Barrett Tillman, *Why Our Next President May Keep His or Her Senate Seat,* 4 Duke J. Const. L. & Pub. Pol'y 107 (2009) (arguing that elected offices are not "under the United States"); Seth Barrett Tillman & Steven G. Calabresi, Debate, *The Great Divorce: The Current Understanding of Separation of Powers and the Original Meaning of the Incompatibility Clause,* 157 U. Pa. L. Rev. PENNumbra 134, 137–40, 146–53 (2008). For strong contrary views, see Tillman & Calabresi, *supra,* at 141–45, 154–59 (response to Tillman by Steven Calabresi); Saikrishna Bangalore Prakash, *Why the Incompatibility Clause Applies to the Office of President,* 4 Duke J. Const. L. & Pub. Pol'y 143 (2009) (responding directly to Tillman, *supra*). In any case, Tillman's argument does not speak directly to the issue at the heart of this chapter: whether the Speaker and PPT count as "officers" in the Succession Clause.

officer qualified to act as president. The 1792 law got past the Catch-22 by dismissing the former problem, and the current law gets past it by dismissing the latter. In either case, though, having the Speaker and PPT in the line of succession causes some constitutional discomfort.[27]

Conclusion

As a legal matter, the secretary of state has a strong case. If nothing else, putting the Speaker and PPT in the line of succession clashes with the rest of the constitutional structure. The Speaker's arguments are not legally frivolous—they should be more than enough to satisfy anybody inclined to support her for other reasons. The problem is, they are not strong enough on their own to provide the *certainty* needed to head off our potential disaster. Only practical considerations could do that.

Practical Considerations

A Bird in the Hand

> Some people disagree with the policies that I intend to pursue as acting president. But the continuity of the presidency is more important than what the polls say about any one policy issue. We have clear succession laws, and we follow them, because the alternative is that the awesome powers of the presidency—including the command of our military in the middle of a war—are up in the air. That would be unacceptable.
>
> Today's horrible tragedy has been disheartening to anyone who loves this country. We cannot let these foul murders tear our nation apart. My foremost goal as acting president is to bring us together at this difficult time. One thing that we have always agreed on is respect for the rule of law. Right now, that means that Secretary Allen must stand down.
>
> —SPEAKER WILTON

Most of the cliffhangers in this book are supposed to be close calls. In this chapter, though, there is a scholarly consensus that the Speaker's argument is weaker than the secretary of state's. Therefore, there must be something *else* strong on the Speaker's side. And there is: the succession law. Obviously, as a legal matter, it is not enough that the Speaker has the statute behind her—the point of the Constitution is to void statutes that conflict with it, and the whole basis of the secretary of state's argument is that the succession law is unconstitutional. As a *practical* matter, though, it would make a big difference to the Speaker to have the statute on her side.

The purpose of a detailed succession law is to provide swift, certain continuity of government. This is no trivial matter. It is not exaggerating much to say that the fate of the world could rest on minute-to-minute control of the presidency. Having two people fighting for control—over the government, the military, or physical custody of the White House—is a truly horrifying prospect.[28]

That is precisely why Congress should remove the Speaker and PPT from the line of succession: to eliminate constitutional doubt. But until and unless that happens, the Speaker has the important advantage of having a real live statute on her side. The succession law is a bird in the hand; citing it, the Speaker could take office immediately and easily find someone to administer the oath of office. The secretary of state would face a heavy burden of proof.

As discussed previously, the succession law is three generations old now and has acquired a patina of legitimacy over the decades. Moreover, the principle of Speaker and PPT succession dates back to the 1792 act, passed by lawmakers who had just lived through the Constitution's ratification, and who therefore have some extra credibility on such questions (even if, as we have seen, they shouldn't). All this would give courts—and thus the secretary of state—some pause. If the situation were extreme enough to overcome this natural reluctance, the secretary of state could still challenge the law in court, but he would have to establish that the law is unconstitutional. Even if his constitutional argument carried the day, it could take a while for the courts to say so. The secretary might seek a preliminary injunction, but even that could take too long. The quick alternative for the secretary would be to use extra-legal methods—like taking over the White House—but that would open the secretary up to charges of being lawless, or even treasonous.

Circumstances might change the secretary's situation. The opening scenario in this chapter was designed to make the secretary's practical position better and expose the Speaker's inherent conflicts of interest. Perhaps more importantly, in such a tremendously volatile situation, the courts might do anything. By contrast, if it were peacetime, the vice presidency were vacant, the president were sedated for a routine colonoscopy, and the Speaker took over for three hours with her blessing, the secretary of state would not look very good barreling in to contest the presidency.[29]

One famous case underlines all this. In the confusion following the attempt on President Reagan's life in 1981, Secretary of State Haig famously stated: "Constitutionally, gentlemen, you have the president, the vice president and the secretary of state in that order, and should the president decide he wants to transfer the helm to the vice president, he will do so. He has not done that. As of now, I am in control here, in the White House, pending return of the vice president and in close touch with him. If something came up, I would check with him, of course." Haig probably meant only that he was physically "minding the store" pending the vice president's return, not that he was assuming the constitutional powers and duties of the presidency. After all, he noted that the president was still president, and that the vice president was being kept in the loop. But by using the word "constitutionally," and ignoring the Speaker and PPT, Haig came across as a power grabber at a very inopportune moment. If, as Reagan lay bleeding, Haig had said, "Constitutionally, gentlemen, you have the president, the vice president and the secretary of state in that order, *because the law putting the Speaker of the House and president pro tempore of the Senate in line is unconstitutional*," he would have seemed even worse.[30]

Unless conditions are just so, the secretary of state would not challenge the Speaker, regardless of the strength of the constitutional arguments against Speaker succession. Then, the uncontested transfer to the Speaker would provide a precedent and make it much less likely that anyone would ever challenge the succession law after that. An analogy: When President Harrison died and Vice President Tyler succeeded him, Tyler asserted that he was president, not merely acting president. This was controversial, and contested, but eventually Congress acceded. Subsequent vice presidents assumed the title of president without controversy, and the Tyler precedent was eventually enshrined in the Twenty-Fifth Amendment.[31]

On the other hand, if conditions *are* just so . . .

Practical Problems with Speaker Succession

President Truman was right about a lot of things, but not this. Why would the Constitution allow Congress to exalt itself in the line of succession? Why would it allow such a jarring break in continuity and party control?
—PRO-ALLEN PUNDIT

The current succession law sprang from President Truman's personal preferences. Truman saw the Speaker as the elected leader of the popularly elected House, and the secretary of state as a mere appointee. Truman disliked the idea of a president designating his own successor. But Truman's points are disputable, and he overlooked some problems with Speaker succession.[32]

The Speaker is an elected national leader, but her election is not quite as "national" as Truman said. Technically, the Speaker represents only one House district. Moreover, as a practical matter, while she is the leader of the whole House, she is chosen only by her own party, not by the whole House in a free vote.* For their part, cabinet secretaries have national reach too. Furthermore, they are chosen by the nation's president, and approved by a majority of the entire Senate in a free vote. Not as democratic as if they were elected, to be sure, but hardly illegitimate either.[33]

The PPT has an even weaker claim than the Speaker. By tradition, the PPT is the most senior senator of the majority party. This means that he is generally very old: between 1947 and 2010, the median age for PPTs was over eighty, with many in their nineties. As such, it is a ceremonial post, not

* While the entire House votes on whom the Speaker should be, the parties caucus beforehand and each nominates a single candidate. The vote for Speaker is one in which party discipline is enforced with unusual firmness. (When Democrat James Traficant voted for Republican Speaker Denny Hastert in 2001, his party stripped him of his committee assignments.) If the majority party didn't do it this way, a centrist challenger to the Speaker might prevail by winning some votes from his own party, and most of the votes from the minority. Such a Speaker would more truly represent the entire House. Even then, the general electorate would be voting mainly for their individual representatives, and not for the likely candidates for Speaker. *See* Howard M. Wasserman, *Structural Principles and Presidential Succession*, 90 Ky. L.J. 345, 403–04 (2002) (describing relatively undemocratic nature of Speaker-selection process).

one that even arguably qualifies someone to step into the presidency—the closest analogue to the Speaker is the Senate majority leader, who is not an "officer."[34]

President Truman's other concern, about it being undemocratic for presidents to appoint their own successors, had been heard in the 1790s and 1880s as well. However, the "successor" is really only a stand-in—he might finish out a dead president's term, but the next election will still be held on schedule. In any case, Truman's objection seems a bit incongruous, given the way that vice presidents are chosen.* And the Twenty-Fifth Amendment demolished Truman's position. Under the amendment, when there is a vice-presidential vacancy, the president nominates someone to fill it. The Constitution thereby *requires* her to choose her own potential successor (subject to confirmation by the full House and Senate). With these principles now woven into the structure of the Constitution, Truman's argument is exactly backward.[35]

In Truman's defense, his proposal would have had the Speaker serve as acting president only for a short time, until there could be a special presidential election to choose someone to fill out the term. This is how the 1792 act worked, and the 1886 act at least allowed for the possibility of a special election. However unconstitutional the 1792 act was, and however undemocratic the 1886 act was, the ability of Americans to elect an acting president significantly mitigated those problems. But Congress stripped the special-election provision from the 1947 act (ironically citing constitutional concerns) and made things correspondingly more unconstitutional and undemocratic.[36]

More significant than what Truman may have gotten wrong is what he disregarded. Continuity, for example, is very important and greatly favors the secretary of state. Continuity will be less than ideal in any succession— only the president and vice president can claim that they were chosen with

---

* Truman himself had been essentially handpicked by President Roosevelt, and while Truman was democratically elected as vice president—something no cabinet member can say—it is not as though many voters in 1944 said, "I'm indifferent between Roosevelt and Dewey, but given how strongly I prefer Harry Truman to John W. Bricker for veep, I'll vote for Roosevelt." *See* Philip Abbott, *Accidental Presidents*, 35 Presidential Stud. Q. 627, 629 (2005) (discussing vice-presidential elections).

the presidency in mind. But the secretary of state is an executive officer, and a key player in the administration who works closely and directly with the president. This would make for a relatively smooth transition if the secretary ever needed to take over. In a time of crisis, the secretary of state's presence at the helm would send a particularly reassuring signal to the rest of the world, for whom the secretary is already the president's designated contact. Following the secretary of state (who has sometimes been a naturalized citizen, and thus statutorily disqualified from acting as president) is the secretary of the treasury, another key executive who would provide a smooth transition and a reassuring signal (in his case, to Wall Street).[37]

By contrast, the Speaker and PPT are legislative officials. Moving the Speaker or PPT from legislation on Capitol Hill to execution at the White House, on a moment's notice, would be more jarring—for the Speaker or PPT themselves, for Congress, for the executive branch, for the country, and for the world. Notably, there have only been four sitting members of Congress elected president, in 1880, 1920, 1960, and 2008, and none of them were Speaker or PPT.* Compare that to the last government job held by other new presidents. Since 1920, there have been six vice presidents, five governors, a general, and a cabinet secretary—all executives. It is true that the Speaker's job is comprehensive in scope, while cabinet secretaries have a narrower portfolio, but when getting a new president, the voters have shown by a wide margin that executive promotions are easier to swallow than lateral moves from the legislature.[38]

An even more jarring possibility is a change in party control. Cabinet secretaries are part of the president's administration and are virtually always a member of her party. The president handpicks them. They work closely

---

* President Polk was a former Speaker but had more recently been a state governor. Three other Speakers—Henry Clay, John Bell, and James Blaine—ran unsuccessfully for president, but only Clay ran as a sitting Speaker, and Blaine had more recently served as secretary of state. No former PPT has ever been elected president, though former PPTs William Crawford and Hugh White ran unsuccessfully for president. Sitting Speakers Schuyler Colfax and John Nance Garner and sitting PPT William King were elected vice president. Former PPTs John Tyler and Charles Curtis were elected vice president, and Tyler succeeded to the presidency upon the death of President William Henry Harrison.

with her. If they oppose her, they get fired. Thus, they embody continuity.*
The Speaker, by contrast, is not part of the administration. Since 1947,
divided government has gotten much more common; the Speaker and president have been from opposite political parties more often than not. At such
times, Speaker succession would be undemocratic, given that the electorate
had given four-year terms to a president and vice president from the other
party. A Speaker who became acting president would also face a cabinet of
political opponents. She could replace them, of course, but that would just
make the transition even more disruptive.[39]

In 1973, Vice President Agnew resigned and Republican President Nixon
nominated Gerald Ford to fill the vacancy. It took nearly two months for the
Democratic-controlled Congress to confirm him. The next year, after Ford
became president, it took Congress nearly four months to confirm his
controversial nominee for vice president, Nelson Rockefeller. To his credit,
Speaker Carl Albert, a Democrat, noticed his conflict of interest. During the
Ford nomination, Albert reportedly promised that if something happened to
Nixon, and Albert became acting president, he would appoint a Republican
vice president and then resign. It would have been unseemly for the
Democrats to take over the presidency because of a congressional delay that
they themselves controlled (the fact that the House could impeach Nixon
was fresh on everybody's mind). It's unclear why, if he felt this way, Speaker
Albert did not press to have the succession law changed. Even so, a secretary
of state fighting with a less principled Speaker could make good use of
Albert's statesmanlike example.[40]

If the legal-political situation is such that the secretary of state would fight
the Speaker, neither side could expect in advance to win. The Speaker would
have the statute and well-settled expectations on her side; the secretary of
state would have the stronger constitutional arguments and all the policy
arguments in this section—a resistible force versus a moveable object. It is

---

* If we switched to pure cabinet succession, some provision would need to be made
for double vacancies that occurred at or before inauguration. Otherwise, if the new
president and vice president were killed before the new cabinet could be confirmed,
the outgoing secretary of state—possibly from the just-defeated party—would become
acting president. This would provide continuity, but the wrong kind; it might seriously
conflict with the recent election results.

impossible to predict how a succession struggle would play out politically. It would depend on the nature of the presidential vacancy, the personas of the Speaker and secretary of state, and various other facts on the ground. Perhaps most importantly, it would depend on who decides.

Who Decides?

As in Chapter 3, it is unclear who would resolve this constitutional crisis. The courts, Congress, the cabinet, the military, and the people could all play roles. In such a highly charged situation, it would be in everybody's interest to declare a winner quickly and definitively. But if both sides were inclined to agree, this issue wouldn't arise in the first place.

There are three possibilities. One is for all hell to break loose, with the winner being whichever contender has the biggest, toughest mobs of supporters mobilized in the streets. The backing of the military could make a big difference too. There is no point discussing this horrifying possibility further—not because it couldn't happen, but because it is impossible to predict in advance which side it would favor. It would be best to avoid such a situation.

The second possibility is that the courts would decide. The mob/military factor might influence the courts (which would put us back to the last paragraph), but ideally it would work the other way, and the legal process would yield a result legitimate enough to calm the losing side. A Supreme Court decision—hopefully a swift and unanimous one—would send a powerful signal to the losing contender to stand down. So would the military and the mobs, but surely the Court, representing the rule of law, is a preferable authority here. In highly politicized cases, the Supreme Court sometimes expresses concern about maintaining its legitimacy and credibility, but this is just the sort of case that it should maintain them *for*.

The third possibility is that the courts would let Congress or the cabinet decide. As discussed in Chapter 3, the courts will refuse to take a case if it is a "political question" that the Constitution gives to Congress or the executive branch to decide. This dispute might be such a case.[41]

It is not the simplest kind of political question, like impeachment or presidential disability, in which the Constitution's text explicitly takes a case away from the courts. The Constitution's Succession Clause does not tell Congress to choose an acting president; it directs Congress to pass legislation setting out the rules in advance. The Constitution limits Congress's range of choices here—it can only put "officers" in the line of succession—so the courts could review the succession law just like any other, making sure that it doesn't violate the Constitution. Political questions can also be found if a dispute is purely a matter of policy, as opposed to a legal question, but there is clearly a legal question for the courts to resolve here.[42]

That leaves one last type of political question: Congress or the cabinet might have an implicit power to decide the issue, and the courts might back off in the name of finality or uniformity, or to respect the separation of powers. So, for instance, in the midst of the crisis, Congress might pass a law; it would then need to decide which putative president to submit it to for a signature. Or one of the would-be presidents might send a nomination to the Senate, which would have to decide if the nominator is legitimate. Similarly, the cabinet could weigh in, if less officially, by obediently reporting to one claimant or the other. If Congress and the cabinet backed the same person (and especially if the military and the larger mobs of people in the streets agreed), there would be uniformity and finality that the courts would be loath to upset.

But the House and Senate might not make a choice right away, or they might not make a definitive one. More problematically, even if Congress did make a clear declaration, it might just back its candidate, the Speaker, while the cabinet backed the secretary of state. Or there could be two cabinets as the putative presidents started firing people. It would be hard—especially in the middle of a war—to expect the military to wait for a few days to see who the commander in chief and secretary of defense are, but the alternative is for the military to operate without civilian control, and that would be unacceptable too. In such a case, the courts would be in a good position to defuse the crisis. From the standpoint of the political-question doctrine, if there were two people claiming to be the acting president, both with significant support from some part of the government and public, there would be no uniformity or finality *until and unless* the courts got involved.

There is a practical side issue here: the oath of office. Traditionally, incoming presidents have the chief justice administer their oaths. The

Constitution does not require this, though, and seven presidents have had other people do it. Besides George Washington (who, at his first inauguration, obviously had not yet appointed a chief justice), the other six were all vice presidents taking over at the spur of the moment after the president died. Notably, though, the other three vice presidents thrust into the presidency managed to have the chief justice administer their oaths. It is a powerful symbol of legitimacy. Both the Speaker and the secretary of state, therefore, would probably scramble to have the chief justice administer their oaths.* It would be very helpful if the highest judicial officer in the country endorsed one side's claim to office that way. Of course, a chief justice might want to avoid taking sides—administering the oath to only one contender might prejudice future litigation or might force him to recuse himself from hearing the case. On the other hand, the chief justice might jump at the chance to get involved and, by adding his weighty support to one side, possibly preempt the conflict early on.[43]

There are an infinite number of ways that Congress, the cabinet, the military, the public, and the courts could line up. If enough of them lined up the same way, and quickly, it could avert a conflict. If not, the courts' role could be crucial. The only certainty here is that all these players might matter, and the contenders for the presidency would do well to remember that.

Can We Fix It?

Even if most theorists think that the Speaker should lose, she might win in a real case. As mentioned already, an uncontested transfer of power to a Speaker would set a precedent and greatly reduce the chances of any future controversy. But there is no guarantee that our first Speaker-president would take power so quietly.

The problem is not that the Speaker could win; maybe she should win. The problem is the uncertainty—and the potential cataclysm—that might

---

* The Constitution can be interpreted as not requiring acting presidents to take the oath of office. *See* U.S. Const. art. II, § 1, cl. 8. Nevertheless, it doesn't forbid them from taking the oath, and the powerful symbolism it would afford would almost certainly lead someone to take the oath if he or she was claiming the presidency for the rest of the term.

precede her victory. As Clinton Rossiter once told Congress, "No man should be expected to, no man should be permitted to, wield the power of the Presidency without the clearest of titles to it." *That's* the point of this chapter. Luckily, this potential disaster is easy to avoid; Congress just needs to rewrite the law. The succession law in effect from 1886 to 1947 excluded congressional leaders and included only the cabinet, and it worked just fine. It would be relatively simple to return to cabinet succession, with one or two minor tweaks.[44]

Then again, passing legislation is never simple. The 1886 act passed only after back-to-back near misses in which Presidents Arthur and Cleveland had no backups. The 1947 act passed only when President Truman scrupulously maintained his demand for Speaker succession even after his Republican opponents took over Congress. Since 1947, several members of Congress have tried to overhaul the succession law, and some of them have tried to remove the Speaker and PPT from the line of succession. They have all been defeated. One reason is competing priorities, and a sense that Congress can handle, at most, one thing at a time.* Another is personal pique: a sense that removing the Speaker from the line of succession is insulting to the Speaker, and to the House in general. These are not substantial justifications. Regardless of whether the current law is unconstitutional, having the Speaker and PPT in the line of succession is hardly so vital to the functioning of government that it is worth courting disaster. It may only be a remote risk, but it is a needless one.[45]

Happily (and unhappily), legal scholars and politicians have identified many other places where the current succession law can be improved and strengthened. With motivated leadership—which arises from time to time—such other problems might spur Congress to act and then, while it is rewriting the succession law anyway, to fix the constitutional problems too.[46]

---

* As an example of this tunnel vision, consider this statement by Senator Feingold at a hearing on succession laws: "Our most dedicated efforts should be devoted to preventing the next terrorist attack. . . . [W]e must not be distracted from the task at hand by too much attention to what will most likely be only theoretical questions." *Ensuring the Continuity of the United States Government: The Presidency: Joint Hearing Before the S. Comm. on the Judiciary and Comm. on Rules and Admin.*, 108th Cong. 16 (2003). Perhaps he thought he was at a different hearing.

Failing all this, if the succession law ever comes into play, Congress could mitigate some of its practical problems. If the presidency was ever about to pass to the Speaker, she could step down as Speaker. The House could then select someone from the president's party to be Speaker. That person would then resign from the House* and the speakership and become acting president. Then the House could restore the old Speaker. Alternatively, the Speaker could let the acting presidency pass to the PPT. The Senate could then choose a PPT especially for that purpose who would be a more appropriate acting president—like someone thirty years younger, and from the president's party.

Such maneuvers would be tricky. There might not be advance notice. If the House tried to plan too far ahead—say, replacing the Speaker whenever the vice presidency was vacant—it would be far too disruptive to the House's business. Regardless, the need for all this noodling around underscores just how bad an idea it is to put the Speaker and PPT in the line of succession in the first place. And if the House consciously choosing the next president is not unconstitutional outright, it certainly doesn't sit comfortably in the constitutional structure.

The optimal solution is simple, if unlikely: Congress must change the succession law. If it fails to do so and the country splits in two, Congress will have no one to blame but itself.

---

* The Constitution does not formally require that the Speaker be a member of the House, so theoretically, the House could select the most presidential person in the country to be its Speaker. Then, that person would become acting president. But there is no precedent for having a non-member Speaker, so this seems unlikely. *See* Akhil Reed Amar & Vikram David Amar, *Is the Presidential Succession Law Constitutional?*, 48 Stan. L. Rev. 113, 120 n.48 (1995) (discussing Speaker's House membership).

5

Impeaching an Ex-President

It's among the worst scandals in presidential history. Ted McGee, a longtime friend of President Jack Martin, collected tens of millions of dollars in "lobbying fees" and forwarded half of the money to President Martin. As desired by McGee's clients, Martin promoted or vetoed legislation, appointed or fired officials, and more. Caught red handed, Martin looks certain to be quickly impeached, removed from office, criminally prosecuted, and convicted. Seeing the handwriting on the wall, he resigns before he can be impeached. He is soon indicted and prepares to defend himself in court.

The new president, maverick Norman Barker, was not involved in the scandal and does not plan to seek a full term. In his first week, he pardons President Martin, on condition that Martin surrender all the money mentioned in his indictment (almost twelve million dollars), plus five million more, to the government. President Barker explains that "a presidential prosecution would produce more spectacle than justice. It would badly distract us when we need to refocus on the real problems facing Americans." Martin accepts the deal.

The country is in an uproar. A few people agree with Barker, and they are satisfied that Martin has suffered enough. Most Americans vehemently disagree, though, and want Martin in prison. But with the pardon, and with no prospect of a state prosecution, prison is not an option. Luckily for the disgruntled majority, the opposition party controls Congress, and it keeps the Martin scandal alive. The opposition has two motivations: investigating the unanswered questions about Martin's conduct that would have emerged in a criminal trial, and exploiting Martin's crimes for political purposes.

Subpoenaed by three separate congressional committees, ex-president Martin refuses to respond. He submits a written statement arguing that the

separation of powers precludes Congress from forcing him to testify under oath
about his actions as president. To vindicate its authority, and to hold Martin
accountable, the House leadership decides to revive Martin's impeachment;
impeachment trumps Martin's separation-of-powers argument, and it is beyond the
reach of Barker's pardon.

Because he has already left office, though, this "late" impeachment divides the
anti-Martin camp. Some question whether Congress has the power to impeach an
ex-president. Others don't worry about the legalities but wonder what the point is.
One obvious answer—that it will keep Martin in the news during the upcoming
election campaign—turns off millions of voters who would like Congress to do
something more productive. Nevertheless, there are still many more angry voters
who want to see Martin pilloried. They argue that it is perfectly constitutional to
impeach an ex-president, and that it is worthwhile to investigate Martin's crimes, to
disqualify him from ever holding federal office in the future, and to brand him with
a mark of shame.

The legal question of late impeachment has to be settled before the case can go
anywhere. The hottest political issue in the country is now a constitutional-law
issue, and the nation's top politicians—and maybe its top judges—gear up to
adjudicate it.

CAN PRESIDENTS BE IMPEACHED EVEN after they have left office? There is no
simple constitutional answer. Congress has conducted a late-impeachment
trial, but with ambiguous results. Scholarly opinion on the question is
divided. There can be only one answer, though; either Congress can
impeach and try former presidents or it can't.[1]

Unlike in previous chapters, the stakes are relatively low here; we are not
talking about two presidents wrestling for control of the White House, or
even a president going to prison. Moreover, Congress will rarely want to
impeach an ex-president anyway. But contemplating late impeachment
gives us insight into the deeper meaning of impeachment in general. As
leading impeachment scholar Michael Gerhardt put it, "[i]mpeachment
proceedings test every institution with which they come into contact." The
question is bigger than just what happens to Jack Martin. That said, what
happens to Jack Martin might matter some day too.[2]

Impeachment Basics

The House of Representatives has "the sole Power" to impeach (accuse) federal executive and judicial officers. The Senate has "the sole Power" to try them, with a two-thirds majority needed to convict, and with the chief justice presiding when the president is on trial. Two sitting presidents—Andrew Johnson and Bill Clinton—have been impeached. Both were acquitted by the Senate.[3]

The maximum allowable "judgment" upon conviction by the Senate is "removal from Office, and disqualification to hold and enjoy any Office of honor, Trust, or Profit under the United States." Criminal prosecution and impeachment are separate—someone who has been impeached is still subject to regular criminal prosecution. Similarly, a presidential pardon can stop or undo a criminal prosecution, but it cannot stop or undo an impeachment.[4]

The most important constitutional clause touching late impeachability is Article II, Section 4: "The President, Vice President and all civil Officers of the United States, shall be removed from Office on Impeachment for, and Conviction of, Treason, Bribery, or other high Crimes and Misdemeanors." The crux of the legal arguments center on this clause—most prominently, on whether "President" refers to the offender at the time of the offense, the time of the impeachment, or both.[5]

Before getting to the constitutional arguments, this chapter will consider whether (and when) late impeachment might be sensible.

Practical Politics

> This is ridiculous. Jack Martin has left office and he'll never work in this town again. Why are we wasting our time with this pointless case? We're impeaching a dead horse.
> —ANTI-IMPEACHMENT SENATOR

> We're not wasting our time. The only thing making this take so long is all the hand-wringing. If we would just get on with it, the whole thing could be done in a few weeks. We already know Jack Martin is guilty as sin, and we know that this is the only chance we have to hold him accountable and to send a message.

> The alternative would give this crook control over the impeachment process and let him make a further mockery of our government.
>
> —PRO-IMPEACHMENT SENATOR

Why would Congress ever want to impeach and try an ex-president? It usually wouldn't; impeachment proceedings are generally dropped if the target resigns. Whatever the theoretical purposes of impeachment may be, the primary practical purpose has been to remove the target from office, and once removal has been accomplished—by whatever means—there is generally little point in continuing. Moreover, the fact that late impeachment is on shaky legal ground means that the ex-president would have some thumbs on the scale in his favor: to avoid impeachment or conviction, he would need a critical mass that *either* rejects the accusations against him *or* concludes that late impeachment is unconstitutional *or* concludes that it is pointless. There are, however, some factors that could make Congress more likely to pursue a late impeachment.

The most important practical consideration is punishment. The maximum constitutional penalty in impeachment cases is removal and disqualification. Removal is required when sitting officers are convicted, but it is moot in late-impeachment cases, which just leaves disqualification.*

Admittedly, disqualification from being a federal judge or executive officer† does not sound like much. If someone disgraces himself so

---

* It is possible that somebody could commit an impeachable offense, leave office, and occupy a different office at the time of the trial, in which case removal might still be on the table. However, as discussed later, there are alternative interpretations of the impeachment power that would allow such cases while barring other late impeachments.

† The disqualification penalty probably does not prevent the convict from being elected to Congress, because the Constitution treats "offices under the United States" as distinct from seats in Congress. *See, e.g.,* U.S. Const. art. II, § 1, cl. 2 ("[N]o Senator or Representative, or Person holding an Office of Trust or Profit under the United States, shall be appointed an Elector."); *id.* art. I, § 6, cl. 2 ("[N]o Person holding any Office under the United States, shall be a Member of either House [of Congress] during his Continuance in Office."). *But see* Michael J. Gerhardt, The Federal Impeachment Process 60–61 (2d ed. 2000) (implying contrary view); Ronald D. Rotunda, *Rethinking Term Limits for Federal Legislators in Light of the Structure of the Constitution,* 73 Or. L. Rev. 561, 573 (1994) (stating contrary view).

thoroughly that two-thirds of the Senate votes to convict him, his chances of getting back into office are pretty slim anyway, especially for offices that require Senate confirmation. (As discussed later, the Senate has not even bothered to disqualify most of the people it has convicted.) Still, disqualification might sometimes be worthwhile. For instance, the prospect of the ex-president staging a comeback might be likely enough*—and undesirable enough—to warrant pursuing the late impeachment. Alternatively, the ex-president's offense might be so heinous that it is appropriate to declare formally to the nation that he is constitutionally unworthy of "honor, trust, or profit."

In another sense, the smaller and more flexible penalties of a late impeachment are an advantage. In a regular presidential impeachment case, removal from office is so momentous and disruptive and potentially disproportionate that senators might decline to convict even an obviously guilty person. But unlike removal, disqualification is never mandatory. In a late-impeachment case, therefore, the punishment could be disqualification, limited disqualification, or even no punishment at all. Because the stakes of the late impeachment would be so much lower, and because the question of punishment could be separated from the question of guilt, it would be comparatively easier for the ex-president's opponents to move their case forward.[6]

As an aside, disqualification may not be the only consequence facing an impeached ex-president. When Senator Arlen Specter suggested in February 2001 that ex-president Clinton could be impeached for his questionable last-minute pardons, Specter did not even mention the possibility of disqualifying Clinton from future office. Instead, Specter indicated that if convicted, Clinton could lose things like his pension and his

---

* President Andrew Johnson was impeached and acquitted by one vote, but he was later elected to the Senate. Secretary of War William Belknap—who was impeached after leaving office and avoided conviction only because he had resigned—had a successful Washington law practice after his impeachment. See Eleanore Bushnell, Crimes, Follies, and Misfortunes: The Federal Impeachment Trials 160, 189 (1992) (describing post-impeachment careers of Johnson and Belknap). Currently, impeached and convicted Judge Alcee Hastings is serving in the House of Representatives. Hastings was not disqualified upon conviction, but disqualification should not apply to election to Congress anyway (a point discussed in the last footnote).

government-provided security. Specter was not quite right; federal law provides that a president who is impeached and convicted loses his pension and other benefits, but only if he is impeached *while in office*. Congress could always change that law, though. In doing so, it would protect the country from malfeasant officers who commit their offenses shortly before leaving office, and it would add teeth to late impeachment, thereby making it more likely to be a worthwhile exercise.[7]

Another practical consideration is precedent. Impeachment cases not only affect the person being impeached and tried; they also can establish principles that guide future cases. As one congressman put it in a late-impeachment case, the House's "great object" was "that [the target's] infamy might be rendered conspicuous, historic, eternal, in order to prevent the occurrence of like offenses in the future." If the president in question had left office, late impeachment would be the only way to do this successfully.[8]

Impeachment might also be the only way to pursue certain conduct. In the waning days of George W. Bush's presidency, some Democrats in Congress made noises about impeaching Bush and his subordinates over torture and surveillance issues arising out of the War on Terror. The Obama administration seemed uninterested in prosecuting any Bush officials, let alone Bush himself. Impeachment would have been a way for Congress to investigate the Bush Administration's conduct seriously, going a step beyond mere hearings (which Bush more easily might have stiff-armed, citing the separation of powers). The threat to impeach Bush faded after he left office, but there had never been much political support for impeachment even before that. If things had been somewhat different—if the facts had been worse but the new administration still did not want to prosecute, if the Democrats' electoral victories in Congress had depended more heavily on the support of the vocal pro-impeachment crowd, if strong evidence had emerged that the Bush administration had willfully concealed and misrepresented material information—this might have been a good fit for late impeachment.

Late impeachment will be more attractive to Congress when the ex-president's actions threaten the impeachment process itself. For instance, a president might thumb his nose at his would-be impeachers, letting them proceed with their case without paying it any mind, and then resigning right before they are about to do something meaningful. Sometimes, Congress would be satisfied with the president's resignation in such a case and would not continue just to protect its turf. But if the president clearly was resigning just to avoid the harsh light that impeachment would shine on his conduct, or if he quit to avoid conviction and disqualification (imagine him resigning seconds before the sixty-seventh senator voted to convict), Congress would be more likely to assert itself and continue with a late impeachment.

Late impeachment could also make sense when the ex-president has been convicted of a crime. This might seem counterintuitive; if the criminal justice system can handle the case, why bother with a cumbersome impeachment? But sometimes it would be worthwhile. A convicted ex-president already would have been found guilty beyond a reasonable doubt, so Congress could piggyback the record developed by the court and perform the impeachment and trial very quickly and cheaply.

Another factor that might affect late impeachment is timing. Ideally, all other things being equal, an offense committed near the end of a president's tenure should be treated the same as one occurring at the beginning. At the beginning, if the president commits an impeachable offense, he can be impeached, removed, disqualified, and prosecuted. Near the end, unless late impeachment is possible, he can only be prosecuted. Thus Congress might want to use the threat of late impeachment as a way to add incentives for presidents to stay honest throughout their terms, and not to cover things up when they go astray. As discussed more later, the main importance of impeachment is seen not in the number of times it has been used, but in the incentives provided by the *possibility* of its use. Disqualification might not be the biggest incentive in the world, but it's something. For its part, Congress might be motivated to keep that incentive in place.

Counterintuitively, late impeachment might be broached by an ex-president himself, to call his opponents' bluff. Vice President John C. Calhoun sought such vindication in 1827, when opponents circulated rumors of his misconduct in an earlier cabinet post. Calhoun appealed to the House as the "grand inquest of the nation" to investigate the accusations; the House did so, and Calhoun was officially cleared. Decades later, former president John Quincy Adams was a member of the House when former secretary of state (and current senator) Daniel Webster faced a similar situation. Adams supported both Webster and the idea of late impeachability, saying, "I hold myself, so long as I have the breath of life in my body, amenable to impeachment by this House for everything I did during the time I held any public office." Adams claimed that "every officer impeachable by the laws of the country, is as liable, twenty years after his office has expired, as he is whilst he continues in office."[9]

Last but not least, party politics could make late impeachment more likely. Votes on executive impeachments tend to track party lines. The House has only impeached three executive officers (Secretary of War William Belknap, and Presidents Andrew Johnson and Bill Clinton), and in all three cases the House was controlled by the party opposed to the president. All three men were acquitted in the Senate, but the closest case—when President Johnson was acquitted by a single vote—occurred at the only time in American history in which the opposition party had a two-thirds majority in the Senate. Notably, though, there have been several times when one party had a majority in the House and a two-thirds majority in the Senate while there were living *ex*-presidents of the other party. The party balance in Congress matters a lot for impeachment, in other words, and the balance is more likely to favor impeachment after a president has left office than it is when he is still there.[10]

While late impeachment is usually not worth pursuing, this section has sketched out some factors that could shorten the odds. One could sum it up by saying that late impeachment is most likely when Congress really, really hates the ex-president and sees a political advantage in acting accordingly. In most cases, though, late impeachment just isn't very likely. But "unlikely" does not mean "unconstitutional"; after all, regular impeachment is very rare as well. These practical considerations are separate from the question covered next: whether late impeachment is legal.[11]

The Basic Argument Against Late Impeachability

Impeach an ex-president? The Constitution talks about impeaching the president, and Jack Martin isn't the president anymore. The point of the impeachment process is removal from office, so once someone is out of office, there is nothing left for Congress to do. This is all just politics—a bunch of partisans trying to drum up votes before the election, and abusing the Constitution to do it.

—EX-PRESIDENT MARTIN'S SPOKESMAN

Those who believe that late impeachment is unconstitutional rely on a particular reading of Article II, Section 4 of the Constitution. They say that when Section 4 limits impeachment to "[t]he President, Vice President, and all civil Officers," it excludes former occupants of those posts. As one lawyer put it during an actual late-impeachment case: "A half-grown boy reads in a newspaper that *the* President occupies the *White House*; if he would understand from that that all Ex-Presidents are in it together he would be considered a very unpromising lad."[12]

Also important is that Section 4 makes removal mandatory upon conviction. From this, opponents infer that *removability* is mandatory for impeachment. Because there is no way to remove an ex-president from office, late impeachability makes no sense. In a broader sense, the removal requirement suggests that impeachment is about protecting the office from a bad person, not punishing that person. Some, like impeachment expert Charles Black, even define impeachable offenses as only those acts that warrant removal. To these people, no proper purpose for impeachment remains once the offender is out of office. Disqualification is possible too, but it isn't necessary for keeping someone like Jack Martin out; if he somehow clawed his way back into service, he would be an "officer" again and could be impeached at that point.[13]

These critics sometimes go further and argue that if Article II, Section 4, permitted late impeachment, it would permit impeachment of every person in the world, because late impeachability requires that Section 4's language of "officers" and "remov[al]" be ignored. That leaves no basis to distinguish between a person who once held office and one who didn't, since neither is an officer and neither can be removed.[14]

That's the simple argument that late impeachability is not just pointless but actually constitutionally inappropriate. The complicated argument emerges in the following pages, in various rebuttals to the arguments on the other side.

The Argument for Late Impeachability: Text and Structure

> It's true that the Constitution limits impeachment to officers, but the point is that they are officers at the time they offend, not that they remain officers for the entirety of the lengthy impeachment process. This isn't about getting Jack Martin out of office, obviously. It's about checks and balances. The Constitution gives us our impeachment authority so that we can hold presidents accountable for their actions and deter them from bad acts. That is exactly what we are trying to do here. What kind of check on the president would impeachment be if a president can stop us from using it?
>
> —HOUSE IMPEACHMENT MANAGER

Proponents of late impeachability have a few arguments of their own, which are more complicated than the arguments on the other side. They can be broken down into two parts: First, the text and structure of the Constitution support late impeachability. Second, history and precedent also favor it.

Text

As seen already, the text of the Constitution specifies several limits on the impeachment power. Article II, Section 4, is generally interpreted as allowing impeachment to reach only "the president, vice president, and all civil officers" (which, to oversimplify, I'll lump together as "officers"). But knowing that impeachment only applies to "officers" leaves questions about the possible timing of the offense and the possible timing of the impeachment proceedings.[15]

There are four possible combinations:

		Must the offender be in office now?	
		Y	N
Must the offense have occurred when the offender was in office?	Y	Conservative	Late
	N	Protective	Radical

The Radical interpretation says that any person can be impeached at any time, because Article II, Section 4, does not purport to define impeachable offenders or offenses. While that is technically true, and while the Radical view has had public proponents, there is ample authority and precedent for reading Article II, Section 4, as the constitutional definition of impeachability. Regardless, impeachments must be "impeachments," and pursuing a private citizen for a private act would not be an "impeachment." Some people conflate the Radical interpretation with the Late interpretation and consider the Late interpretation equally untenable. But as the chart here makes clear, the Radical and Late interpretations are distinct.[16]

The Late, Protective, and Conservative interpretations are more plausible, and this section will only discuss them, not choose between them. Other considerations—structure, history, and precedent—need to be considered too.

The Late interpretation limits the timing of the offense, but not the timing of the impeachment. A person can be impeached at any time, as long as he was an officer when he committed the offense. This describes every person ever impeached under the federal system.*

The principal benefit of the Late interpretation is that it reinforces the notion that "impeachment" for "high crimes and misdemeanors" is supposed to apply to offenses committed by public officers qua public officers. As *The Federalist* put it, impeachment is about offenses that "proceed from the misconduct of public men" and that "may with peculiar propriety be denominated POLITICAL." Thus, it would make sense that the term "officer" refers to the offender at the time of the offense, regardless of what has happened to him in the potentially lengthy stretch of time between the commission of the offense, discovery of it, accusation, debate in the House, impeachment, more debate in the Senate, and judgment.[17]

The Late interpretation is unconvincing to those who think that "officer" means "officer at the time of impeachment and trial." It also clashes with

---

* It is also consistent with how Congress treats its own members. Article I, Section 5, Clause 2, provides that the House and Senate can "punish [their] Members for disorderly Behaviour." Congress has used this power to discipline members who had already left office. *See* Brian C. Kalt, *The Constitutional Case for the Impeachability of Former Federal Officials: An Analysis of the Law, History, and Practice of Late Impeachment*, 6 Tex. Rev. L. & Pol. 13, 92–93 (2001) (discussing Whittemore and Deweese cases).

Section 4's requirement that anyone convicted be removed from office; ex-officers have no office to be removed from. But the other possible penalty, disqualification, still looms for ex-officers. And on its face, the removal requirement does not purport to describe who is impeachable.* Put another way, the Late interpretation sees the removal requirement as protecting offices from bad officers, not protecting bad people from impeachment.[18]

Some opponents of late impeachability endorse the Protective interpretation, which limits the timing of the impeachment, but not the offense; a person can be impeached regardless of whether he was an officer when he committed the offense as long as he is currently a civil officer. Protective interpreters can be comfortable that "officers" never means "ex-officers," and that the mandatory removal penalty can always be carried out. Under this view, impeachment is about protecting the office from bad occupants, regardless of when their badness manifested itself. An officer who commits a high crime and leaves office would only face impeachment if he returns to office. Similarly, a private citizen who commits a high crime (the two examples of high crimes in the Constitution—treason and bribery—can both be committed by private citizens) could be impeached if he subsequently enters office. The Protective interpretation is a plausible enough textual reading of Article II, Section 4, even if it ignores all the purposes of impeachment besides removal.

The Late and Protective interpretations are not mutually exclusive; one might combine them and allow impeachment if the offender was a civil officer when he committed the offense *or* he is a civil officer now. Adding

---

* By analogy, consider the federal law against bribing meat inspectors, which specifies its scope and penalties in a similar way: any inspector or "other officer" with inspection responsibilities who accepts a bribe "shall be deemed guilty of a felony and shall, upon conviction thereof, be summarily discharged from office," and fined and imprisoned. 21 U.S.C. § 622 (1994). The statute mentions inspectors and officers, not ex-inspectors and ex-officers. It specifies removal from office as a mandatory punishment. But ex-officers can still be prosecuted under the statute as long as they were officers when they offended; even though they cannot be removed from office, other penalties are available. Indeed, former agriculture secretary Mike Espy was indicted under this statute three years after leaving office. *See* Bill Miller, *Espy Acquitted in Gifts Case*, Wash. Post, Dec. 3, 1998, at A1 (summarizing chronology of Espy case). He was acquitted, but not because he'd already left. *See* United States v. Espy, 145 F.3d 1369, 1370–72 (D.C. Cir. 1998) (attaching no legal significance to fact that Espy, as ex-secretary, was no longer subject to removal).

this possibility does not tell us whether late impeachment is constitutional, though.

The main competitor to the Late interpretation is the Conservative interpretation, which limits the timing of both the offense and the impeachment: a person can only be impeached and tried if he was a civil officer when he committed the offense and is a civil officer now. This describes every person ever impeached *and convicted* under the federal system.* The Conservative interpretation takes full stock of the word "officer" and of the removal requirement, and respects the contextual notion that impeachment is about public officials qua public officials. That said, it overemphasizes removal just like the Protective interpretation does. Moreover, it opens up a potential textual dilemma: can a president be impeached for something he did in a prior office? A prior term as president? To the extent that such a president is impeachable under the Conservative interpretation, it becomes less tenable to distinguish among it, the Late interpretation, and the Protective interpretation. In all, though, the Conservative interpretation is another plausible reading of the text.

It is easy for opponents of late impeachability to argue that, if the Constitution had meant to allow late impeachment, it would have made that point much more clearly. On the other hand, the same can be said about *precluding* late impeachment. Proponents of late impeachability have a good argument that, at the very least, the constitutional text does not clearly and directly address the proper timing of impeachment, and that there are multiple possible interpretations. With that, it's time to consult structure, history, and precedent.[19]

Constitutional Structure

The Constitution's structure—its internal, recurrent themes and connections—provides more fodder for discussion. Late impeachment is

---

* As this chapter was being edited, the House impeached and the Senate convicted Judge Thomas Porteous. Article II of Porteous's impeachment centered on a course of corrupt conduct that began when he was a state judge, though it continued after he became a federal judge. Article IV dealt with false statements Porteous made during his Senate confirmation proceedings, technically before he was an officer, but inextricably linked with his officer status. *See* H.R. Res. 1031, 111th Cong. (2010).

consistent with a deterrence-centered view of impeachment, it makes disqualification a meaningful penalty, and it protects Congress's control over the process. But it is less consistent with a removal-centered view of impeachment, and it arguably makes too much out of disqualification.

First, deterrence. With impeachment, the Constitution gives Congress a powerful check on the president. Impeachment is available to get rid of malfeasing presidents, but it also serves to deter them from doing bad things in the first place. As future Supreme Court justice James Iredell put it during the North Carolina ratifying convention, impeachment "will not only be the means of punishing misconduct, but it will prevent misconduct. A man in public office who knows that there is no tribunal to punish him, may be ready to deviate from his duty; but if he knows there is a tribunal for that purpose, although he may be a man of no principle, the very terror of punishment will perhaps deter him." Without late impeachment, there is effectively "no tribunal to punish" a president who does bad things late in his term, which makes it more likely that he will "deviate from his duty."[20]

By analogy, consider the president's power to appoint officers, subject to Senate confirmation. The main effect of the Senate confirmation process is not that it leads the Senate to reject nominees—it almost never does that—but rather that it pushes the president to nominate acceptable people in the first place. Imagine the sorts of appointments that presidents might make if Senate confirmation were not required. Now consider impeachment. The House rarely impeaches anyone. But think of the power of the *availability* of impeachment. Picture a United States in which the president knew that no matter what he did, he would be able to remain in office for four years. It seems obvious that presidents would not always resist the temptation to abuse power—particularly to get reelected—nearly as well in that system as they have in our real one. No president has ever been removed from office through impeachment, but every president has been constrained by the possibility.[21]

By the same token, late impeachment will rarely be worth pursuing, but its availability can deter presidents from bad acts, especially toward the end of their terms. If impeachment cannot touch an ex-president, then it only provides an incentive to behave early in his term and encourages him to conceal his wrongdoing (which is much easier for him to do while he is still president). By contrast, if presidents can be impeached after leaving office, they will have more incentive to conduct themselves appropriately to the very end. If this incentive is not enough to prevent a president from doing bad things, it still gives Congress the power to pursue him and deter his successors.[22]

Some say that late impeachment is unnecessary because ex-presidents can be criminally prosecuted in ordinary court. But sitting presidents can face criminal prosecution too (even if, as discussed in Chapter 1, the prosecutors might need to wait until they leave office). The criminal law provides an important deterrent to presidents, which impeachment neither reduces nor increases; prosecutability doesn't protect sitting presidents from being impeached, so it should not preclude ex-presidents from being impeached either.

The next structural issue is disqualification. If removal says, "Get out!" disqualification adds an emphatic and irreversible "And stay out!" The Constitution's Framers considered it a serious blot to be "sentenced to a perpetual ostracism from the esteem and confidence and honors and emoluments" of the United States without hope of pardon. Later, even a critic of late impeachment conceded that disqualification was a weighty thing, because it made the convict "a living, moving infamy," and "a moral leper."[23]

A critic might argue that disqualification functions mainly as leverage: if removal were the only possible penalty, impeachees would have nothing to lose by fighting impeachment tooth and nail. With disqualification on the table, impeachees have an incentive to resign, dealing themselves a de facto plea bargain down to simple removal—the real point of impeachment, to these critics—and saving Congress significant resources. Sure enough, only three officers have ever been disqualified by the Senate, but dozens of others facing impeachment have resigned.[24]

But disqualification is either a significant punishment or it isn't. If it isn't, then it would not spur these "plea bargains." If it is a significant punishment, it should not be so easy to evade; without late impeachability, any impeachee can avoid conviction and disqualification simply by resigning at the last moment. Some might fight it out, but those who know that they will be convicted—the worst offenders, ironically—would have every reason to resign and thus would always avoid disqualification.[25]

"Checks and balances" are another structural support for late impeachability. Congress is the grand inquest of the United States, with the explicit power to investigate the conduct of the executive branch outside the confines of the criminal law. Congress can call witnesses and hold hearings, but presidents can stonewall them with relative impunity. By contrast, impeachment guarantees Congress the constitutional power to investigate abuses of the public trust and render a formal verdict on them. The president cannot stop an impeachment—the Constitution precludes him from using the pardon power against them—so it would be strange if he could subvert the process simply by quitting.* Congress has the *option* of declaring victory and ending proceedings if a target resigns, but that is a far cry from the president having the power to *force* Congress to stop. Barring late impeachment, one senator marveled in a late-impeachment case, would make the Senate "the only court in Christendom whose jurisdiction . . . depends on the volition of the accused."[26]

Some critics of late impeachability concede that an impeachee cannot strip the House or Senate of jurisdiction once the impeachment process has begun, but they insist that any other late impeachment is forbidden. This distinction (which essentially creates a separate interpretive category) makes sense as a matter of institutional design, but it has no basis in the Constitution's text. If the Constitution really does limit impeachment in the House and trial in the Senate to current, removable "officers," then the impeachee can end the proceedings any time he chooses by resigning. Opponents of late impeachment might not like that, but if they are limiting their argument to the Constitution's text, they have to live with it.[27]

Opponents can move beyond the text, though; there are structural arguments against late impeachability. If impeachment is mainly about removal, for instance, then the Protective interpretation fulfills that objective in the broadest possible way: Congress can remove an unfit president, regardless of when he committed his offense. As Jorge E. Souss put it in 2001: "[A]re we supposed to believe that . . . if George W. Bush robbed a jewelry store on the morning of January 20, a few hours before being sworn in, that he

---

* Similarly, without late impeachability, the president could subvert impeachments of lower-ranking officers by firing them.

would not be subject to impeachment [and removal] for such behavior?" A fair question.[28]

But there is a more probable problem on the flip side. Suppose a president issued a corrupt pardon a few hours before his *successor* was inaugurated. The Protective interpretation would say that he could not be impeached unless and until he returned to office. What worked for Souss's jewelry-store owner is cold comfort once one returns to the principal focus of impeachment: public offenses. Unless it was combined with the Late interpretation, the Protective interpretation would do nothing about such an abuse of power, and it might go unpunished. (Abuses of the public trust often are not prosecuted criminally—some because they technically aren't crimes; others because the president's successor is unwilling to pursue them. It is no coincidence that neither William Blount nor William Belknap—the two men whom the House has late-impeached—was criminally prosecuted for his offense.)[29]

As Alexander Hamilton wrote in *The Federalist*, the very nature of impeachable offenses makes them automatically politicized, so that Congress—not regular prosecutors and judges—is the proper body to take the lead. This is why impeachment is supposed to be limited to *high* crimes and misdemeanors, a term of art for offenses against the state. By saying that impeachment is for current officers and that anyone else is left to the criminal law alone, the Protective interpretation misses these points. Impeachment draws its institutional reason for being from the nature of the offense, not the nature of the defendant's employment when the Senate trial date rolls around. That, at least, is what proponents of late impeachability would argue, with some confidence.[30]

The Late interpretation gets many structural points right. It lets Congress use impeachment to inquire "into the conduct of public men," however late in the president's term the offenses occur, and however long he has covered them up. In doing so, it gives the president a more complete incentive to do his job honestly. It takes disqualification seriously. It lets Congress fulfill its constitutional duty to deter, investigate, rule upon, and fully punish high crimes and misdemeanors, regardless of how much the president would like to subvert Congress's jurisdiction. But there is no certainty here. Anyone who favors different structural considerations—like removal instead of deterrence—can still conclude quite reasonably that late impeachment clashes with the structure of the Constitution.

The Argument for Late Impeachability: History and Precedent

> We need to remember history. In England, late impeachment was the norm; there was a late impeachment going on in Britain at the very moment that the Framers were drafting the Constitution in Philadelphia. In America, several state constitutions preferred or even required late impeachments, and no states forbade them.
>
> The Constitution added several specific limits on impeachment, to depart from English and state practice, but it said nothing about preventing late impeachment. At the Constitutional Convention, the big argument was whether to make the president impeachable while in office; being able to impeach him after he was gone went without saying.
>
> Most importantly, the House and Senate have already answered this question. The House unanimously impeached the ex-secretary of war in 1876 even though he had already resigned. The Senate seriously debated late impeachability, and voted "yes" on it. The answer is still yes.
>
> —HOUSE IMPEACHMENT MANAGER

Impeaching an ex-president is admittedly an odd thing to do, and the possibility doesn't exactly leap out from the text or structure of the Constitution, as the less-than-conclusive arguments in the last section showed. The strongest arguments for late impeachability are rooted in history and precedent, and while these arguments are not unassailable, the ex-president's opponents would lean on them heavily.

History

English impeachment is the ultimate foundation of American federal impeachment (the drafters of the Constitution were also influenced by colonial and state experiences, but English impeachment informed those too). English impeachment was essentially a criminal prosecution that went through Parliament instead of the courts. By 1787, though, it was perceived as limited to public offenders or public offenses—cases that "the ordinary magistrate either dare[d] not or [could] not punish." Most cases were about mismanagement by government officials, or treason by nobles.[31]

Late impeachment was never problematic in England, because the bounds of impeachment were so expansive. Punishments went so far beyond removal—loss of property and even death were not uncommon— that impeachments were still very weighty matters after the target left office. But even after impeachment penalties became more restrained, late impeachment remained as a sensible option. Impeachment was more about guaranteeing accountability than it was about removing bad men from office; late impeachment exemplified this fact.[32]

At the time of the constitutional convention, the two most recent British officers to be impeached were Lord Chancellor Macclesfield (impeached and convicted in 1725), and Warren Hastings (governor-general of India, impeached in 1787—shortly before the Constitutional Convention—and acquitted in 1795). Both Macclesfield and Hastings were impeached after they had left office, but that fact prompted no objections. Viewed from Britain in 1787, late impeachment was not only acceptable, it was the norm.[33]

In America too, "impeachment" had become a process for the legislature to pursue public offenses by public officials. In contrast to England, American impeachment was more widely practiced, and it developed its own characteristics. Late impeachment was less firmly established in pre-constitutional America than it was in England, but it was known and accepted.[34]

Twelve states wrote constitutions before the federal Constitution was drafted in 1787. Ten included impeachment provisions, and in all ten, late impeachment was either required, permitted, or not discussed; nowhere was it explicitly forbidden. Four states explicitly allowed or even required late impeachment. In Virginia, the governor could *only* be impeached after he left office. (In 1781, ex-governor Thomas Jefferson was subjected to preliminary impeachment proceedings for his conduct in office, though in the end he was not impeached.) Delaware had a similar requirement. In Pennsylvania and Vermont, officials could be impeached while in office, or after leaving office if they had resigned. Thus in these states impeachment was designed, at least in part, as a means of ensuring accountability for official action, and not just as a mechanism for removing bad people from office.[35]

Five other states wrote their constitutions after Virginia, Delaware, and Pennsylvania and said nothing for or against late impeachment. Given the backdrop—England making late impeachment the norm, and the other states allowing or requiring late impeachment—one would think that these newer constitutions would have said something if they wanted to bar late impeachment. New York invented—and spelled out—the requirements of two-thirds majorities, a special oath for impeachment judges, and a ban on punishments greater than removal and disqualification. South Carolina, Massachusetts, and New Hampshire adopted very similar impeachment provisions, as did the federal Constitution. But while these constitutional drafters added these explicit new restrictions on impeachment, they did not touch late impeachment.[36]

Delegates came to the Constitutional Convention in 1787 aware of their own state constitutions and precedents, and of English cases like Hastings's. They discussed impeachment at length and on several separate occasions at the convention. Late impeachability never arose directly, but some discussions provide oblique hints as to the Framers' understanding of it.[37]

The working draft of the Constitution had a general impeachment provision that applied to all executive and judicial officers, presumably including the president. The Framers' main bone of contention was whether the president should be impeachable *while* in office; they may thus have presupposed that ex-presidents could be impeached. Their debate highlighted the idea that impeachment is about accountability and deterrence (providing "essential security for the good behaviour of the Executive," as one put it) and not just removability.[38]

The ratification debates shed little light on late impeachability. For instance, Alexander Hamilton wrote in *Federalist 69* that, regarding impeachment, the president "would stand upon no better ground than a governor of New York, and upon worse ground than the governors of Virginia and Delaware" (who, as noted earlier, could only be impeached after they left office). Hamilton may or may not have believed in late impeachability; it is unclear whether the "worse ground" was being removable *and* late-impeachable, or being removable *instead* of being late-impeachable.[39]

Similarly uncertain is a statement from the North Carolina ratification debates. While discussing who exactly could be impeached, delegates worried that *state* officers and even private citizens might be susceptible to federal impeachment. Governor Samuel Johnston rejected this notion, stating: "Removal from office is the punishment—to which is added future disqualification. How could a man be removed from office who had no office?" Opponents of late impeachability could read Johnston's interpretation as precluding late impeachment. But Johnston was trying to dispel the notion that state officers or ordinary citizens could be impeached and was not discussing the timing of impeachment trials.[40]

Both sides would use this (and other) historical evidence, despite the fact that it is vague, oblique, and disputable. Luckily for them, all the other evidence—constitutional text, structure, and precedent—is vague, oblique, and disputable too. But proponents can make a strong case that when the Constitution's impeachment clauses were drafted, late impeachment was in the air, and while the Constitution conspicuously cast off many features of English and state impeachment practice, late impeachment was not one of them.[41]

Precedent

Unlike the speculative and inferential arguments featured so far, arguments from precedent are concrete and take the issue of late impeachment head on. Official House precedent, citing the *Blount* and *Belknap* cases discussed in the following pages, indicates that the "[a]ccused may be tried after resignation." Old impeachment cases do not bind future Congresses, but they can carry a lot of weight. Still, none of the precedents are clear enough to be definitive.[42]

The nation's first federal impeachment case was a late impeachment. The House hastily impeached Senator William Blount on July 7, 1797. The next day, the Senate expelled Blount for his "high misdemeanor" and adjourned. The House continued work on the case after Blount's expulsion, approving the actual articles of impeachment much later, and the Senate trial began in December 1798. Blount's lawyers objected to the fact that he was being tried even though he was no longer in office, but their argument "was easily disposed of, and [they] did not press it." More successful was their claim that senators are not "officers" subject to impeachment in the first place—after a lengthy debate on the issue, the Senate voted fourteen to eleven to dismiss the case.[43]

The next precedent*—and the most important one—is the 1876 case of ex–secretary of war William Belknap. Belknap was connected to a kickback scheme involving western trading posts. When the arrangement was uncovered by a House committee, Belknap learned that he was about to be impeached. He wanted to avoid the infamy of a national inquest, as well as the penalty of disqualification from future office, so he hurried to President Grant's office and resigned.[44]

House members, aware that Belknap had resigned that day, nevertheless decided unanimously to impeach the "late Secretary of War" for offenses committed "while he was in office." To be sure, the House members were not motivated solely by their lawyerly views of the Constitution; 1876 was an election year. The Democrats had taken over the House in 1874, helped by outrage over corruption in the Republican Grant administration, and they wanted to repeat their success. This pressured congressional Republicans to come out strongly against executive corruption as well.[45]

Once the case reached the Republican-controlled Senate, however, motives changed. The vote in the House had been a quick, costless way for members of both parties to condemn Belknap, but the Senate had to actually try the case. Belknap's lawyers argued that Belknap's resignation deprived the Senate of jurisdiction, and the Senate had to settle that issue before putting Belknap on trial—it debated late impeachability for over a month. The discussion covered every legal and practical point raised in this chapter, and many more. Whatever political motivations informed the final vote, no senator could complain that there hadn't been a thorough constitutional dialogue.[46]

In addition to textual and structural arguments, the two sides tussled over precedents and commentaries. Both sides made use of the records of the

* Some claim that Judge West Humphreys, who was impeached and convicted in 1862, was late-impeached. See, e.g., 3 Cong. Rec. 324 (1875) (statement of Rep. Butler). Humphreys had abandoned his judicial post to accept another one in the Confederacy. But he had not actually resigned, and the Senate purported to remove him when it convicted him. See Eleanore Bushnell, Crimes, Follies, and Misfortunes: The Federal Impeachment Trials 115–24 (1992) (describing Humphreys case).

Constitutional Convention, the state ratification debates, and Blount's case. Also prominent was Justice Joseph Story's *Commentaries on the Constitution*. Opponents latched onto Story's arguments against late impeachment almost gleefully. This spurred proponents to cite Story's caveats and mitigation of his own comments, and to trot out statements in favor of late impeachment from William Rawle and John Quincy Adams.[47]

In the end, the Senate voted thirty-seven to twenty-nine in favor of late impeachability. Republicans split thirteen to twenty-seven against, while Democrats supported it twenty-four to two. Some might take the near unanimity among Democrats, coupled with the significant support among Republicans, as a sign of the strength of the *Belknap* precedent. On the other hand, the Senate vote might just have ended up reflecting the same political considerations that had driven the House to impeach Belknap.[48]

With the jurisdictional question out of the way, the trial proceeded for two more months before Belknap was acquitted. The vote on the closest charge was thirty-seven to twenty-five, five votes shy of the two-thirds majority needed to convict. Of the twenty-five senators voting to acquit, only three said that they thought Belknap was not guilty of an impeachable offense; the other twenty-two based their acquittal votes solely on the fact that Belknap had already left office. So on one hand, the House and Senate specifically voted in favor of late impeachability. On the other hand, Belknap avoided conviction only because his impeachment was late.[49]

In defense of late impeachability, there is a big difference between the dismissal Belknap sought and the acquittal he got. The trial was an embarrassing ordeal, and it established Belknap's factual guilt. By deciding only after a full trial to acquit Belknap, the Senate essentially decided that he shouldn't be convicted, not that he *couldn't* be. Bearing this out are several practical factors in the case. If Belknap had presented more of a danger to the Republic—say, if his crime had been more treasonous than venal, or if he had seemed likely to return to federal office—some of the twenty-two senators voting against jurisdiction and conviction might have changed their minds. If everyone had agreed on Belknap's factual guilt, it would have taken just two senators changing their jurisdictional votes for him to be convicted. Some senators were swayed by the fact that Belknap faced criminal liability with a potential sentence of disqualification; if they had seen the future (Belknap was never prosecuted), they might have changed their votes. What if it hadn't been an election year? What if the partisan balance in the Senate had been slightly different? What if Belknap had resigned just after the House impeached him rather than just before? With slightly different facts, Belknap's case could have been a definitive precedent rather than just a tantalizing, muddled one.[50]

One other Senate precedent is noteworthy. Judge George W. English was impeached in 1926 for tyrannical, corrupt, partial, and abusive conduct on the bench. He resigned six days before his trial was set to begin in the Senate. The House resolved that, in light of the resignation, it "d[id] not desire further to urge the articles of impeachment." The House managers told the Senate that while they recommended terminating the proceedings, they believed that "the resignation of Judge English in no way affects the right of the Senate, sitting as a court of impeachment, to hear and determine" the charges against English. No senator suggested that it would have been impossible or unconstitutional to proceed; one senator noted, without contradiction, that he wanted it "distinctly understood" that the case was not a precedent against late impeachability. Indeed, nearly everyone acted as though they *could* have proceeded with the trial. But English was old, his government career was over, and his offenses were relatively mild given the energy that would have been required to pursue them. The Senate dismissed the case, voting seventy to nine.*[51]

In numerous other cases—the most famous being President Nixon's— the target of an impeachment inquiry resigned before the House could vote. Besides Belknap's, the House dropped every one of these cases. This series of cases clearly shows that late impeachment will rarely be deemed worthwhile. But none of these cases reflects a consensus against the *power* of late impeachment. There is a ready analogy: the vast majority of criminal

---

* Congress has handled other impeachees' resignations consistently. One example occurred as this chapter was being edited, when impeached (and convicted felon) Judge Samuel Kent resigned. The House resolved that it did not "desire" to pursue the case, and the Senate dismissed it, agreeing that it was not "useful" to continue. H.R. Res. 661, 111th Cong. (2009); 155 Cong. Rec. S7832–33 (daily ed. July 22, 2009) (Senate dismissal). These careful word choices made clear that Congress simply chose to drop the case, but did not feel legally bound to do so.

prosecutions in this country end in guilty pleas, with no trial and with reduced sentences, and with a tremendous savings of resources for prosecutors and courts. Like criminal jury trials, full-blown impeachment proceedings are expensive and cumbersome. Thus, it is no surprise that late impeachment usually isn't worth the effort once the accused removes himself from office. But just as prosecutors can still take a criminal case to trial even though they usually don't, the pattern of aborted impeachments does not change the legality of late impeachment.[52]

Precedent is the best thing proponents of late impeachability have going for them: late impeachment has been done before, and Congress has stuck up for it on other occasions too. Like all the other evidence favoring late impeachability, it is contestable, but in a way that establishes that late impeachment is hard, not that it is unconstitutional.

Don't Forget the Courts

To all the hurdles—legal and practical—that late impeachment would face in Congress, add the further hurdle it would face in court. For the most part, matters relating to impeachment are off limits to the courts, under the political-question doctrine. In *Nixon v. United States*, federal judge Walter Nixon challenged the procedures that the Senate used to try him. The Supreme Court ruled that because the Constitution specifically gives the Senate "the sole Power to try all Impeachments," there was no room for the Court to get involved in the details of Senate trials. In the realm of impeachment, Congress has the first word, the last word, and all the words in between.[53]

Late impeachability is different, though, because the whole question is whether it *is* "in the realm of impeachment." It is thus more analogous to *Powell v. McCormack* than it is to *Nixon*. *Powell* dealt with another area over which the Constitution makes the House and Senate the sole judge: the qualifications of their members. The House ruled that duly elected Representative Adam Clayton Powell, Jr., was unfit, based on alleged corruption, to take his seat in the House. The Supreme Court, however, declared that the House had no power to exclude Powell. The Constitution, the Court ruled, establishes a limited number of specific qualifications: age, citizenship, residency, and loyalty. The House could judge whether a would-be representative met those qualifications, but this did not give the House the power to insert new ones (like non-corruption). The House was supreme within the bounds set by the Constitution, but it could not redraw those bounds.[54]

The question, then, is whether late impeachment is within the powers granted to Congress in the Constitution. If a late impeachment is properly considered an "impeachment," or if it seems to be within Congress's sole power to decide that issue, then late impeachability is a political question and the courts cannot entertain any challenge to it. But if a late impeachment is not a valid impeachment under the Constitution (as non-corruption was not a valid qualification in *Powell*), then the courts can get involved. (This is somewhat backward—the courts would decide the merits in order to decide whether they can consider the case—but that's how it goes.) Even if the courts are inclined to defer heavily to Congress's interpretation of its own impeachment powers, the courts could still step in if they felt that Congress exceeded its bounds. The result is that the foregoing arguments in favor of late impeachability might have to convince the courts as well as Congress.[55]

Nothing to Worry About

Late impeachment was discussed after President Nixon's ignominious exit from office, and the question reemerged when President Clinton issued several controversial pardons in his last hours in office (however rare it may be for late impeachment to be worth pursuing, it is less rare for it to be worth considering). The late-impeachment question will never be resolved, though, unless and until Congress actually tries to carry one out.[56]

As stated at the outset of this chapter, the stakes for this constitutional cliffhanger are relatively low. Some might worry—as I have, elsewhere—that Congress could abuse and overuse late impeachment, especially given that impeachment is not checked by any other powers of any other branches. But the same potential for abuse exists for regular impeachments. In both cases, there is one very powerful check: elections. If it is good in a particular case to impeach an ex-president, then there is nothing to worry about. If it is bad, our worry is tempered by the fact that it would be hard for the impeachment to succeed. If Congress decides (with the courts' approval) that it can and should go forward with a late impeachment, it becomes a matter between Congress and the voters. In any case, the Republic and the presidency would survive.[57]

On the flip side, one might argue that late impeachability is so important that there is a different sort of problem here: that late impeachability is not clear enough. It is hard to see this as a problem either, though. To the extent that a president would ever be worried about the possibility of late impeachment, one cannot imagine him breathing easy and saying, "That's OK, I like my odds." Theoretically, Congress could concede its power of late impeachment, but a president engaged in an interbranch conflict should never rely on Congress to meekly deny itself power.

There is no plausible way to preempt the issue anyway. No court would rule on this question in the absence of an actual case, or possibly even *with* an actual case. Until a real late impeachment arises, Congress could only offer non-binding or indirect commentary, such as by legislating that officials who have been late-impeached and convicted lose their pensions. This would send a clear signal that Congress favors late impeachability, but it would not bind anyone until and unless an actual late impeachment occurred.

The only way to resolve whether late impeachment is constitutional without actually executing one would be to amend the Constitution, and it strains credulity to imagine an amendment like that moving to the top of the national political agenda. Between (1) the members of Congress who would not want to call their impeachment powers into question, (2) the members of Congress and state legislatures who would rank countless other matters much higher on their priority lists, and (3) the opponents of late impeachability who could raise plausible objections, the effort would surely fail.

As long as it is a possibility, late impeachment can help to curb potential presidential excesses. At the same time, the uncertainty surrounding late impeachment might curb Congress's potential excesses too. Unlike the cases in other chapters in this book, it would not be worthwhile for us to "fix" the late-impeachment cliffhanger, even if we could.

6

The Third-Term Controversy

President Frederick is three years into his second term. He remains so popular that some pundits have floated the idea of repealing the Twenty-Second Amendment and letting him run for a third term. Frederick laughs off such talk, and a national opinion poll shows that only 12 percent of voters support repeal. Still, Frederick casts a large shadow; on the eve of primary season, his Democrats have no clear front-runner for the nomination to replace him.

Then disaster strikes: a treacherous terrorist attack kills tens of thousands of Americans. The country rallies behind President Frederick as he leads a strong offensive against the terrorists and their sponsors. His approval rating shoots into the nineties. While the country is badly rattled by the attack, people feel safer with Frederick in charge.

Frederick feels pretty good being in charge too. Now, when the Twenty-Second Amendment comes up, he sounds increasingly coy. Support for repeal rises to almost 50 percent in the polls. But Republicans—and several prominent Democrats— argue against amending the Constitution in the heat of the moment, so the congressional and state supermajorities needed for an amendment are well out of reach.

At this point, a startling idea gains traction among Democrats: President Frederick can run for vice president. Many people would find Frederick's mere presence reassuring. Others envision a figurehead president who would leave VP Frederick in charge or perhaps even resign and let Frederick become president again. This last maneuver would be constitutional, they say, because the Twenty-Second Amendment only says that no one "shall be elected to the office of the President more than twice," and Frederick would not be "elected" president. The amendment says nothing about a two-term president "succeeding" to the presidency, or "serving" as *president. Buoyed by Frederick's stratospheric popularity and the atmosphere of crisis, the plan steadily gains support, and Frederick's anointed surrogate, Representative Stevens, sweeps the Democratic presidential primaries.*

The Republicans object forcefully. As one senator puts it on a Sunday morning talk show, "We're all grateful to President Frederick for his leadership during these difficult months, but everybody knows we have a two-term limit. We shouldn't let the Constitution be a casualty of this war." Frederick is officially nominated for vice president at the Democratic convention, and the litigation floodgates open.

EVERYBODY KNOWS THAT THE PRESIDENT OF the United States is limited to serving two terms. The Twenty-Second Amendment, ratified in 1951, spells it out: "No person shall be elected to the office of the President more than twice. . . ."* The Twelfth Amendment keeps two-termers out of the vice presidency too: "no person constitutionally ineligible to the office of President shall be eligible to that of Vice-President."

The law is funny, though. When people have strong enough incentives and good enough lawyers, they may take things that everybody knows aren't legal and find a way to make them legal after all. Politics can be funny too. In the right political climate, "everybody knows" can quickly become "everybody thought," and half the country can decide overnight that it now "knows" something quite different. And so, a president could perhaps serve a third term as president—and a fourth term, and a fifth—by performing the legal maneuver described here. His opponents (invoking the conventional understanding of presidential term limits) would fight back but, as this chapter will show, if the politics were just so, the courts, Congress, and the voters really could put a two-term president back in office.

---

* The amendment continues: ". . . and no person who has held the office of President, or acted as President, for more than two years of a term to which some other person was elected President shall be elected to the office of the President more than once." Thus a nitpicker could say that a president can serve more than two terms if he inherits just under two years of someone else's term and then gets elected twice in his own right. A top-flight nitpicker might add that a president could conceivably serve *multiple* partial terms before being elected twice in his own right. For simplicity's sake, this chapter will refer to anyone barred by the amendment from reelection as a "two-termer."

A president would have to be very popular to try this, but if he is, he might be popular enough to succeed. In the last half century, many executives in the United States and around the world have used their power and popularity to circumvent term limits. Some got the law changed or used brute force, but others exploited loopholes to stay in power. It is easy today to distinguish U.S. presidents from New York mayors (Bloomberg), Colombian presidents (Uribe), and Russian presidents/prime ministers (Putin), but political culture can change quickly and dramatically.[1]

Some History and Perspective

There was a two-term tradition before the Twenty-Second Amendment, but it was informal and shaky. A few presidents—most seriously Ulysses Grant and Theodore Roosevelt—tried to win third terms but failed. Numerous policy makers tried to formally ban third terms, but they failed as well.[2]

This chapter's opening scenario somewhat resembles the climate in 1940, when conditions were perfect for a breach. President Franklin Roosevelt wanted a third term (though publicly he was demure). The opposition Republicans had a popular candidate, Wendell Willkie, while Democrats had no one remotely as compelling as Roosevelt. World War II had broken out, and anxious voters in the still-neutral United States put a premium on keeping Roosevelt at the helm. Willkie pressed the third-term issue, warning that it was a prelude to dictatorship, but to no avail. Roosevelt's comfortable margin of victory meant that the two-term tradition was officially dead. In 1944 he easily won a fourth term.[3]

Roosevelt died in 1945, and the Republicans retook the House and Senate in the next congressional election. In 1947, on their first day in power, Republican leaders introduced the Twenty-Second Amendment, to limit presidents to two terms. Within a couple of months it passed both houses. The states were not exactly thirsting for term limits—ratification took an unprecedented four years—but they did approve them.[4]

Even before the amendment, it was hard for presidents to win third terms; Franklin Roosevelt was only able to succeed during a global crisis. Now that the Twenty-Second Amendment seemingly bans third terms, it seems unlikely that any president would be able to evade term limits unless circumstances were much more calamitous. Unfortunately, it is not as hard as it used to be to imagine such a thing.[5]

In such a calamity, Americans might just repeal the Twenty-Second Amendment outright. But the Constitution is not designed to be amended quickly or easily. For our hypothetical President Frederick to get a new amendment, he would need the support of two-thirds majorities in the House and Senate, plus three-fourths of the states—something Roosevelt probably would not have been able to muster quickly in 1940 had term limits existed at that point. By contrast, Frederick could circumvent term limits simply by winning a court case (and then the election). President Frederick's evasion of term limits might require an extraordinary crisis, but a made-to-order repeal of the Twenty-Second Amendment would require an even greater one.[6]

The Twenty-Second Amendment has so far barred Presidents Eisenhower, Nixon, Reagan, Clinton, and Bush from running for third terms. Each man has nonetheless inspired low-level talk of future presidential or vice-presidential service—mostly proposals to repeal the Twenty-Second Amendment, but sometimes ideas for circumventing the amendment, using legal arguments like the ones in this chapter. The time has just never been right—yet.[7]

The Twenty-Second Amendment

After Representative Stevens wins the Democratic presidential nomination and picks President Frederick as his running mate, the campaign drops subtle hints that if Stevens wins, he will resign and let Frederick become president again.

In October, Frederick faces his opponent for the vice presidency, Senator Green, in a televised debate.

Moderator: Senator Green, do you think it would be legal for President Frederick to become president again?

Green: No. George Washington established the tradition that after a president serves two terms, he goes home. When President Roosevelt broke that tradition, Americans said, "Never again," and put the two-term limit in the Constitution. Since then, when our presidents have served two terms, they've understood this. We've all understood it. Why would the Constitution force men like President Reagan and President Clinton to retire but let President Frederick sneak back into office?

Moderator: President Frederick, how do you respond? Isn't the Twenty-Second Amendment supposed to keep people in your position from being president again?

Frederick: When the Republicans pushed the amendment through, they were just striking back at the late President Roosevelt, who had beaten them four times in a row. I guess they thought World War II would have gone better if Wendell Willkie had been president. [Audience laughs.] Look, it doesn't matter what they were thinking, it matters what they said. They said a two-termer can't get elected president again. But I'm not running for president. The amendment doesn't speak to my situation.

Moderator: Senator Green, your rebuttal?

Green: President Frederick is asking the voters to keep him in power. He says he's not running for president, but you can almost see him winking. My fellow Americans, if the only way our nation can survive is to make Jim Frederick president for life—while pretending the Constitution is OK with that—then this is not the America I fought two wars to defend.

The third-term controversy is a media sensation. There is no shortage of lawyers and law professors making their constitutional arguments on cable news shows. Here is a relatively calm pair.

Professor Scott: Look, I can't tell you why the drafters of the Twenty-Second Amendment limited it this way. But they did. When they wrote the first draft of the amendment, they said two-termers couldn't "hold the office." But then, they changed it from "hold the office" to "be elected." You see? They initially banned what President Frederick is trying to do, but then they changed the language until it didn't say that anymore. They said "elected" only, they said it on purpose, and that's that.

Professor McCulloch: The Twenty-Second Amendment was written to keep two-termers out. The Twelfth Amendment says two-termers can't run for *vice president either. Frederick is a two-termer. It's not that complicated, and people know it. Professor Scott likes talking about the "plain meaning of the text" here, but that just means he wants to ignore the context, and ignore the clear purpose of the amendment, and ignore the way people have understood this language for generations. If the Twenty-Second Amendment is this easy to avoid, then it means nothing, and judges don't like to interpret the Constitution as an exercise in futility. I think Professor Scott and I agree on one thing, though: if the courts don't prevent this, the people will still get to decide. Lots of voters who would otherwise vote for President Frederick are going to vote against him, because they recognize how inappropriate this is.*

Our hypothetical President Frederick has two main bars to clear. The courts might keep him off of the ballot; if not, the voters could keep him from winning the election. (A third possible bar will arise in the following pages: Congress could weigh in.) Because the voters get a say here, Frederick would need to pitch his legal arguments not just to hair-splitting judges but also to millions of plain folks.

The clever legalistic logic and intricate historical evidence that might convince a judge is less likely to move the average voter. For them, the legal arguments would be inextricably bound with political choices. If Frederick loses the election, it only means that the voters did not want him in office; it says nothing direct about how they interpreted the Twelfth or Twenty-Second Amendment. Even voters who based their choice solely on the term-limit issue would fall into a fuzzy middle: some might be saying that electing a two-termer would be unconstitutional, but others might be saying only that electing a two-termer is a bad idea. This chapter will concentrate more on the former—the legal arguments—but that should not obscure the fact that "the barriers to a third presidential term are stronger than just the constitutional provision itself," and that the voters' policy preferences (whatever they may be) would matter a lot in our fictional election.[8]

It might seem ironic that President Frederick, whom I have made a Democrat, is using a "plain meaning" interpretation of the Twenty-Second

Amendment, since that approach is usually associated more with conservatives. Frederick's Republican opponents favor a looser interpretation of the Twenty-Second Amendment, going beyond the text to vindicate a particular legislative purpose, even though that approach is more often associated with liberals. In reality, though, there is nothing new or ironic about constitutional interpretation being driven by high-stakes political expediency rather than philosophical purity.

The Argument for Continued Eligibility

Many people, most prominently Bruce Peabody and Scott Gant, have made the argument that two-termers can serve again as president. The argument has two main parts. First, the Twenty-Second Amendment explicitly limits itself to preventing another *election* but says nothing about becoming president by *succession*. Second, earlier versions of the amendment barred any sort of service, not just being elected, but that language was knowingly changed. Proponents can say that if the result of their interpretation seems foolish, it is only because the amendment's drafters and ratifiers were foolish. (A third part, relating to the Twelfth Amendment and the vice presidency, will be discussed in a later section.)[9]

The key distinction—between being elected to the presidency and succeeding to it—is not subtle. Nine of our forty-four presidents entered office by succession, and five of them were never elected president. At the very moment that the Twenty-Second Amendment was written in 1947, the incumbent president was Harry Truman, who had succeeded to the office and had not (yet) been elected in his own right. At that time, every generation in living memory had featured unelected presidents, with successions occurring in 1841, 1850, 1865, 1881, 1901, 1923, and 1945.*

---

* On these occasions, pursuant to Article II, Section 1 (as later clarified by the Twenty-Fifth Amendment), the vice president succeeded to the presidency when the president died. The Twentieth Amendment presents another possibility: if a president-elect is removed from the picture, the vice president elect takes the oath of office as president. When this chapter talks about the vice president "succeeding" to the presidency, it does not distinguish between these two methods. *Cf.* Bruce G. Peabody & Scott E. Gant, *The Twice and Future President*, 83 Minn. L. Rev. 565, 568, 619 (1999) (distinguishing between methods of succession).

Succession clearly was on Congress's mind during the debates on the Twenty-Second Amendment. One contentious point during the drafting was whether and how to count partial terms toward the two-term limit. The final amendment only counts an unelected term—defined as when someone "held the office" or "acted as President" during the time for which "some other person was elected"—if it lasts more than two years. As Peabody and Gant note, this suggests that the drafters were aware of how "holding the office" is distinct from being "elected."[10]

While the drafters addressed both elected and unelected presidents on the "who gets limited?" side of the amendment, they opted to cover only elected presidents on the "limited from what?" side. It didn't start out that way, though. As originally written, the amendment was conscious of our potential loophole, and it guarded against it. The first version of the amendment, introduced in the House, said that no one "shall be chosen *or serve* as President of the United States for any term, or be *eligible to hold the office* of President during any term, if such person shall have heretofore served as President during the whole or any part of each of any two separate terms." The House Judiciary Committee made the language more concise without changing its effect: "Any person who has served as President of the United States during all, or portions, of any two terms, shall thereafter be *ineligible to hold the office* of President." After limited debate, this language passed the House and went to the Senate. During the debate, Representative Earl Michener, who introduced the resolution that became the amendment, made the following apt statement: "[T]he language of a constitutional amendment is most important, more so than in the case of ordinary legislation. Every comma, every semicolon, every capital letter, every word means something in a constitutional amendment, and under these circumstances we should not lightly adopt language in a constitutional amendment that has not been thoroughly weighed."[11]

The Senate Judiciary Committee limited successions even more, consciously closing a loophole for two-termers who might say that they are "acting" as president and not actually holding the office. Its language read: "A person who has held the office of President, or acted as President, on three hundred and sixty-five calendar days or more in each of two terms shall not be *eligible to hold the office* of President, *or to act* as President, for any part of another term."[12]

When the amendment reached the Senate floor, Senator Warren Magnuson piped up. He was against counting any partial terms toward the two-term limit, and he wanted to use more straightforward language to avoid "complicated legal questions." He also worried that the Judiciary Committee's language was "very complicated," such that he "doubt[ed] if many State legislators could really understand its wording." Thus, Magnuson proposed that the amendment simply provide: "No person shall be elected to the office of President more than twice."[13]

This is the point where successions got removed from the "limited from what?" side. Magnuson could have avoided this by saying something like: "No person elected to the office of President twice shall be eligible to hold the office of President, or to act as President, in any subsequent term." But maybe Magnuson wasn't worried about two-term presidents returning to office through succession. The only federal offices ever held by ex-presidents (John Quincy Adams in the House, Andrew Johnson in the Senate, and Taft on the Supreme Court) have been outside the line of succession. No former president has ever run for vice president, let alone gotten elected vice president, let alone succeeded to the presidency. Perhaps the prospect of it happening in the future seemed too remote to Magnuson to justify doubling the length of his concise amendment.

However, the Senate's final text (which the House later accepted) added plenty of clutter. It began with Magnuson's draft, but it continued with a clause counting partial terms toward the limit if they exceeded two years (a compromise between the House version, which counted any partial term, and Magnuson's language, which counted none of them). Then, it concluded with some awkward language to exempt then-president Truman from the amendment. Magnuson's 13 elegant words were stretched to 121— but without restoring the language cut by Magnuson that would have avoided the controversies in this chapter.[14]

The bottom line for proponents of continued presidential eligibility is that the draft language changed from barring two-termers from any presidential service to barring them only from being elected. The Senate opened up a loophole, the House and the states approved it, and the problematic text is in there, whether we like it or not. Under this reading, the Twenty-Second Amendment does not totally prevent third terms; it just raises the bar. Specifically, it requires that a would-be third termer have enough political support not just for a third term but for the constitutional tricks required to win it. That barrier has been high enough to prevent anyone from even attempting to clear it. So far.

The Argument Against Continued Eligibility

Nobody has set out the argument against the loophole as carefully as Peabody and Gant have set out the argument for it. Partly, this reflects political reality. Even before the amendment, there was a powerful presumption against third terms; the common understanding of the amendment makes that presumption much, much more powerful. Two-termers like Eisenhower and Clinton have inspired talk of skirting the amendment, but never much more than idle speculation. Therefore, there has been no incentive to develop a legally rigorous argument against the loophole. But any president who made a serious attempt to use the loophole would have to be riding a powerful wave of political popularity—the worst possible time to start constructing a complex legal case against him.[15]

Given how strongly the general public and some experts presume that two-term presidents cannot continue to serve as president, it is surprisingly complicated to argue that the Twenty-Second Amendment requires that result. The core of the argument rests on a bit of a bootstrap: the similarly strong presumption among the framers of the amendment that this is what they were accomplishing, even if it isn't exactly what they said.[16]

The amendment's text does not rule out succeeding to the presidency; it really does only stop two-termers from being "elected." It does, however, set up an important textual argument: that the Twelfth Amendment bars two-termers from being elected *vice* president. This argument would stop our hypothetical President Frederick's plan, and it might explain why the framers of the Twenty-Second Amendment did not worry about the loophole. In 1947, there had been only two kinds of presidents: those elected president, and those elected vice president who stepped up when the president died. The Twelfth Amendment states that "no person constitutionally ineligible to the office of President shall be eligible to that of Vice-President," so people could have read the Twelfth and Twenty-Second Amendments together to make two-termers ineligible to be elected president or vice president. But—as discussed in more detail in the next section—this interpretation of the Twelfth Amendment argument is disputable. Even if it works, moreover, it provides only partial protection. For one thing, the Twenty-Fifth Amendment (ratified in 1967) provides an alternative path to the vice presidency. Indeed, the last person to succeed to the presidency, Gerald Ford, was appointed vice president—not elected—under the Twenty-Fifth Amendment procedure for filling a vacancy. Additionally, as discussed in Chapter 4, the line of succession extends past the vice president, leaving other possible paths to the presidency. Preventing someone from being *elected* president or vice president only makes it harder—not impossible—for that person to *be* president.

There is still an argument that the Twenty-Second Amendment bars successions as well as elections; the point is just that that argument has to reach beyond the amendment's plain text, into its purpose.

It may well be that the framers of the Twenty-Second Amendment—who had been so careful in their wording initially—knew that they were creating a loophole and just felt that it was too small to worry about. It certainly appears, though, that they did not create the loophole consciously. When Senator Magnuson opened the door to unlimited terms by succession, nobody on either side in the Senate (or the House, or the state legislatures) made a peep. Everyone continued under the assumption that two terms was the limit.[17]

By any measure, the whole point of the amendment was to send presidents home after two terms, and it looks as though this is what Congress and the states thought they were doing. Parsing the text to mean that presidents can stay in power forever—making the amendment accomplish the exact opposite of what it was supposed to—is precisely the sort of result that leads legal interpreters to go beyond the text in response (and that leads people to dislike lawyers).[18]

But there are different ways to "go beyond the text." Using intent to resolve ambiguity is simple. Recall Chapter 3, and the constitutional clauses on presidential disability. There, the language was ambiguous (did it mean *A* or *B*?), but everyone present knew what it meant (*A*, not *B*), so the argument that the language actually means *A* is very strong in light of the clear intent. As a general matter, constitutional interpreters prefer a "second-best" reading of the text that vindicates a provision's purpose, over a reading that parses the text perfectly while missing the point of the provision. But the Twenty-Second Amendment presents us with an omission, not an ambiguity, making it harder to use intent this way. The senators used a clear term (*A*) and completely overlooked an implication of that clear term (*A* does not include *B*). While there is ample evidence that that implication was unwelcome, it is harder to rely on that intent evidence to *trump* the text than it was in Chapter 3 to use intent evidence to *clarify* the text.[19]

Still, is it really immaterial that nobody voting on the amendment wanted our loophole? Or noticed it? These things are hard to get past, and they are at the heart of the vehement arguments that commentators have offered against continued presidential eligibility. The point of the Twenty-Second Amendment is clearly to limit presidential service, and it should be interpreted that way, even in the face of seemingly clear text to the contrary. The unacceptable alternative, notwithstanding the plain meaning of the text, is to apply the amendment to reach a result that subverts the amendment's purpose, and to allow a president who is barred from a straightforward reelection to become president through ponderous constitutional convolutions.

The notion that a constitutional provision should be interpreted foremost in a way that vindicates its intended purpose is a powerful one in American law. It is not hard to get a few votes for the proposition on the Supreme Court, and not uncommon to get a majority for it. It is a satisfying technique as well: One looks at the fact that the Twenty-Second Amendment was meant to close the door on further presidential service, not at the fact that the precise text used could be interpreted as leaving the door slightly ajar. Then, because the amendment was so clearly meant to close the door, and because the slight opening is so far from—indeed, so opposite to—these intentions, the door is interpreted as being completely closed.[20]

Of course, as discussed already in this chapter, it might be harder to get judges to go along with the purposive interpretation, given that the text is not ambiguous. It may be that the "purposive" approach is not powerful enough to lead the Supreme Court to declare President Frederick's presence on the ballot unconstitutional, especially since the dispute here is not over a flexible term (like "liberty" or "due process") that cries out for a loose inter-pretation. Another reason they might read the amendment narrowly is that it is anti-democratic—indeed, it is the only amendment in the Constitution that directly restricts citizens in the exercise of their political rights.[21]

If the Supreme Court read the amendment restrictively, to preserve voters' power to the maximum extent possible, it is important to remember that the voters could use that power to defeat our would-be third-termer. If enough voters react to Frederick's interpretation of the Twenty-Second Amendment by saying, "Hey! Frederick can't do that!" then he will lose the election. The voters will have made themselves right: Frederick couldn't do it.

The Twelfth Amendment and Vice-Presidential Eligibility of Two-Term Presidents

The question in this chapter is whether the Twenty-Second Amendment allows a two-term president to subsequently succeed to the office; everyone agrees that it bars him from being elected directly to a third term. Thus, our scenario is actually fought out in a different arena: since President Frederick can't be elected president, can he be elected *vice* president?

Under the original Constitution, the qualifications for vice president and president were identical, because the vice president was always a (runner-up) presidential candidate. When the Twelfth Amendment made the vice presidency a separately elected office, it needed to make this implicit symmetry explicit. Thus, the amendment says, "no person constitutionally ineligible to the office of President shall be eligible to that of Vice-President of the United States."[22]

At the time, it was clear what the Twelfth Amendment meant: the original Constitution said that to "be eligible to the Office of President," a person must be a natural-born citizen, at least thirty-five years old, and a U.S. resi-dent for at least fourteen years. (A loyalty requirement was added later.) The Twelfth Amendment simply required that a vice president meet these same three requirements, using the same "eligibility" phrasing.[23]

The framers of the Twenty-Second Amendment clouded the issue. As seen above, their initial drafts talked about being "eligible to the office," a phrasing that would have avoided any confusion, but their final version instead says only that no two-termer "shall be elected to the office." The question is whether that makes two-termers "constitutionally ineligible" to *be* president—and thus ineligible to be a vice president under the Twelfth Amendment.

For those who believe that the Twenty-Second Amendment bars two-termers from any service as president, the answer is easy: two-termers are completely ineligible to be president, so they are completely ineligible to be vice president too. But for those who believe that the Twenty-Second Amendment allows two-termers to serve as president, things are not as clear cut.[24]

The answer turns on the intertwined meanings of electability and eligibility. Some people argue that they are synonymous. This means that when the Twenty-Second Amendment makes two-termers presidentially unelectable, it also makes them "ineligible" to *be* president, and thus ineligible to *be* vice president, under the Twelfth Amendment. If this interpretation is correct, then it makes it much more difficult (though not impossible) for a two-termer to return to office.[25]

But others shoot back that eligibility is broader, with electability as only one of its parts: because the Twenty-Second Amendment stops short of making two-termers totally ineligible to serve as president, the Twelfth Amendment does not restrict them in any way from becoming vice president either.[26]

Another, more subtle interpretation is that, by precluding their election, the Twenty-Second Amendment makes two-termers *partially* ineligible to be president. The Twelfth Amendment defines vice-presidential eligibility as identical to presidential eligibility. Therefore, the Twelfth Amendment precludes two-termers from being *elected* vice president. Put another way, Judge Richard Posner once wrote, one could argue that "[e]lecting a vice president means electing a vice president and *contingently* electing him as president. That interpretation, though a little bold, would honor the intention behind the 22nd Amendment." When the Twenty-Second Amendment was written, such an interpretation would have constituted a total bar on becoming vice president, because election was the only way to become vice president. Subsequently, though, the Twenty-Fifth Amendment provided for vice-presidential vacancies to be filled by presidential appointment and congressional confirmation. This opened the vice-presidential door back up for two-termers under this interpretation. If President Frederick's partisans are willing to run a stand-in for president who would then resign, surely they would be willing to run a stand-in for vice president and have him resign too, leaving the vice presidency open for Frederick to be appointed to it.[27]

All these interpretations are possible. Significantly, though, even the ones that would shut President Frederick out of the vice presidency would still permit a determined nation to bring him back into the White House through a more complicated path, from further down in the line of succession (a prospect discussed later in this chapter). But who is "the nation" here, and how would it decide any of this?

Who Decides?

In this chapter, for the first time in this book, the voters would have a direct role in resolving a constitutional cliffhanger. The voters' sense of the Constitution would be intertwined with their ordinary political judgment, but the fact remains that their constitutional judgment would carry great weight: if Frederick lost the election, he could not be vice president or ascend from there to the presidency; if Frederick won the election, Congress and the courts would challenge that result at their peril. That does not mean that the courts and Congress would be shut out of the process. Rather, it means that they would need to get involved early—something that is much more feasible for the courts than for Congress.

The Courts

There is no question that, if a two-term president like Frederick was nominated by his party to run for vice president, people would file lawsuits—some in support, some in opposition. Finding a proper plaintiff would be relatively easy. If a state decided that Frederick was constitutionally disqualified and kept him off of the ballot, he would then have standing to sue to get on the ballot. If the state instead decided to put him on the ballot, Frederick's opponent would probably have standing to sue to get him removed. More helpfully, given that time would be short, the state or either candidate could seek a declaratory judgment before the state even made its decision.[28]

Different states (and D.C.) have different standards for ballot access, and for litigating disputes over ballot access, so the candidates might need to file fifty-one separate lawsuits to preserve their rights and avoid procedural problems. Nevertheless, the question here is over the proper interpretation of the federal constitution, so ultimately—ideally—the litigation would get funneled up to the Supreme Court very quickly for a unified and definitive ruling. President Frederick should welcome the certainty that such a decision would provide. A positive court judgment would undermine a big campaign issue against him, but even a negative court ruling would be helpful, since it would let him give up early and cheaply (unless he wanted to resist, in which case the legal discussion in this chapter would probably be irrelevant anyway).[29]

Having the courts rule before the election, instead of leaving it for Congress to decide afterward, would prevent a painful no-win situation. Assume that Frederick ran for vice president, state officials let him on the ballot, and the courts didn't get involved. If Frederick won and Congress objected, it might throw the vice-presidential election into the Senate* and potentially void millions of people's votes—an awkward proposition, both legally and politically. On the flip side, assume that state officials left Frederick off the ballot, the courts didn't get involved, and the election went on without him. In such a case, Congress would have no way to provide Frederick with a remedy after the fact. Prompt action in court would circumvent both dilemmas.

As the cases worked their way up to the Supreme Court, whichever side lost below could add an argument: that the issue is a non-justiciable "political

---

* If no candidate wins an electoral-vote majority (which would be the case if Frederick won but his votes were thrown out), the Senate elects a vice president from the top two finishers. Frederick's Democrats could have a few electors cast their votes for someone else, to ensure that one Democrat was among the top two finishers, but this would be pointless. If the Republicans had enough votes to exclude Frederick's electoral votes, they would have enough votes to elect the Republican vice-presidential candidate; the addition of a replacement Democrat into the mix would make no difference. A better course, if Congress objected to the vice president elect's eligibility, would be for it to declare him the winner but also declare him ineligible. It could then declare the vice presidency vacant—similar to what would happen if the electoral college chose someone who then died. This would avoid the problems just discussed. The new president would simply nominate a vice president, to be confirmed by Congress, as specified in the Twenty-Fifth Amendment.

question." While it would be better to win outright than on a technicality like this, the stakes are high and either side would likely take any court victory it could get.*

The political-question analysis has appeared in multiple chapters already. The first issue would be whether the Constitution's text expressly gives Congress the sole power—to the exclusion of the courts—to judge the qualifications of vice-presidential candidates. The Twelfth Amendment says that "The President of the Senate shall, in the presence of the Senate and House of Representatives, open all the certificates [containing the states' electoral votes] and *the votes shall then be counted*." Congress has interpreted this passive-voice passage to mean that Congress counts the votes, and that when votes are questionable, Congress decides which ones are valid. But even if this gives Congress the authority to resolve electoral disputes, it is a far cry from giving Congress the *sole* power to interpret the Twenty-Second Amendment and the rest of the Twelfth. Consider, by contrast, one unmistakable example of a "textual commission" political question: qualification disputes in congressional elections. The Constitution says that each house of Congress "shall be *the* Judge of the . . . Qualifications of its own members," which more clearly excludes the courts from playing a role.[30]

There is precedent for Congress resolving electoral-vote disputes, and not the courts. In 1872, candidate Horace Greeley died after Election Day, and Congress decided not to count his electoral votes, without the courts getting involved. In 1876, four states had disputed electoral votes, and the result of the election hung in the balance. Congress formed a commission to resolve the dispute, again without litigation interfering. In 1887, Congress passed a statute to govern future disputes, in which it underlined its view: Congress gets the last word (even if, as we will see, it generally chooses to defer to the states).[31]

But these cases are distinguishable. In 1872, there was no case to litigate, because Greeley had lost the election anyway. More importantly, in both

---

* Since state courts do not necessarily follow the same standards as federal courts for things like political questions, it is possible that getting a federal court to dismiss the case as a political question would not be a complete victory. Individual states might reach the merits, possibly yielding a fragmented patchwork of results until and unless the Supreme Court intervened.

1872 and 1876, the complications arose only after Election Day. There was nothing to litigate before. There was also no problem with Congress taking complete authority, because Congress was in a good position to use that authority promptly and decisively. In our case, though, the term-limit issue would arise months before the election, quite a while before the matter could reach Congress. Only the courts would be in a position to settle the issue promptly and thereby prevent problems from arising in the first place. Moreover, *Bush v. Gore* showed that the Supreme Court is willing nowadays to intervene even in post-election disputes; as Rachel Barkow put it, "the unmistakable trend is toward a view that all constitutional questions are matters for independent judicial interpretation." Given that the *Bush* Court was unwilling to wait three weeks for Congress to resolve that case, it is hard to imagine in our case that the Court would wait for months, ducking the case and allowing the election to go forward shadowed by such doubt. To be sure, *Bush v. Gore* is far from the Court's most prestigious precedent, and much of the negative commentary about *Bush* (including Justice Breyer's dissent) argued that the case *did* present a political question, which the Supreme Court should not have heard. But President Frederick's issue presents a much more compelling case for judicial action; if they could act quickly enough, the courts would merely be enabling a candidacy rather than anointing one.[32]

Political questions can also arise when a case turns on a matter of pure policy, as opposed to something within the court's usual legal bailiwick; or when it is important to respect the decisions of the political branches for the sake of finality, uniformity, or the separation of powers. But in our case, just as in other chapters, the issue is one of constitutional interpretation, not merely policy. Moreover (and as discussed further in this chapter), the likely sequence of events would make congressional action, not a court decision, the real threat to stability and finality.[33]

Overall, the dispute in this chapter is easily reducible to a question of ballot access, something that courts routinely resolve. Even for congressional elections, where Congress is supposedly the sole venue for resolving disputes, state officials can keep unqualified candidates off of the ballot beforehand, and courts can hear and resolve challenges to those decisions. It would be the best course of action here.

Congress

Congress's involvement in presidential elections is usually ceremonial. After Election Day, the electoral college meets to cast its votes, and Congress convenes to count those votes on January 6. As discussed earlier in this chapter, Congress considers its duty to count electoral votes as including the resolution of disputes over *which* votes count. Under current law, in place since 1887, if a state resolves any issues regarding its electoral votes six days before Electoral College Day (currently in mid-December), Congress must accept that state's votes, so long as the votes were "regularly given." Unfortunately, nobody knows what constitutes "irregular giving" here. It is unclear, therefore, what Congress could, should, or would do about a two-term president running for vice president.[34]

Congress has dealt with several disputes under the 1887 law, but it has always simply deferred to the conclusions of the states submitting the votes, and to those states' courts. This reflects the mild nature of the disputes more than it does the bounds of Congress's powers, however. Consider a tougher case: a state, observing all the requisite procedures, casts its electoral votes for a clearly unconstitutional candidate—say, a thirty-year-old. If the state certified and submitted the votes on time, and settled any litigation over the young candidate more than six days before that, the 1887 law might preclude Congress from rejecting the votes. But Congress also could very plausibly declare these votes to be "irregularly given" and refuse to count them.[35]

Congress has judged the qualifications of electoral-vote recipients before. As mentioned above, Democratic candidate Horace Greeley died in 1872, between Election Day and Electoral College Day (then in January). All the Democratic members of the electoral college voted for other (living) people, except for three ultra-faithful electors in Georgia who voted for the dead Greeley. It was a moot point—Greeley had lost anyway—but Congress ruled that dead people cannot get electoral votes, and it refused to count the Greeley votes from Georgia. In doing so, it asserted its power to judge presidential candidates' eligibility. The 1887 law later seemed to accept this power, and so not much stands in Congress's way if it wishes to exercise this power again.[36]

After the 2000 election, regardless of whether the Supreme Court was right or wrong to get involved, Congress still had a chance to rule on the issue in January 2001. On Counting Day, Vice President Al Gore officially declared himself the loser after presiding over the counting and rejecting protests from some House members about the Florida votes being not "regularly given." Significantly, he didn't reject the protests for being out of order. He rejected them because the 1887 law required the protests to have the support of a senator before they could go forward. Had any senator objected to George W. Bush's Florida victory, Congress could have considered Bush's fate then and there. Whatever everyone else does, Congress can still get the last word, or at least a fair shot at it.[37]

In practical reality, though, Congress's role has been small. Electoral votes and presidential qualifications are rarely disputed. In 2008, when questions arose regarding Senator John McCain's status as a natural-born citizen, the Senate passed a resolution declaring him to be one, but the resolution was non-binding. Questions also arose about Senator Barack Obama's status as a natural-born citizen, but Congress opted not to dignify the questions with a response, and nobody with standing to sue took the issue to court. Still, in an extreme case like President Frederick's, it is easy to imagine some members of Congress blanching at counting votes for him. They could argue that if a successful candidate is not constitutionally qualified for office, the Twelfth Amendment makes Congress the last line of defense and gives it the legal authority to throw out unconstitutional votes. Even if Congress's *authority* under the Constitution is debatable, Congress clearly has the *power* to interject itself and, at the very least, to complicate things.[38]

If this happened—if Congress refused to approve Frederick's vice-presidential election even after the courts and voters had—Frederick would be stuck. He could sue, but it seems unlikely that the courts would hear the case; besides the political-question doctrine, the courts would also struggle with finding a proper defendant and a viable remedy. It would be politically perilous for Congress to defy the courts and voters this way, but if Congress wanted badly enough to keep Frederick out, there might not be anyone to stop them legally.

None of this changes the fact that the best time to rule on the two-term question is before the vote, not after, and that the best place is in court, not Congress. Even though Congress has the ability to storm in at the end, the courts must not abdicate their role here. The cleanest result, and the one that best respects the voters, is for the courts to step up, and for Congress to step back.

Variations on the Theme

There are plenty of potential twists to add to our scenario. Some would make the political posture of the case different. For instance, if President Frederick were sincerely running for vice president, with every intention of serving only in that office, he would have an easier time prevailing. Similarly, if President Frederick had been out of office for four, eight, or twelve years and therefore was not using the power of incumbency to entrench himself in office, the political arguments against him would be diminished somewhat. To some extent, any legal arguments based on the intent of the Twenty-Second Amendment would be too.[39]

Another scenario was broached earlier, when it was posited that—in parallel to the loophole view of the Twenty-Second Amendment—the Twelfth Amendment might bar two-termers from being elected vice president, but not from *being* vice president. Thus, Frederick could have a second surrogate get elected vice president. The surrogate could then resign, allowing the president to nominate Frederick to fill the vice-presidential vacancy. The voters would have no direct say; under the Twenty-Fifth Amendment, Frederick's nomination would just need to be approved by simple majorities in the House and Senate. If both chambers agreed that the Twelfth Amendment allowed Frederick to serve as vice president, the courts would be very unlikely to overturn that decision. First of all, it would be hard to find a plaintiff with standing to challenge Congress's decision. Second, even if someone did have standing, the courts would likely declare that the Twenty-Fifth Amendment gives Congress the last word here, making the confirmation a political question that the courts cannot review.

A more complicated variation would be for a two-term president to return to office from lower down on the line of succession. Under current law, if the president and vice president are both out of commission, the Speaker of the House, president pro tempore of the Senate, and members of the cabinet are next in line. Thus, President Frederick could serve in one of these other offices and ascend to the presidency—through either catastrophe or design.⁴⁰

The succession statute currently on the books specifies that only people who are "eligible to the office" can act as president.* Thus, the same Twenty-Second Amendment issue would have to be resolved before a two-termer could reenter the office this way. But there is nothing legally problematic about filling jobs that are in the line of succession with people who are not presidentially eligible—former secretaries of state Henry Kissinger and Madeline Albright were not natural-born citizens, for instance—because if their turn ever comes up, they just get skipped. Under current law, then, President Frederick unquestionably could become Speaker of the House or secretary of state; it's just that if the succession worked its way down to him, and he tried to act as president, his presidential eligibility would need to be addressed.⁴¹

In the main scenario in this chapter, President Frederick tries to win the vice presidency, which requires him to win a national election. To win the speakership, by contrast, he would need only the support of a majority of the House of Representatives, and he would not need to wait until a quadrennial election. Of course, going from the speakership to the presidency raises all sorts of issues, including the constitutional ones from Chapter 4. If the Speaker happened to be a former two-term president, the controversy would be heightened, to put it mildly.

Another dramatic possibility could arise from an undone or unsettled presidential election. The Twentieth Amendment covers situations in which there is no one prepared to take the oath of office when the new presidential term begins. This could happen for several reasons: the president-elect and

---

* Some have argued that an acting president (someone standing in temporarily rather than formally taking over the office) does not need to meet *any* of the qualifications for the presidency. *See, e.g.,* James C. Ho, *Unnatural Born Citizens and Acting Presidents,* 17 Const. Comment. 575 (2000); Mark Tushnet, *Resolving the Paradox of Democratic Constitutionalism,* 3 Green Bag 2d 225, 226 n.1 (2000). The qualifications in Article II, Section 1, Clause 5, are expressed as eligibility "to the Office," but acting presidents do not actually assume the office of president. Thus, an underage naturalized citizen could, under this argument, act as president. By extension, a two-termer could too. For any of this to happen, though, Congress would have to amend the succession statute along these lines.

vice president elect could both be dead, disabled, or unwilling to take the oath; they could turn out to be constitutionally unqualified for office; the election could still be in dispute; or the election could have been delayed by a natural disaster or terrorist attack. The amendment gives Congress very broad power to legislate who should act as president in such a situation—broad enough, in fact, to avoid Chapter 4's "officer" problems. To date, Congress has not exercised that expanded power, electing instead to just use the "regular" succession law. But Congress could pass a law on the fly to let the incumbent president stay on as acting president.[42]

This very possibility arose during the 2000 election crisis, when it still looked like the dispute might not be resolved in time; a *New York Times* op-ed suggested that Congress provide for two-termer Bill Clinton to stay in power until the election could be properly resolved. As in the rest of this chapter, this sort of presidential service would not entail being "elected" again, so it might be constitutional. Moreover, the bar might be lower for someone acting as president only until a new choice could be made, as opposed to filling out the rest of the term.[43]

As a final note, to put things in perspective, there are ways for a two-term president to retain power in ways that would not implicate any constitutional concerns at all. The most obvious is the "Lurleen" method. When George Wallace was elected governor of Alabama in 1962, the state constitution barred him from seeking a second consecutive term. After failing to amend the state constitution in time, Wallace had his wife, Lurleen, get elected in his stead. The Wallaces made it clear to the voters that George would continue to run things, and he essentially did until Lurleen died of cancer midterm. There is no legal reason that a president could not do something similar; if the voters could be politically persuaded to vote for a stand-in as president, the Twenty-Second Amendment would have nothing to say about it.[44]

Of course, not every wife would be as submissive as Lurleen Wallace. The presidential candidacy of Hillary Clinton certainly did not come across as a subterfuge for putting her husband back in power. Furthermore, as the case of Presidents Theodore Roosevelt and William Taft demonstrated, even handpicked protégés can go their own way once in office. The only way for an American president to be absolutely sure to retain presidential power is for him to stay president.

Still, some possibility of a puppet presidency exists. Anyone who confi-dently dismisses the constitutional arguments in this chapter needs to remember that the Twenty-Second Amendment is not the only thing protecting the country from a two-term president retaining power.

What to Do?

Just as in previous chapters, there is no real hope—or precedent—for amending the Constitution to edit a single phrase just because a few persnickety professors think that the current language is less than perfect. When the Constitution is amended to make a technical fix, it tends to be in the wake of an actual problem. The rest of the time, we rely on the Constitution's backstop—the political process, which here would make it very hard for President Frederick to succeed—to keep us out of trouble. Conversely, as Senator Lodge put it (during a 1913 debate over a proposed term-limit amendment), "If we should reach the point where the people were ready to have a perpetual President or dictator, no constitutional provi-sion would stand in the way. . . . [P]aper barriers will not prevent the calamity."[45]

There are, however, a few things that could be done to bolster our current paper barrier, the Twenty-Second Amendment. For instance, Congress is in charge of the presidential succession law, and it has chosen to require that people in the line of succession be "eligible to the office of president." Congress could elaborate in the statute that eligibility includes not just the age, citizenship, residency, and loyalty requirements, but also not being a two-term former president. Congress's constitutional interpretations are not binding on courts—especially when they appear tangentially like this—but they also aren't completely meaningless. Such a statute would reinforce the sense that history, practice, and common understanding all favor barring two-termers from service, and in any case it would shrink our Twenty-Second Amendment loophole.[46]

It would also be helpful for two-term presidents to address their hypothet-ical eligibility, and to squash such talk. Former president Clinton appeared on a talk show a few years after leaving office and, when asked about it, offered an off-the-cuff constitutional argument why he could not run for vice president. Clinton sounded convincing, but his legal argument was a bit thin. It would have been easy for the White House counsel to issue a more official and thoroughly argued follow-up. If every two-termer did this when asked, the "history, practice, and common understanding" argument would be even weightier.[47]

Stephen Carter has written of the concept of the "constitutional impropriety": a thing that conflicts with the Constitution's spirit, even if the Constitution provides no legal avenue to prevent it. This is a useful idea in our case, and one that Peabody and Gant, the leading exponents of the loophole, concede may apply. The concept is not a perfect fit—the whole point of this chapter is that it isn't quite clear what the Twenty-Second Amendment means—but it emphasizes the power of the voters to enforce a constitutional norm by exercising their will, instead of relying on courts and Congress. The more that Congress and presidents reinforce the constitutional impropriety of serving more than two terms, the more that voters will be inclined to vote against a candidate trying to exploit the careless loophole left in the Twenty-Second Amendment, and the smaller that loophole will become.[48]

A distinguished commentator, discussing the possibility of a two-term president running for vice president, offered that it was "more unlikely than unconstitutional." By taking simple actions like those described in this section, Congress and presidents could make it even less likely. Still, they could not eliminate the possibility altogether. A third term might not happen soon, or ever, but it could. Constitutional disputes do not arise in a vacuum, and our democracy has had its weak moments. It would be foolish to assume that the United States will never have a president who is more popular than the Constitution—or, more to the point, more popular than one disputable interpretation of it.[49]

7

Getting Out of Trouble

SOME OF THE CLIFFHANGERS IN THIS BOOK are more likely to occur; others are less likely. Some would cause a "crisis"; others would only rise to the level of "interesting predicament." Some would be resolved in court; others in Congress, the White House, or the streets. Some would be easy to prevent or fix; others would be practically impossible. With all of them set out, we can identify some common threads and some lessons learned.

This chapter focuses on three areas: (1) ways that law interacts with politics when constitutional cliffhangers are resolved; (2) ways that constitutional weak spots get patched up, either before or after they cause problems; and (3) ways to improve constitutional and legislative drafting to prevent such weak spots from developing in the first place.

Resolution: Law and Politics

Constitutional cliffhangers like the ones in this book are dramatic for two reasons. First, they are rare, so they are startling when they happen. Second, they take place in the high-stakes realm of presidential power.

An important effect of this is engagement. Take the 2000 Florida recount. If such electoral meltdowns were routine, or if the deadlocked election had been for the state agriculture commissioner rather than for president, the recount would not have transfixed the nation for six weeks and beyond. When the public is engaged in a legal issue in this way, it is no longer a matter just for lawyers to resolve, with just their lawyerly techniques. Politics is front and center. This can have noteworthy effects, depending on the forum in which the cliffhanger plays out. It also illuminates some interesting features of Congress and the courts, not just the presidency.

Politics in Court

Two of our cliffhangers would be resolved in court, simply because that's where they would arise in the first place, as a prosecutor pursues a sitting president (Chapter 1) or pursues an ex-president who had pardoned himself (Chapter 2). The presidential defendant would assert his constitutional defenses in both cases, and the courts would have to decide if the case against him could go forward.

One would hope that a case that is completely in the courts' domain would be decided as a matter of law, not politics. Another way to express this is to hope that these cases would come out the same way in court regardless of whether the president was a Democrat or a Republican. When President Clinton argued that he was immune from Paula Jones's civil suit against him, for example, all nine justices disagreed, including the four "liberal" justices. Similarly, when President Nixon refused to turn over the Watergate tapes, the Supreme Court—much of which Nixon had appointed—was unanimous in ordering him to.[1]

There are problems with trying to keep politics out of law, though. It can be hard to draw a bright line dividing law from politics. The starting point for most cliffhangers is that the law is unclear; legally, the case could go either way. When the law is in equipoise but the politics are not—when the politics are, in fact, screamingly unbalanced—then the court's decision will be inextricably linked with its political context. Here, the example is not *Clinton v. Jones* or *United States v. Nixon*, but *Bush v. Gore*. *Bush v. Gore* dealt with several complicated legal issues: election law, equal protection, federalism, the political-question doctrine, and more. The lawyers stuck to legal arguments as the case bubbled up through Florida state courts to the U.S. Supreme Court. None of them said, "My client should win because he belongs to your political party, your honor." But it was evident that if George W. Bush won the case, he would win the presidency. That political ramification, and the short deadline for resolving it, overwhelmed the legal issues in the case. Few believe that all nine justices would have voted the same way in *Bush* if the parties had been reversed. When politics infuses the courts like that, the moral authority of the judicial system suffers. There is an added incentive, then, to prevent any constitutional cliffhanger that would play out in court in such a politicized manner.[2]

The question is, which court cases get politicized? One important factor is the stakes. The situation in Chapter 2 (adjudicating the fate of an ex-president who had pardoned himself) would surely be a less politicized, cooler-headed affair than the one in Chapter 4 (deciding whether the Speaker of the House or the secretary of state is the rightful acting president). There are legitimate legal issues in both cases, but the high-stakes power struggle in Chapter 4 would much more easily overwhelm the legal considerations.

Another factor in politicization is the likelihood of repetition. The Supreme Court in Chapter 1 (deciding whether the president can be prosecuted while in office) would know that its decision could easily concern every single president from both parties, given how unfortunately common presidential investigations have become. The immediate political consequences of prosecuting the current president would be substantial, but the possibility of a future partisan turnabout would at least dampen their effect. By contrast, Chapter 6 (a popular two-term president trying to retain power) might seem more like a one-time deal—like *Bush v. Gore*—leaving less to mitigate the effect of the intense politics of the moment.[3]

Even when politics intrudes, though, the law still matters. A strong precedent or a strong legal argument may be enough to outweigh political considerations. Even without clear legal guidance, judges generally think that they are following the law, or at least they act like they think they are. It is not as though judges self-consciously discard all pretense of legal analysis and make their decisions explicitly political. Politics might drive judges to choose one legal argument over another, but they are still choosing from among a small set of *legal* arguments, and they still couch their decisions in legal terms. Understanding the legal issues would be essential to understanding a cliffhanger as it played out, and to evaluating how badly politics actually intruded into the process.[4]

A long-standing and vigorous debate in American law asks whether and how politics drives judicial decisions. Many substantive legal issues (like abortion, the death penalty, affirmative action, the War on Terror) are highly politicized. They turn on nebulous and intentionally vague constitutional phrases ("liberty," "cruel and unusual punishment," "equal protection," "executive power") that leave lots of room for politics to intrude into the interpretive process. But our cliffhangers turn on structural and procedural issues, where such wide-open interpretive techniques do not fit as well,* and where the political choices will not be as clear. Politically, any abortion decision is easy to render as left or right; not so with most of our cliff-hangers. To take Chapter 1 as an example, who can say whether it is liberal or conservative to allow a president to be prosecuted? It might be liberal or conservative to answer a certain way if the *president in the particular case* is liberal or conservative, but that didn't spare Nixon and Clinton from losing their cases unanimously. All this adds an interesting dimension to this vital jurisprudential debate—a dimension whose full exploration is, unfortunately, beyond the scope of this book.[5]

Finally, constitutional cliffhangers complicate another contentious issue: the political-question doctrine. In the last four chapters, we saw that at least one of the parties would argue for the courts to defer to Congress and not interfere. As also seen in those chapters, though, the political-question doctrine is not overly clear. Moreover, the doctrine seems to have been weakened lately as federal courts have grown more assertive about inserting themselves into conflicts like these. Compare the disputed 1876 presidential election, in which Congress's ad hoc resolution carried the day with nary a peep from the Supreme Court, to the disputed 2000 presidential election, in which the Supreme Court's ad hoc resolution carried the day with nary a

---

* In this book, I have not advanced a consistent constitutional strategy for dealing with cliffhangers. This is for three reasons. First, as I hope this book has shown, cliff-hangers are diverse—any given interpretive technique will play out very differently from cliffhanger to cliffhanger—so there is little hope for a unified approach. Second, even if that weren't so, there are so many different ways that people can interpret the Constitution that it's not realistic to expect a decisive majority to pick just one, especially not on the say-so of a lone law professor. Third, it would usually be hard to maintain any sort of pure interpretive intentions during a cliffhanger, with its overwhelming political pressures. It is even harder to do so in advance, in a discussion as speculative as the ones in this book must necessarily be. Thus, it is not useful to attempt any systematic new theories of constitutional interpretation here. Sorry.

peep from Congress.* Elizabeth Garrett has cogently described the lack of faith that the public and the Court had in Congress's ability to resolve the 2000 election, and how unwarranted and damaging that lack of faith is. Nevertheless, that lack of faith is a fact.[6]

For most of our cliffhangers, letting the courts get involved would be perceived as a good thing. Garrett's critique aside, we saw how courts might provide faster and more decisive action in a crisis than Congress could. The Court is, justifiably or not, currently exalted as the nation's ultimate authority over the Constitution. Additionally, courts offer a more neutral forum for disputes, like those in Chapters 4 and 5, in which Congress itself is one of the combatants. Sometimes it makes sense to leave a particular constitutional decision to Congress; ordinary impeachment, for example, belongs in Congress because impeachment requires political accountability. But often there are no such structural or institutional considerations. Instead, we have constitutional disputes like the succession controversy in Chapter 4—arising out of Congress's failure to set aside politics, its own interests, and expedience long enough to think carefully about the Constitution and steer clear of constitutional obstacles. When that spawns a cliffhanger, the courts have much less incentive, and much less basis, to give Congress the last word in resolving it.[7]

Politics in Congress

When constitutional cliffhangers play out in Congress—as in Chapters 3 (disability) and 5 (late impeachment), and maybe also in Chapters 4 (succession) and 6 (term limits)—the presence of politics seems less controversial. Congress is full of politicians, after all, so politics clearly "belongs" there. To return to *Bush v. Gore*, if a dispute is going to be resolved by a party-line vote,

---

* To be sure, the 1876–2000 contrast is not quite as stark as it seems. Congress's plan to resolve the election in 1876 was to form a commission; Supreme Court justice Joseph Bradley ended up being the swing vote on the commission. Congress's plan also allowed for the defeated candidate (Samuel Tilden) to take his case to the Supreme Court. *See* Michael F. Holt, By One Vote 243 (2008) (discussing possibility of Tilden suing). Tilden chose not to, possibly because he lacked sufficient support there to win anyway. In 2000–01, as described in Chapter 6, Al Gore could have challenged the Supreme Court's decision in Congress, but he too lacked sufficient support to make such a gambit worthwhile. Nevertheless, the Supreme Court's recent assertiveness is striking.

isn't it better to have that vote in Congress than in the Supreme Court? Even a seemingly objective issue like presidential disability will be infused with politics, as both sides carefully weigh the political ramifications of their choices and ponder who might deserve the benefit of the doubt. The Constitution assigns lots of tasks to Congress, from the mundane (passing laws, confirming presidential nominees) to the exceptional (impeachment, presidential disability disputes, winner-less presidential elections). The Constitution's Framers opted for flexibility, painstakingly creating a structure through which these matters—often matters of great constitutional import—can be settled by ordinary political actors being ordinary and political. This system works well and would work even better if we gave it more of a chance.[8]

But if matters are assigned to Congress because it is representative and accountable, this presents a problem when Congress falls short on either score. An imperfect Congress cannot resolve constitutional cliffhangers with the same legitimacy as a "better" Congress. And there are plenty of imperfections in Congress's representativeness and accountability. Setting aside corruption and our questionable campaign-finance system, even well-meaning Congresses have problems: gerrymandered House districts, the disproportionate influence of small states in the Senate, having a Senate in the first place, and more. These dysfunctions are not necessarily fatal. Just providing certainty and stability is worth something, after all.* But they are problems.[9]

As a general matter, the two-party system can deliver decisive, binary, majoritarian results, especially in the modern era, in which the parties are more distinct ideologically. But narrow majorities, the continued toleration of filibusters, congressional self-interest, and the sheer inefficiency of Congress undermine this. There are too many opportunities for Congress to get things wrong. When it comes to situations like the one in Chapter 4 (deciding which of two contenders is the rightful acting president) there is a dangerous possibility that Congress would thwart the will of the people rather than promote it. In ordinary times, the people can reassert their

---

* Certainty and stability are not so simple. A strong majority can head off some cliffhangers—having a decent legal argument and a clear upper hand politically might prevent the other side from even bothering to raise an issue. By the same token, though, if a majority is strong enough politically, it might be able to press a *weak* legal argument enough to create a cliffhanger.

control in an orderly manner every two years when they vote in congressional elections. But in the middle of a struggle over control of the White House, waiting for the next election would be insufficient. If the stakes are this high, and if Congress is so unrepresentative that its actions lack legitimacy, Congress would be skating on very thin ice, and (as discussed more in the next section) the people could mobilize in worrisome ways.

Even to the extent that the two-party system successfully delivers stability and legitimacy, its existence cannot be taken for granted. The Constitution does not guarantee a two-party system—the Framers did not want to have *any* political parties. Thus, to paraphrase this book's introduction, if the United States ever devolved into a more fractious, multiparty system, the Constitution's reliance on ordinary politics to solve extraordinary problems could become a defect rather than a feature.

The President and the People

Running through all our cliffhangers was a sense that the president's political position—the strength of his allies in Congress and his personal popularity in the country—would affect how things played out. In each chapter, the more popular the president (or would-be president) was, the more likely he or she would be to emerge victorious, or not to get in trouble in the first place. This is worth a closer look, particularly in light of the president's commander-in-chief power, and his populist power to mobilize the public.

In Chapters 3 (disability) and 4 (succession), two people claimed control of the presidency, and it mattered whose side the military took. This is troubling; the Constitution creates a norm of civilian control of the military, which is threatened if the military starts choosing presidents. On the flip side, civilian control could paralyze the military if there were two people claiming to be commander in chief, with two putative secretaries of defense. Chapters 3 and 4 both take place in wartime, and the military might not have the luxury of standing down while politicians and judges sort through the controversy. Therefore, it would be intolerable for the military to choose sides, but also for it not to choose sides. Perhaps worst of all is a third possibility: the military could be divided and choose *both* sides. There is no good answer here, just more incentive to prevent the cliffhangers.

Also potentially decisive is the relationship between the president and the public. In Chapter 6, for instance, the president could not even think about avoiding term limits unless he had strong popular support. If that support translated into an electoral victory in November, it would confer a unique legitimacy on him. It is unclear how well suited "populist constitutional law" is for interpreting narrow procedural provisions like this, as opposed to broad rights provisions, but Congress and the courts resist the people at their peril.[10]

Less comforting is the possible role of the people "out of doors." Citizen-mobs who take to the streets can be decisive, whether because they galvanize opinion, frighten opponents, or provoke a reaction from the state. We are in the midst of a relatively quiet period in American history, mob-wise, but this potential is never far from the surface, and angry assemblages have played an important part in American constitutional history.[11]

This book has not analyzed the role of mobs much; if a struggle between competing constitutional theories comes down to which side is backed by the biggest, baddest throngs, there is little point in splitting hairs to find the best legal theory. But mobs matter in this chapter, because the ability of mobs to decide an outcome relies on the corresponding inability of Congress and the courts to decide it. For instance, in Chapter 4's struggle between the Speaker of the House and secretary of state for control of the White House, rival mobs might start fighting in the streets right away, but it seems more likely that order could be maintained for a little while as the courts and Congress worked through the problem. The more credible the courts and Congress are, the longer the mobs would hold off, and the more likely a formal decision would be to quiet things down. Conversely, if Congress and the courts are delegitimized, public demonstrations might actually be the *most* legitimate way to resolve the conflict. This sounds more like other countries—Egypt in 2011 or Ukraine in 2004—than anything in recent U.S. history. Looking further back in history, though, and thinking about possible futures, we should not dismiss out of hand the potential contributions of an American public that is mobilized (the etymological source of the word "mob") and exercising its First Amendment right to assemble.

All this highlights an interesting characteristic of the presidency. Presidents draw their power from the people, because of the way that presidents are elected and reelected (or not). At the same time, though, presidents have tremendous power *over* the people; they control the country's biggest bully pulpit, and they control the increasingly pervasive power of the federal government over people's lives. Nobody is in a better position to whip the public into a frenzy—to inspire mobs to form, and to move them to action all over the country—than the president. The problem is that in many constitutional cliffhangers, nobody will have a better *incentive* to do so than the president. This is inconsistent with our current political culture; in calmer times, the political cost of being a shameless demagogue is high enough to keep these pressures contained. When a cliffhanger occurs, however, that balance could change and those pressures could explode.

As with the military, to the extent that the role of mobs is troubling, it gives us yet another incentive to fix and avoid constitutional cliffhangers. Strong and legitimate institutions, bounded by effective rules and processes, can resolve conflicts that would otherwise be decided in the streets—or perhaps the battlefield. This is a good note on which to switch the discussion to repairing these dangerous weak spots in the Constitution.

Installing Guardrails

This book is somewhat unfair. Rather than condemn the Constitution, its Framers, and generations of lawmakers for their creation and maintenance of a few odd weak spots, a more balanced account would consider all the places where the Constitution is well designed, or at least adequate. Of course, it wouldn't make sense to write a book about, say, the September 11 attacks and give equal time to each airplane that terrorists *didn't* crash that year. But it is important to keep some perspective, and to respect the distinction between actual failures and merely possible failures.

The previous section showed how our system can work through constitutional cliffhangers peacefully and decisively—and sometimes even correctly. As Sanford Levinson and Jack Balkin have put it, "[d]isagreement and conflict are natural features of politics. The goal of constitutions is to manage them within acceptable boundaries. When constitutional design functions properly—even if people strongly disagree with and threaten each other—there is no crisis." Other than those that gave rise to the Civil War (admittedly a big "other than"), every structural wrinkle that has arisen has been ironed out without the country falling apart. But while this is better than the alternative, there is little room for self-congratulation. Our constitutional structure is not perfect. We have been lucky, and luck always runs out eventually. Thus it is worth considering how to strengthen our foundations and reduce our risk from these rare but momentous events.[12]

How Congress Acts

> This condition has, it is true, never happened in the history of the country, and while it may never happen, it does seem very important that some constitutional provision be enacted by which this most dangerous emergency may be avoided.
> —SENATOR GEORGE W. NORRIS, DISCUSSING AN OBSCURE PORTION
> OF WHAT BECAME THE TWENTIETH AMENDMENT[13]

Scholars have long debated how much Congress worries about the constitutionality of the laws it writes. Here, however, we are dealing with the different matter of Congress's *direct* handling of the Constitution: drafting constitutional amendments, and filling in blanks (like the line of succession) that the Constitution tells Congress to deal with.

The Constitution's procedural and technical provisions are often insulated from judicial review. When they are not, they often use black-or-white wording that is not susceptible to creative judicial interpretation. Presidents and courts cannot pass legislation or initiate constitutional amendments. For these reasons, it is usually up to Congress to react when these sorts of provisions present risks.

Congress has two ways to respond: eliminating the risk or ignoring it.* When Congress opts for the former approach, it can be for one of four reasons, listed here in ascending order of proactivity.[14]

---

* Ordinarily, risks like these—low probability of occurring, but high impact if they do—call for a third kind of response: buying insurance. There is no good analogy to insurance here, though. If my house burns down, my insurance will pay me money to build a new one, and to live somewhere else in the meantime. There are no such compensations or substitutions available for the presidency. We can have contingency plans for such events, but that's different. *But see* Sanford Levinson, *Our Undemocratic Constitution* 73 (2006) (using insurance analogy for continuity-of-Congress contingency plan).

Category 1: Congress has no choice. In some cases, a cliffhanger is presented directly to Congress for resolution—it considers an individual case and settles the cliffhanger for the future. An example, discussed in Chapter 5, is the 1790s case of Senator William Blount. The House impeached Blount, so the Senate had to decide whether members of Congress are subject to impeachment. It voted no and settled the issue. Among the cliffhangers in this book, the ones in Chapters 3 (disability), 4 (succession), and 5 (late impeachment) could fall into this category if a case gets sent to Congress and the courts do not resolve it first. It would be irrelevant that Congress lacks foresight and finds it hard to be proactive. Congress would resolve these cliffhangers, because it would be forced to.*

Category 2: Something bad happens. Some cliffhangers would play out somewhere else, but Congress would be shocked into responding. One example (though not really a cliffhanger under my definition) is the election of 1800, discussed in the introduction, in which the House of Representatives struggled to break a deadlock between Thomas Jefferson and his running mate Aaron Burr. Afterward, Congress responded with the Twelfth Amendment, and the states ratified it in time for the next election.† In Category 2 cases, there usually is not a constitutional uncertainty for Congress to resolve as such. Rather, a problem was resolved, but people are unhappy with the result. In 1801, everybody could see that the House of Representatives was capable of deciding a presidential election, but they did not *want* elections thrown

---

* In Chapter 5, Congress's decision in a late-impeachment case might not settle the issue conclusively. The Senate might repeat the Secretary Belknap precedent, in which it decided (by a simple majority) that it could late-impeach but also decided (lacking the two-thirds majority needed for a conviction) to acquit because of the lateness. Moreover, Congress is not formally bound by its precedents—it could decide that late impeachment is fine but change its mind in the next case, or vice versa, especially to the extent that it thinks a precedent was based on politics rather than law. *See* Neal Kumar Katyal, *Legislative Constitutional Interpretation,* 50 Duke L.J. 1335, 1387–88 (2001) (discussing role of congressional constitutional precedent in impeachment).
† Congress is not always so prompt; as discussed in Chapter 3, for example, it took decades and numerous troublesome episodes before Congress passed the Twenty-Fifth Amendment to address presidential disability.

into the House when one party had won a clear victory. Similarly, in Chapter 1, if the courts found that presidents are not constitutionally immune from prosecution, and Congress was unhappy with that result, it could legislate immunity. In every chapter (and in any Category 1 case), if the result of a cliffhanger was politically unpopular enough, Congress could respond with a constitutional amendment to rewrite the rules. This category requires some political initiative, but little foresight.

Category 3: A near miss. Sometimes, Congress is moved to act when something nearly happens but misses the mark. We saw this in Chapter 4 with the 1886 presidential-succession law, passed after presidents were left with no backup in 1881 and 1885. Near misses could occur for any of the chapters in this book and have already occurred for Chapters 1 and 2. The point here is that the near miss alerts Congress to the existence of the cliffhanger, and Congress is conscientious enough to act even though nothing actually happened. This category requires rather more initiative, but still not much foresight.

Category 4: Congress is completely proactive. This category requires both foresight and substantial initiative. As a result, it is not well populated. A rare example is Section 4 of the Twentieth Amendment, ratified in 1933. If a winner-less presidential election is thrown into the House of Representatives, and one of the finalists dies, his faction would be unfairly deprived of its chance to win. But this has never happened. Still, Congress was concerned enough about it to pass Section 4.* The situations in any chapters in this book that do not qualify for Category 3 could fit here, if Congress were motivated enough to address them. The line between Categories 3 and 4 is somewhat fuzzy, though. For example, Section 3 of the Twentieth Amendment covers the death of a president-elect, or the failure to elect a president before Inauguration Day, neither of which has ever happened—this is what Senator Norris was referring to in the quotation that opened this section. But in 1853, President-Elect Franklin Pierce was in an accident in which his son was killed; in 1872 candidate

---

* Section 4 does not specify what to do when a finalist dies. Instead, it empowers Congress to pass legislation to specify what to do. Ironically, though, Congress has never done so; proactivity has its limits.

Horace Greeley died, but he had lost and the electoral college had not yet met; in 1877, the disputed election was settled just two days before Inauguration Day. Near misses are a matter of degree.

When Congress Acts

With these four categories set out, we can consider what things lead Congress to be more or less proactive. Many factors converge; each one makes a difference if all other things are equal—though with so many factors in play, all other things are never equal. The following is a ramble through some of those factors.

Amendments versus statutes. It takes dogged leadership to get anything done in Congress, but more so for constitutional amendments than for statutes. Even though the U.S. Constitution has been measured as the hardest in the world to amend, legal scholars sometimes identify a real but very minor problem and conclude blithely that a constitutional amendment is in order. This is almost always an unrealistic suggestion. Statutory fixes are no picnic either, but they are not as hard to pass.[15]

Real versus abstract (part 1). If a cliffhanger is still just hypothetical, it makes it easier to reach consensus on a solution, because the parties will be less focused on who benefits. To be sure, the parties might still perceive winners or losers—there might not be any real case pending, but the president might appreciate winning temporary immunity from any criminal prosecution, or the Speaker of the House might resent being taken out of the line of succession. Even if the fix would only matter in the future, when we cannot be sure who the president or Speaker will be, it can be hard to shift one's political imagination away from the current cast of characters. Still, this is nothing compared to what happens in a real case. In 1997, members of Congress could have had a real debate about what constitutes an impeachable offense; in 1998, their opinions miraculously lined up based on their party and on what they thought of Bill Clinton.[16]

Real versus abstract (part 2). Keeping things hypothetical makes consensus easier, but it makes motivation harder. The political system is driven by self-interest; unless a party or interest group expects to benefit from a particular reform, there often will be nobody willing to lead it through the legislative process. Good ideas never hurt, but unless there is a payoff for someone, a good solution to a hypothetical problem will have a harder time getting on the agenda ahead of more immediate priorities. Sometimes the advantages of reality outweigh the advantages of abstractness discussed in the last paragraph, and sometimes the opposite is true; assessing this more thoroughly is a matter for another day.[17]

Volume discounts. As discussed above, the Twentieth Amendment (passed in the 1930s, at the tail end of a burst of amendments) was unusually proactive. Nobody was clamoring for the reforms in Sections 3 and 4 of the amendment, and nobody benefited directly from their passage. So how did it happen? Because enough people *were* clamoring for the reforms in Sections 1 and 2. Those sections shortened the lengthy "lame duck" period, during which the old Congress and president retained power after the new Congress and president had been elected. While they were at it, some reformers in the House realized that they had a chance—and a responsibility—to change some other, somewhat related things. The Senate eventually agreed. You can't cram everything through such a window of opportunity (the Twentieth Amendment leaves other related issues untouched) but the more that gets done, the better. When Congress is in a reforming mood, savvy reformers take advantage.[18]

Specialization. Congress's committee structure should make it easier to get Congress to consider arcane constitutional minutiae. The nation may be facing all sorts of more direct and pressing crises, but each subcommittee in the House and Senate has the luxury of worrying just about its little corner of the universe. The main reason that the Twenty-Fifth Amendment came to fruition was that Birch Bayh, an energetic first-term senator, was made chairman of the Senate subcommittee in charge of constitutional amendments.* This point should not be taken too far, though. For one thing, the House and Senate still have to give their final approval, and specialization does nothing to increase their limited time for floor debate and final votes.

---

* Interestingly, the effort to pass the Twentieth Amendment was led by progressive Senator George Norris after a proposal was referred to his Agriculture and Forestry Committee (to laughter in the Senate) instead of the less sympathetic Judiciary Committee. Dogged leadership sometimes trumps specialization. *See* 63 Cong. Rec. 26 (1922) (statement of Sen. Caraway); George W. Norris, Fighting Liberal 329–30 (1945).

For another thing, subcommittees' jurisdictions are not that narrow. Bayh's old subcommittee, for example, deals not just with amending the Constitution but also with separation of powers, federalism, interstate compacts, and the enforcement and protection of rights and liberties. Another example: presidential succession is the bailiwick of the Senate Rules Committee, which has no subcommittees and which deals with many other weighty matters. As a final note, given how stridently contested the Constitution is, the relevant committees are particularly polarized politically, which makes it harder to muster the bipartisan consensus that constitutional amendments usually need.[19]

Bad results. There are two kinds of cliffhangers: those in which the main problem is a bad result, and those in which the main problem is uncertainty. An example of the former is given in Chapter 1, where a sitting president might get prosecuted (with the attendant disruption) or might not (with the attendant injustice). The fact that, in the meantime, presidents and prosecutors go about their days unsure of the answer is less of a problem. Legislating requires energized consensus, but while part of the country thinks that prosecuting a president would be horrible, another part thinks that immunity would be horrible, and another (big) part doesn't really care. This makes it very hard to be proactive. When, as in Chapters 1, 2, and 5, the uncertainty causes little harm, it should be no surprise when Congress declines to be proactive. Better to wait for an actual case to deliver a final resolution—either an acceptable result or an unacceptable one that motivates Congress to act.

Bad uncertainty. When the problem is uncertainty, by contrast, the case for proactivity is strong. In Chapters 3 and 4, constitutional uncertainty could rip the country in half, with two people claiming presidential power, issuing contradictory orders to the military, and purporting to fire cabinet members. It might be politically problematic to take congressional leaders out of the line of succession, but surely it would be much more problematic to not know *who* is president. The cost of resolving such cliffhangers "the hard way" is so high that it should soften opposition and make it easier—if not easy—to reach a consensus and fix things ahead of time.

Half measures in Congress. Several chapters suggested that Congress address a cliffhanger indirectly. Instead of proposing a sweeping solution (like a full-blown constitutional amendment), Congress could make minor, helpful changes by tweaking statutes or internal rules. Sometimes, even just holding hearings and discussing things could help, by pinning down opinions and making it harder for everyone to switch their legal theories for partisan advantage when a cliffhanger later occurs. This lesser level of congressional action would still not be easy, though. Indeed, given that the payoffs would be smaller and subtler, it might actually be *harder* to motivate Congress to execute one of these half measures.

Half measures by the president. Separately, in some chapters, we saw that the president and his legal team could help matters by issuing certain official statements. These too would be half measures, nudging the result rather than fully foreclosing a cliffhanger. But some of these presidential pronouncements would be very helpful. They also would be much easier to execute than congressional action would, because of the unitary nature of the presidency.

Pulling It Together

With these considerations in mind, and reflecting back on the last six chapters, we can recap the prospects for fixing our six cliffhangers. Chapter 1 proposed legislation to make sitting presidents temporarily immune from criminal prosecution, with various protections and caveats. Ideally, this would be done proactively. Realistically, though, it would probably follow an unpopular and damaging prosecution that the courts declared constitutional.

In Chapter 2, on self-pardons, a fix would require a constitutional amendment. This would almost certainly require a real case, like a court approving an egregious self-pardon, or some other sort of abusive pardon that prodded Congress to revisit the pardon power more generally.

The best bet in Chapter 3's disability crisis was for a president to endorse the proper interpretation of Section 4 of the Twenty-Fifth Amendment. This could easily be added to a disability contingency plan, which new presidents routinely issue. By cementing a proper understanding of Section 4, it would minimize the risk of Chapter 3's disastrous uncertainty.

The issues discussed in Chapter 4 might fade away; if the first transfer of presidential power to a Speaker of the House is uncontroversial, it would provide a quieting precedent. But the potential controversy—two people claiming control of the White House—is just too dangerous. Congress needs to swallow its pride and take its leaders out of the line of succession or at least move them down. Hopefully, the recent attention paid to making the line of succession more robust (extending it beyond Washington, D.C., for instance) will pay off and will accommodate a piggybacking effort to make the line of succession more constitutionally robust as well. At present, however, prospects for action seem dim.

Chapter 5, on late impeachments, is the least fretful in the book; the conclusion even noted some benefits to leaving things unresolved. The country will not suffer too badly if it waits for an actual case to settle whether late impeachment is constitutional. Nor will it suffer if the outcome of that case stands, or alternatively, if it is somehow reversed with a constitutional amendment. That's good, because there is virtually no hope for any proactive solutions.

Chapter 6's potential third term is hard to fix, because it presupposes a president who is more popular than the conventional understanding of the Constitution. The populist pressures fueling this cliffhanger would mean that no half measures—no subtle legislation, no strongly worded legal interpretations from a previous White House—would be enough. Chapter 6 is a perfect candidate for proactivity (act now, before such a president arises!), but it would require a constitutional amendment, and there is no precedent and little hope for passing one that is so persnickety.

This note of relative hopelessness provides a good segue to the final section: how to avoid creating potential constitutional cliffhangers in the first place.

Making Amendments Better

An ounce of prevention is worth a pound of cure. The problem is that for the most part, it is too late for prevention. There is no way to go back in time to 1787 and help the Framers write a better Succession Clause or help them specify whether presidents can be prosecuted, can pardon themselves, or can be impeached after leaving office. There is no way to go back to 1947 to help the Twenty-Second Amendment's drafters tighten up their wording, or to 1965 to help the Twenty-Fifth Amendment's drafters with theirs. Congress will probably draft procedural constitutional amendments in the future, though. This section offers some modest suggestions for drafting them better.

What to Do

The rules and procedures surrounding the presidency are no place to be casual. These provisions should be hyper-precise, even if it means losing some of the public accessibility that is otherwise ideal for the Constitution's language. Chapter 6's sad tale of Senator Magnuson's attempt at simplicity in the Twenty-Second Amendment shows that sacrificing exactitude for punchiness can cost you both. Those two ideals are not mutually exclusive anyway; a better-drafted version of the Twenty-Second Amendment wouldn't have sounded *that* much worse.

Relatedly, as seen in Chapter 3, on displacing a disabled president, it is risky to rely on legislative history as a substitute for clarity. To be sure, it is helpful when the record clearly establishes what the drafters intended. But as Chapter 3 discussed, not every constitutional dispute is settled by lawyers and judges coolly analyzing such legal sources. If you are drafting the rules that will apply to the transfer of presidential power during a crisis, you should make it extra simple for frantic people wrestling for supreme power to read them correctly. It would have been easy to draft the constitutional waiting-period language in Chapter 3 better; the drafters probably just needed more motivation. They were too confident that their intentions would be consulted, and this may have made them too relaxed about getting the text just right.[20]

Next, Congress should be attentive to future uncertainty. Admittedly, it isn't overly helpful to admonish Congress to be more clairvoyant, but Congress should at least be mindful. Background assumptions can change, and that can cause problems. It doesn't always take that long. The Twenty-Fifth Amendment, drafted in 1965, talks about the "death" of a president, but medical technology has complicated the definition of "death"; in a debate over whether a president is alive for constitutional purposes, one can imagine squabbles over the latest research on the different varieties of brain death. Another part of the amendment requires people to "transmit" a "written declaration" to leaders in Congress; if the writer is half a world away, would a "signed" e-mail suffice? It is worth thinking about what would happen in an unclear case before blithely deciding that it doesn't matter. In the case of the Twenty-Fifth Amendment, a maybe-death would not be too troubling, because the "disability" provisions provide a backstop. By contrast, the written transmission issue has no such safeguard and could conceivably cause a problem. Believing that we can rely on "the system"— Congress, presidents, and courts acting in good faith—is a valid assumption most of the time, but it may still be a needlessly risky one.

Finally, constitutional drafters should be careful and clear when they allocate decision-making authority. If they want courts to have a possible role in resolving disputes—and we have seen several reasons why they should— they should say so clearly enough to fend off the political-question doctrine. Another problem is when amendments leave it to Congress to write standards through ordinary legislation. There is virtue in leaving things nimble and flexible, but Congress does not always execute these constitutional assignments adequately. Sometimes it implements things poorly (as in Chapter 4), and other times it shirks its duties altogether (as with Section 4 of the Twentieth Amendment, which it has never implemented). Thus, if they are delegating choices to future Congresses, constitutional drafters should be clear about any restrictions they want to apply. The drafters should also consider default provisions, to provide rules when Congress fails to act. An example of this is the Twenty-Fifth Amendment, which gives the cabinet a default role in assessing the president's disability, but which allows Congress to substitute another group.[21]

The suggestions in this section must seem obvious: "Hey Congress, be careful and mindful and smart, OK?" But if this advice is obvious, it is nevertheless necessary. Congress gets amendments mostly right but can still get little details wrong. How can it do better?

One Way to Do It

As discussed in the introduction, and as seen in the most recent examples (the Twenty-Second and Twenty-Fifth Amendments), the process of drafting technical amendments is an odd combination of painful slowness and reckless speed. It typically takes years and multiple attempts to get a proposed constitutional amendment introduced, through committee in one house of Congress, onto the floor, approved by two-thirds, through committee in the other house, onto the floor there, and approved by two-thirds there. Each step presents an opportunity to change the text. Especially at the final stages, though, there is a strong sense of impatience and urgency. Having gotten as far as they have, proponents are reluctant to allow anything that might stop the proposal's forward progress. Moreover, having fought so much and for so long over the details, they distrust any attempt to unravel their craftsmanship.[22]

To a large extent, they are right. Getting things through Congress is hard, and there are a lot of ducks to keep in a row. Often, proposed last-minute changes represent arguments that were already considered at the committee level and either were shot down there or were the subject of a carefully wrought compromise. Even to the extent that some changes are new, any proposal that stops long enough to get pecked at by hundreds of individual members of Congress will have a hard time ever getting through. If the proposed change is picky and it concerns an unlikely series of events—the stuff of constitutional cliffhangers—it will be hard to defeat the floor leaders' natural desire to ignore it.[23]

As discussed in Chapter 3, it took years for Senator Bayh to build a consensus for the presidential disability provisions in Section 4 of the Twenty-Fifth Amendment. The debate combined several elements: the concept itself (what should we do?), the execution (why the cabinet? what about bringing in doctors?), the details (should the waiting period be two, four, or seven days?), and the text (should we say it this way or that way?). The further along things got, the more reluctant Bayh and his allies were to change anything. They treated attempted changes in any of these categories as equally threatening to their goal.[24]

But the last category, the text, is different. Disagreements over concept, execution, and details may be matters of true opposition. Once there is a consensus on them, though, an argument that is solely about the text is a discussion about how best to achieve a common goal. To be sure, when somebody on the floor of the Senate identifies a phrase that could be drafted better and proposes redrafting it, that *is* inimical to the goal of final passage. Sending the language back through committee could take weeks or months—an unavailable luxury near the end of a congressional term. Drafting by the full Senate on the spot doesn't work very well either. Still, sometimes a late change really is called for. Realistically, it's the last chance; once Congress has approved a proposed amendment, it has no real opportunity to do any redrafting.[25]

Congress thus needs ways to identify mistakes earlier in the process,* and to fix late-discovered mistakes in a way that doesn't unravel years of careful work. The key is to separate the process for agreeing on an amendment's purpose from the process for finalizing the text. I have a modest suggestion: add two steps to the process, drawing upon wisdom in the general public and using modern collaborative technology to perform a sort of "wiki government."[26]

When people or committees have been working with a text for too long, it becomes difficult for them to see the problems with it. A fresh pair of eyes— or better yet, millions of fresh pairs—can be very valuable. One successful wiki-government endeavor, the Peer-to-Patent project, has demonstrated that some government decision making (there, reviewing patent applications) can be improved by drawing upon the knowledge and judgment of interested experts outside the government. Peer-to-Patent is an imperfect model for drafting constitutional amendments, which, unlike patents, do not require gathering a mountain of widely dispersed data, and which do not have as many moving parts to break up and distribute to separate groups of helpers. However, Peer-to-Patent has shown that the public contributes well as self-selected, engaged collaborators (as they would be here) rather than as atomized commenters (as they are in the "notice-and-comment" regulatory process, where the Internet has made little difference). A closer analogy to constitutional amendments is the process by which software

* Elizabeth Garrett and Adrian Vermeule have offered some interesting suggestions on how to structure Congress's internal structures and rules to bring constitutional concerns to the foreground in the legislative process. *See* Elizabeth Garrett & Adrian Vermeule, *Institutional Design of a Thayerian Congress*, 50 Duke L.J. 1277, 1309–30 (2001) (suggesting, among other things, constitutional-impact statements, centralized and neutral constitutional-expert staff, and expanded use of points of order). These ideas are directed at preventing constitutional problems with statutes (relevant in Chapter 4 and perhaps Chapter 1), but some of their principles might be helpful for drafting constitutional amendments too.

companies use open-source collaboration to write and debug software—extremely effectively—with the help of people outside the company. Experts have started to think seriously about collaborative public legislative drafting. Constitutional amendments can be complicated, but they are less so than legislation and software. Thus, there is good reason to think that with the right collaborative technology, interested members of the public would be very helpful at "debugging" and optimizing proposed constitutional amendments.[27]

When a committee debates a proposed constitutional amendment, and it makes changes to the concept, execution, or details, it obviously must change the proposal's text in order to do so. It is counterproductive, however, to try to polish the text perfectly every time it makes a change. Instead, when the committee has reached a final, clear consensus on the concept, execution, and details, it should give the text one more run-through. The goal: to make any improvements to the text that better vindicate the agreed-upon concept, execution, and details.

The committee could take, say, five days to optimize the text with the help of an online process through which interested members of the public could propose, discuss, and rate alternatives. Working together, the interested public can quickly discover previously unnoticed loopholes and pitfalls, can identify the best ways to prevent them, and can optimize the text. Textual optimization is not easy, but that's precisely the point. Members of Congress and their staffs, even at their most able, intelligent, and hardworking, cannot match the "wisdom of crowds."[28]

The "crowd" might find bugs that affect the details in ways the committee had not clearly addressed, but the collaborative process could provide multiple optimized texts, each one reflecting a different set of substantive choices. The committee would still be deciding what to do vis-à-vis those substantive choices; the public process would just flag issues and offer good language to deal with them. (The committee could get public input at an earlier stage, when it is discussing execution and details in the first place, but there is reason to doubt that this would work as well.)[29]

Once the proposal moves from committee to the full House or Senate, there might be new debate about the concept, execution, and details. Changes at this stage would require changes to the text that the first round of public input might not have covered. But at that point, a similar (and shorter) public process could help to smooth the text over again. Because the textual changes would be working toward a common goal, and because it need not entail rejecting or tabling or sending the item back to committee, the public process would not need to slow things down much at all.

Congress would still maintain its voting power, of course; the public would have influence, not direct authority. But public influence would be a welcome addition to the process, even aside from its effectiveness. The Constitution represents the voice of the People with a capital P, not just that of their representatives, in a way that is not the case in the less concise, less accessible world of statutes. When it comes to writing new words into the Constitution, this sort of public participation has a nice symbolic value to it.

A Final Thought

It seems more appropriate to end on this positive note than with the thread of doom and gloom that has run through this book. This chapter rests on a notion that, in addition to our six constitutional cliffhangers, there are others lurking out there. Some are known but neglected, some are undiscovered, and some are yet to be created. But the catalog of responses to the doom and gloom—the reasons not to fret about all these constitutional cliffhangers—is quite encouraging. Cliffhangers are scarce, because the Constitution is generally well designed. When cliffhangers happen, our institutions typically settle them bloodlessly and often fix them so that they don't happen again.

It's still worthwhile—indeed, crucial—to take these potential problems seriously. But at the end of the day, thinking about cliffhangers is not about doom and gloom, it's about venerating the Constitution: Thinking about it deeply, first of all. Getting acquainted with all of the Constitution's nooks and crannies. Wrestling with all its permutations. Probing its limits until these minor flaws emerge. Then, caring deeply about the Constitution. Not writing off its flaws as "minor." Being unwilling to ignore what it says just because it causes headaches. Most of all, wanting always to improve the Constitution. It deserves no less.

NOTES

Introduction

1. Nassim Nicholas Taleb, The Black Swan (2007); *see also* Akhil Reed Amar & Vikram David Amar, *Constitutional Vices*, FindLaw.com (July 26, 2002), http://writ.news.findlaw.com/amar/20020726.html (noting that "Americans are slow to imagine the unimaginable—even after it happens").

2. Sanford Levinson, Bush v. Gore *and the French Revolution*, Law & Contemp. Probs., Summer 2002, at 7, 32. On the terminology of constitutional crises and chaos, see William N. Eskridge, Jr. & Sanford Levinson, *How Stupid Can a Coasean Constitution Be?, in* Constitutional Stupidities, Constitutional Tragedies 107, 108 (1998) (using "constitutional landmine" to describe a clear-rule/bad-result situation); Eric A. Posner & Adrian Vermeule, *Constitutional Showdowns*, 156 U. Pa. L. Rev. 991 (2008) (using "constitutional showdown" to describe certain interbranch struggles over constitutional powers).

3. The justices in 1877 played a decisive role as part of a commission convened by Congress to settle the disputed election. The rest of the commission was politically balanced, but the five justices on the commission included three Republicans, and all issues were decided by party-line votes. There was a lot more going on in 1876, of course, including disputes in other states, and the suspension of the old rules for resolving disputed electoral votes. *See generally* Michael F. Holt, By One Vote: The Disputed Presidential Election of 1876 (2008).

4. *See* U.S. Const. art. II, § 1, cl. 5 (Natural-Born Citizen Clause); S. Res. 511, 110th Cong. (2008) (resolving, in non-binding fashion, that John McCain is a "natural born Citizen"); Gabriel J. Chin, *Why Senator John McCain Cannot Be President: Eleven Months and a Hundred Yards Short of Citizenship*, 107 Mich. L. Rev. First Impressions 1 (2008), *available at* http://www.michiganlawreview.org/assets/fi/107/chin.pdf (arguing that McCain is not a natural-born citizen).

5. *See* Eskridge & Levinson, *supra* note 2, at 109 (arguing, in similar context, that it would be "foolhardy to believe that absolutely none" of what they call constitutional landmines "will detonate in our lifetime").

6. To compare, Sections 2 and 3 of Article II, defining presidential power, contain 320 words. Clauses 2 through 4 of Article II, Section 1, describing the presidential election process, contain 374 words. The latter were superseded by the Twelfth Amendment, which contains 399 words (though it also covers vice-presidential elections).

7. *See* Victoria F. Nourse & Jane S. Schacter, *The Politics of Legislative Drafting*, 77 N.Y.U. L. Rev. 575, 594–96 (2002) (positing time pressure, deliberate ambiguity, and political necessity as leading causes of lack of clarity in legislative drafting). There are some vague procedural provisions, such as the "natural born citizen" requirement for presidents. *See* Sarah Helen Duggin & Mary Beth Collins, *"Natural Born" in the USA*, 85 B.U. L. Rev. 53 (2005).

8. *See* Sanford Levinson & Jack Balkin, *Constitutional Crises*, 157 U. Pa. L. Rev. 707, 751 (2009) ("[E]nough lawyers, given enough time, are likely to attempt every logical argument to its fullest extent on behalf of the interests of their clients, including power-seeking presidents of the United States.").

9. The typo is discussed in a footnote in Chapter 4. *Cf.* Nourse & Schacter, *supra* note 7, at 585–87 (discussing how senators are not normally involved in the actual drafting of legislation). Constitutional amendments are not as dauntingly technical as legislation typically is, making it more tempting for any member of Congress to chime in with his or her own edits.

Chapter 1. Prosecuting a President

1. The pro-immunity argument in this chapter draws heavily upon Akhil Reed Amar & Brian C. Kalt, *The Presidential Privilege Against Prosecution*, 2 Nexus 11 (1997), in ways that are both too cumbersome and too subtle to cite or quote point by point. Professor Amar has graciously given his permission for this.

2. *See* Eric M. Freedman, *The Law as King and the King as Law: Is a President Immune from Criminal Prosecution Before Impeachment?*, 20 Hastings Const. L.Q. 7, 10 n.7 (1992) (detailing Jaworski's thinking); *see also* Ken Gormley, *Impeachment and the Independent Counsel*, 51 Stan. L. Rev. 309, 315 (1999) (describing Jaworski's predecessor, Archibald Cox, as concluding that Nixon was immune while in office).

3. Senator Robert Byrd, for instance, thought that President Clinton was guilty of impeachable offenses but nevertheless voted against convicting and removing him. *See* 145 Cong. Rec. 2570 (1999) (statement of Sen. Byrd); *see also* Jonathan Turley, *"From Pillar to Post": The Prosecution of American Presidents*, 37 Am. Crim. L. Rev. 1049, 1103 (2000) (arguing that president's term would probably run out before trial or sentencing for a major crime).

4. *See* Morrison v. Olson, 487 U.S. 654, 727–32 (1988) (Scalia, J., dissenting) (noting dangers of unaccountable prosecutors pursuing single targets of their own choosing); *Impeachment or Indictment: Is a Sitting President Subject to Compulsory*

Criminal Process?: Hearing Before the Subcomm. on the Const., Federalism and Property Rights of the S. Comm. on the Judiciary, 105th Cong. 20 (1998) [hereinafter *Senate Hearing*] (statement of Lawrence E. Walsh) (discussing prosecutorial techniques).

5. *But see* Freedman, *supra* note 2, at 13 ("[T]he dispute over whether the President is immune from criminal liability is not a dispute exclusively, or even primarily, about legal rules. It is . . . a clash over how we conceive of our President and our country.").

6. *See* Memorandum from Robert G. Dixon, Jr., Assistant Attorney General, Office of Legal Counsel 30 (Sept. 24, 1973) [hereinafter Dixon Memo] (on file with author) (making similar argument in real case).

7. *See Senate Hearing, supra* note 4, at 13 (statement of Laurence Tribe) (noting that Constitution's text provides no immunity, but arguing that its structure does).

8. *See* Terry Eastland, *The Power to Control Prosecution*, 2 Nexus 43, 45 (1997) (discussing early roots of this precedent); Freedman, *supra* note 2, at 25–36 (discussing prosecutability of other federal and state officials); Turley, *supra* note 3, at 1072–74 (discussing prosecutions of sitting officers); Memorandum from Randolph D. Moss, Assistant Attorney General, Office of Legal Policy, A Sitting President's Amenability to Indictment and Criminal Prosecution 2 (Oct. 16, 2000) [hereinafter Moss Memo], *available at* http://www.usdoj.gov/olc/sitting_president.htm (noting "constitutional practice since the Founding" of pursuing sitting officers other than the president). As discussed later, members of Congress have partial immunity.

9. *See Senate Hearing, supra* note 4, at 3 (statement of Sen. Ashcroft) (opposing immunity but calling uniqueness "[p]erhaps the best constitutional argument" for immunity); Memorandum for the United States Concerning the Vice President's Claim of Constitutional Immunity at 16–17, *In re* Proceedings of the Grand Jury Impaneled Dec. 5, 1972, Civ. No. 73-965 (D. Md. Oct. 5, 1973) [hereinafter Vice-Presidential Immunity Memo] (discussing negligible effects on their branches of incapacity of judges and members of Congress). A closer analogy to prosecuting the president would be prosecuting the entire Supreme Court, or the entire Senate. *See* Gormley, *supra* note 2, at 322 (offering this analogy); *see also* Clinton v. Jones, 520 U.S. 681, 713 (1997) (Breyer, J., concurring) ("[I]nterference with a President's ability to carry out his public responsibilities is constitutionally equivalent to interference with the ability of the entirety of Congress, or the Judicial Branch, to carry out its public obligations.").

10. *See* Nixon v. Fitzgerald, 457 U.S. 731, 749–50 (1982) (noting, in case granting presidents civil immunity for official acts, that "[t]he President occupies a unique position in the constitutional scheme" that "distinguishes him from other executive officials"); *Senate Hearing, supra* note 4, at 13 (statement of Laurence Tribe); *id.* at 207 (statement of Susan Low Bloch); Vice-Presidential Immunity Memo, *supra* note 9, at 18; Jay S. Bybee, *Who Executes the Executioner?*, 2 Nexus 53, 60 (1997); Eastland, *supra* note 8, at 46; Gormley, *supra* note 2, at 320; Scott W. Howe, *The Prospect of a President Incarcerated*, 2 Nexus 86, 87–88 (1997); Brett M. Kavanaugh, *The President and the Independent Counsel*, 86 Geo. L.J. 2133, 2159 (1998); Dixon

Memo, *supra* note 6, at 28–30 (stating that prosecution "would interfere with the President's unique official duties, most of which cannot be performed by anyone else," and that it "boggles the imagination" to contemplate an indicted president trying to serve); Moss Memo, *supra* note 8, at 16–17 (describing presidential duties); *see also Clinton*, 520 U.S. at 698–99 (rejecting civil immunity but conceding these features of the presidency).

11. Morrison v. Olson, 487 U.S. 654, 691–93 (1988) (using "trammel" and "interference" language); *Nixon*, 457 U.S. at 754 (using balancing-test language and finding president civilly immune for official acts); *see Clinton*, 520 U.S. at 701–02 (rejecting civil immunity for private acts for sitting presidents); United States v. Nixon, 418 U.S. 683, 712–13 (1974) (finding limited executive privilege); *Senate Hearing, supra* note 4, at 210 (statement of Susan Low Bloch) (doubting that Framers "contemplated our country's having to put its national security and domestic agenda on hold while state and/or federal prosecutors, perhaps several at once, ply their trade"); Moss Memo, *supra* note 8, at 11 (arguing that balancing test accounts for cases granting presidents some immunities but denying them others, and is consistent with criminal immunity for sitting presidents). To be sure, *Nixon v. Fitzgerald* based presidential civil immunity for official action on other factors as well, such as the shadow that potential liability would cast over presidential decision making. That factor is less of an issue in our case, which is really a matter of timing, not ultimate liability.

12. Turley, *supra* note 3, at 1078–79, 1080 n.168, 1084, 1089–90; *see Clinton*, 520 U.S. at 694 (noting, in civil context, "we have never suggested that the President, or any other official, has an immunity that extends beyond the scope of any action taken in an official capacity"); *Senate Hearing, supra* note 4, at 35 (statement of Eric M. Freedman) (citing "fundamental concept of the President as an ordinary citizen temporarily exercising power"); Dixon Memo, *supra* note 6, at 22–24 (contrasting amenability of president to judicial process for official activities to amenability for personal, criminal prosecution). *But see* Joel B. Grossman & David A. Yalof, *The "Public" versus the "Private" President: Striking a Balance between Presidential Responsibilities and Immunities*, 28 Presidential Stud. Q. 821, 821 (1998) ("[A] president's private life does not exist in a vacuum outside of his public life, and the law must reflect this reality.").

13. Alexander Bickel, *The Constitutional Tangle*, New Republic, Oct. 6, 1973, at 14–15 (emphasis added); *see Senate Hearing, supra* note 4, at 14 (statement of Laurence Tribe) (distinguishing president's lack of civil immunity); Vice-Presidential Immunity Memo, *supra* note 9, at 18 ("[T]he President is the only officer whose temporary disability while in office incapacitates an entire branch of government."); Moss Memo, *supra* note 8, at 1 (agreeing that "all federal civil officers except the President are subject to indictment and criminal prosecution while still in office"); Akhil Reed Amar, *On Impeaching Presidents*, 28 Hofstra L. Rev. 291, 293 n.2 (1999) (noting different consequences of president-defendant refusing to participate in civil case versus criminal one).

14. *See Senate Hearing, supra* note 4, at 190 (statement of Akhil Reed Amar) (stressing national constituency of Congress); Bybee, *supra* note 10, at 66 (distinguishing civil [non-]immunity because of unavailability of impeachment); *see also* Moss Memo, *supra* note 8, at 23 (praising impeachment process as politically account-able mechanism for policing presidents). Washington, D.C., residents participate in presidential elections but not congressional ones, so the president's constitu-ency isn't precisely the same as Congress's.

15. *See Senate Hearing, supra* note 4, at 11 (statement of Edwin Meese III and Todd Gaziano) (arguing that president in his official capacity could constitutionally prosecute president in his personal capacity); *id.* at 176 (reprinting Memorandum from Carl B. Feldbaum et al. to Leon Jaworski 13 (Feb. 12, 1974)) (arguing against immunity but conceding president's ultimate power to control federal prosecutions); Eastland, *supra* note 8 (arguing that a president may be prosecuted "but only to the extent that he allows himself to be," and noting that Congress could impeach a president who blocks his own prosecution); *cf.* Freedman, *supra* note 2, at 25 (arguing that separation-of-powers immunity argument is weaker for presidents than for members of Congress or judges, because latter are more likely to be cowed by interbranch threat of prosecution). There is a potential conflict of interest if a president consents to be prosecuted by an executive branch that he heads. *See* Dixon Memo, *supra* note 6, at 26 (discussing conflicts of interest).

16. *See Senate Hearing, supra* note 4, at 3 (statement of Sen. Ashcroft) (arguing against immunity given *Morrison*'s rejection of unitary-executive theory); *id.* at 11 (state-ment of Edwin Meese III and Todd Gaziano) (rejecting distinction between ability to subpoena president, approved in *Nixon* without unitary-executive problems, and ability to prosecute him); *id.* at 215 (statement of Akhil Reed Amar) (distin-guishing *Morrison* from case in which president is pursued); Eastland, *supra* note 8, at 51 (arguing that *Morrison* does not prevent president from firing inde-pendent counsels who are prosecuting him). To be precise, the statute in *Morrison* gave the attorney general, not the president, the power to remove the independent counsel; moreover, the attorney general's power to remove was restricted. *See Morrison*, 487 U.S. at 663–64.

    The disruptiveness to President Clinton of the Paula Jones civil case, after the Supreme Court ruled in *Clinton v. Jones* that it should not be so, also weighs in favor of immunity. *See Senate Hearing, supra* note 4, at 207 (statement of Susan Low Bloch).

17. *See* Vice-Presidential Immunity Memo, *supra* note 9, at 20 (alluding to self-pardon argument); Raoul Berger, *The President, Congress, and the Courts*, 83 Yale L.J. 1111, 1130–31 (1974) (rejecting self-pardon argument); Freedman, *supra* note 2, at 57–59 (giving lengthy rejoinder to self-pardon argument); Turley, *supra* note 3, at 1091–92 (discussing and rejecting pardon equity argument); Akhil Reed Amar, *Bringing Justice to Clinton*, N.Y. Times, Mar. 20, 2000, at A23 (arguing that because sitting presidents cannot pardon themselves, and because nobody else can either,

it would be inappropriate to subject them to prosecution); Dixon Memo, *supra* note 6, at 26 (raising pardon issue).

18. *See Senate Hearing, supra* note 4, at 6 (statement of Sen. Torricelli) (arguing for immunity in light of inherently public and political nature of presidency); The Federalist No. 65, at 396–97 (Alexander Hamilton) (Clinton Rossiter ed., 1961) (discussing impeachment as way to handle political crimes by political men); Kavanaugh, *supra* note 10, at 2157–61 (discussing inevitable tremendous politicization of any prosecution, or non-prosecution, and thus aptness of exclusive congressional role); *cf. Senate Hearing, supra* note 4, at 189 (statement of Akhil Reed Amar) ("Once we understand how [the Constitution] was engineered to work, we will see more clearly some of the design flaws of the modern independent counsel statute."). *But see* Dixon Memo, *supra* note 6, at 24–26 (arguing for immunity but rejecting notion that prosecution of presidents is necessarily too political to be handled in court).

19. *See Senate Hearing, supra* note 4, at 178 (reprinting Memorandum from Carl B. Feldbaum et al. to Leon Jaworski 15 (Feb. 12, 1974)) (dismissing disruption argument by comparison to impeachment); *id.* at 190 (statement of Akhil Reed Amar) (praising finality of impeachment relative to criminal process, and noting impeachment's helpful geography); Turley, *supra* note 3, at 1082 (noting how government continued to function during presidential impeachments); Dixon Memo, *supra* note 6, at 28, 31 (distinguishing impeachment disruption as constitutionally acceptable, and minimized by impeachment process's finality); Moss Memo, *supra* note 8, at 16, 23 (comparing accountability and relative burden of impeachment versus prosecution). *But see* Michael J. Gerhardt, *The Perils of Presidential Impeachment*, 67 U. Chi. L. Rev. 293, 305 (2000) (reviewing Richard A. Posner, An Affair of State (1999)) (declaring it "unlikely" that prosecution would impair executive branch any more than impeachment would).

20. Howe, *supra* note 10, at 90; *see Senate Hearing, supra* note 4, at 9 (statement of Edwin Meese III and Todd Gaziano) (noting conflict between immunity and speedy-trial rights); Laurence H. Tribe, 1 American Constitutional Law 756 (3d ed. 2000) (discussing speedy-trial implications); Freedman, *supra* note 2, at 51–52 (noting likelihood that criminal presidents would only avoid impeachment and removal for minor crimes); Turley, *supra* note 3, at 1081–83, 1099–103 (discussing timing of prosecutions and ability of executive branch to function without presidential control, and arguing further that personal distractions are inevitable and no case law "protects the President from distractions caused by his personal conduct"); Moss Memo, *supra* note 8, at 20–21 (noting incongruity of forcing a busy president to waive his speedy-trial rights). Turley also cites President Clinton's claim that his civil lawsuit and impeachment did not distract him from his duties. Turley, *supra* note 3, at 1086.

Two prosecutors of presidents have argued the opposite. Iran-Contra independent counsel Lawrence Walsh testified to Congress that the intensity of the president's duties is such that presidents should not be pursued by independent counsels for their non-official actions until they have left office. *Senate Hearing, supra* note 4, at 16–17 (statement of Lawrence E. Walsh). Brett Kavanaugh, a prominent member of Kenneth Starr's team pursuing President Clinton, argued nearly contemporaneously against prosecuting sitting presidents. *See* Kavanaugh, *supra* note 10, at 2157–61.

21. *Senate Hearing, supra* note 4, at 211 (statement of Susan Low Bloch); *see* Gormley, *supra* note 2, at 322 (discussing criminal defendant's rights and requirement to attend trial); Moss Memo, *supra* note 8, at 18–21 (distinguishing burdens of civil and criminal liability).

22. *See* Eastland, *supra* note 8, at 49 (discussing reasons presidents might choose to be prosecuted); Turley, *supra* note 3, at 1087–88 (arguing that any presidential criminal charges would likely be minor, and attendant procedures minimally intrusive); *cf.* Dixon Memo, *supra* note 6, at 29 (noting weaker case for immunity for minor crimes). Under the Twenty-Fifth Amendment, a president who is "unable to discharge the powers and duties of his office" can hand temporary power to the vice president. As discussed in Chapter 3, the vice president and cabinet can displace an unwilling president this way too.

23. *See Senate Hearing, supra* note 4, at 9–10 (statement of Edwin Meese III and Todd Gaziano) (positing that imprisoned president could be declared disabled under Twenty-Fifth Amendment); *id.* at 227–28 (statement of Frank Tuerkheimer) (noting that staying in office would be a significant bargaining chip in any presidential plea bargaining); *id.* at 225 (statement of Peter F. Rient) (mentioning possibility of presentment to Congress instead of indictment); Richard A. Posner, An Affair of State: The Investigation, Impeachment, and Trial of President Clinton 106 (1999) (making structural argument against allowing prosecutors to preempt impeachment by plea-bargaining a president out of office); Turley, *supra* note 3, at 1081 (rejecting notion that prosecution is "a de facto removal").

24. *See* Clinton v. Jones, 520 U.S. 681, 713 (1997) (Breyer, J., concurring) ("[A] President, though able to delegate duties to others, cannot delegate ultimate responsibility or the active obligation to supervise that goes with it."); Turley, *supra* note 3, at 1081, 1088, 1103–05 (rejecting immunity and noting possibilities of trial or sentence waiting until president leaves office, of sentence not including prison, and of constitutional requirements that president be allowed to perform his duties from prison). Turley is critical of the idea of a prosecutor delaying an indictment, though. *Id.* at 1088 n.195. He also concedes that there are some constitutional limits on the conditions of a president's incarceration. *Id.* at 1102 n.257; *see also* Freedman, *supra* note 2, at 52–53 (noting flexible sentencing powers and rarity of prison sentences); Moss Memo, *supra* note 8, at 17–18 (arguing that imprisonment "would indisputably preclude the executive branch from performing its constitutionally assigned functions").

25. *See Senate Hearing, supra* note 4, at 10 (statement of Edwin Meese III and Todd Gaziano) (rejecting disruption argument for being about policy rather than law).

26. *See* Turley, *supra* note 3, at 1061–62 ("The absence of a textual reference to Presidential immunity from prosecution is a significant omission.").

27. U.S. Const. art. I, § 6, cl. 1; *see Senate Hearing, supra* note 4, at 3 (statement of Sen. Ashcroft) (using congressional immunity as evidence against presidential immunity); Turley, *supra* note 3, at 1054, 1057 (discussing contrast between explicit congressional immunity and lack of such for president).

28. *See* Nixon v. Fitzgerald, 457 U.S. 731, 750 n.31 (1982) (damages immunity for official acts); United States v. Nixon, 418 U.S. 683, 705–06 (1974) (executive privilege); *see also Senate Hearing, supra* note 4, at 187 (statement of Akhil Reed Amar) (making broad-immunity point); *cf.* Vice-Presidential Immunity Memo, *supra* note 9, at 5 (using Congressional Immunity Clause to reject vice-presidential immunity); Dixon Memo, *supra* note 6, at 18–20 (arguing for implicit immunity, with Congressional Immunity Clause limiting, not granting, immunity). *See generally* Josh Chafetz, Democracy's Privileged Few 87–110, 134–43 (2007) (discussing congressional immunity). The presidential immunities that the Court has found are more like Congress's "speech and debate" immunity than Congress's privilege against arrest, and the former seems applicable only to the president's official conduct.

29. U.S. Const. art. I, § 3, cl. 7; *see Senate Hearing, supra* note 4, at 3 (statement of Sen. Ashcroft) (rejecting sequentialist argument in light of lack of immunity for other impeachable officials); *id.* at 9 (statement of Edwin Meese III and Todd Gaziano) (noting that some senators prefer waiting for criminal conviction before removing judges); *id.* at 13–14 (statement of Laurence Tribe) (favoring immunity but rejecting sequentialist argument); Vice-Presidential Immunity Memo, *supra* note 9, at 6 (stating that "the Framers contemplated that this sequence should be mandatory only as to the President"); Susan Low Bloch, *Foreword*, 2 Nexus 7 (1997) (referring to sequentialist and anti-sequentialist theories); Bybee, *supra* note 10 (defending sequentialist theory); George E. Danielson, *Presidential Immunity from Criminal Prosecution*, 63 Geo. L.J. 1065, 1067 (1975) (stating clause does not specify sequence but rather "establishes that courts of impeachment and courts of law are two different and unrelated forums"); Eastland, *supra* note 8, at 44 (discussing sequentialist assertions by Vice President Agnew); Freedman, *supra* note 2, at 41 (discussing separation between impeachment and criminal law); Gormley, *supra* note 2, at 316–17 (discussing rejection of sequentialist theory); Howe, *supra* note 10, at 89 (rejecting sequentialist theory); Turley, *supra* note 3, at 1054–62 (criticizing sequentialist theory); Dixon Memo, *supra* note 6, at 2–17 (rejecting sequentialist theory and citing historical sources).

30. *See Nixon*, 457 U.S. at 748 (finding presidential civil immunity for official acts "implicit in the nature of the President's office").

31. *See Senate Hearing, supra* note 4, at 2 (statement of Sen. Ashcroft) ("The President is subject to the law, not above it. If he violates the law, he can be prosecuted."); Freedman, *supra* note 2, at 46–51 (making rule-of-law argument against immunity); *cf.* Erwin Chemerinsky, *Justice Delayed Is Justice Denied*, 2 Nexus 24, 27–28

(1997) (making similar equality point against presidential civil immunity). For an eloquent statement against exalting the president, see Freedman, *supra* note 2, at 13–15.

32. *See Nixon*, 457 U.S. at 757–58 & n.41 (granting civil immunity for official presidential actions, but noting that impeachment, politics, and history can all punish misconduct, and contending that "[i]t is simply error to characterize an official as 'above the law' because a particular remedy is not available against him"); United States v. Burr, 25 F. Cas. 187, 192 (C.C.D. Va. 1807) (No. 14,694) (expressing sentiment by Chief Justice Marshall—no friend of President Jefferson's—that "[i]n no case of this kind would a court be required to proceed against the president as against an ordinary individual"); *Senate Hearing, supra* note 4, at 9 (statement of Edwin Meese III and Todd Gaziano) (arguing against immunity because "the normal presumption is so strong that no one is above the law"); Howe, *supra* note 10, at 86–87 (making rule-of-law point); Moss Memo, *supra* note 8, at 10, 23 (arguing for temporary immunity and noting that with it, "the President is not above the law, and that he is ultimately accountable for his misconduct").

33. *See* Moss Memo, *supra* note 8, at 22–23 (addressing degradation argument); *cf.* Chemerinsky, *supra* note 31, at 29 (making similar argument against delays due to temporary civil immunity).

34. *See Senate Hearing, supra* note 4, at 9 (statement of Edwin Meese III and Todd Gaziano) (noting statute-of-limitations problems); *id.* at 16 (statement of Lawrence E. Walsh) (arguing for temporary immunity and tolling of statute of limitations); *id.* at 214–15 (1998) (statement of Akhil Reed Amar) (favoring constitutionally automatic tolling but suggesting that clear legislation would be preferable); Howe, *supra* note 10 (arguing that courts should not find immunity in the Constitution but should grant it as a prudential matter); Turley, *supra* note 3, at 1083 (mentioning ways in which judges could accommodate presidential criminal defendants); Dixon Memo, *supra* note 6, at 29 (discussing possibility of allowing indictment but waiting for trial); Moss Memo, *supra* note 8, at 22 (discussing statute of limitations and general "costs of delay"); *cf. Senate Hearing, supra* note 4, at 14–15 (statement of Laurence Tribe) (arguing that allowing sitting presidents to be indicted but not tried violates Constitution's speedy-trial requirement). *But see* Moss Memo, *supra* note 8, at 20 (arguing that criminal cases allow for less flexibility than civil cases); Clinton v. Jones, 520 U.S. 681, 707–08 (1997) (finding in civil case that president had not met his burden for a discretionary stay).

35. McCulloch v. Maryland, 17 U.S. (4 Wheat.) 316, 435–36 (1819); *cf. Clinton*, 520 U.S. at 691 (noting, in civil immunity case, "[i]f this case were being heard in a state forum, instead of advancing a separation-of-powers argument, petitioner would presumably rely on federalism and comity concerns"). Interestingly, a memorandum from his staff to Watergate prosecutor Leon Jaworski argued that while presidents are subject to federal prosecution, state prosecution would be unconstitutional. *See Senate Hearing, supra* note 4, at 176 n.* (reprinting Memorandum from Carl B. Feldbaum et al. to Leon Jaworski 13 n.* (Feb. 12, 1974)).

36. *McCulloch*, 17 U.S. (4 Wheat.) at 432 (emphasis added). Ken Gormley makes this point with some extreme hypotheticals, such as President Kennedy being lured to Mississippi and arrested during the Ole Miss crisis in 1962, and President Clinton being tried for criminal assault against Paula Jones in deeply Republican Texas. Gormley, *supra* note 2, at 321; *see also* Amar & Kalt, *supra* note 1, at 14–15 (hypothesizing about President Lincoln being arrested in Virginia in early 1861).

37. *See* Turley, *supra* note 3, at 1092–93 (criticizing *McCulloch* analogy).

38. *Cf. id.* at 1089 ("Historically, the primary threat of Presidential indictment has come from federal, and not state, prosecutors."). Impeachment can be based on a state criminal violation, of course. *See* Bybee, *supra* note 10, at 57 (arguing that originally, high crimes and misdemeanors "would have largely been [defined by] *state* law").

39. 2 The Debates in the Several States on the Adoption of the Federal Constitution 480 (Jonathan Elliot ed., Washington, 1836); *see* 10 Annals of Cong. 74 (1800) (Pinckney).

40. The Federalist No. 69, *supra* note 18, at 416 (Alexander Hamilton) (emphasis added); 2 The Records of the Federal Convention of 1787, at 64–65 (Max Farrand ed., rev. ed. 1966) (Gouverneur Morris and George Mason implying that only president's "Coadjutors" could be punished for a crime); *id.* at 500 (Morris implying that impeachment would precede trial); *see also* The Federalist No. 77, *supra* note 18, at 464 (Alexander Hamilton) (suggesting prosecution would be "subsequent" to impeachment and removal); Michael J. Gerhardt, The Federal Impeachment Process 16 (2d ed. 2000) (contending that Hamilton's statement on immunity "reflected his personal agenda"); Gormley, *supra* note 2, at 317–18 (discussing statements of Hamilton and Morris); Joseph Isenbergh, *Impeachment and Presidential Immunity from Judicial Process*, 18 Yale L. & Pol'y Rev. 53, 57–58 (1999) (discussing debates); Turley, *supra* note 3, at 1063–64 (discussing Hamilton's likely views on immunity).

41. The Diary of William Maclay and Other Notes on Senate Debates 168 (Kenneth R. Bowling & Helen E. Veit eds., 1988); *see* Clinton v. Jones, 520 U.S. 681, 695–97 & n.23 (1997) (discussing Maclay and other historical materials); Freedman, *supra* note 2, at 15–21 (quoting Maclay and other evidence and finding it inconclusive). Probably the best originalist argument against immunity is Berger, *supra* note 17, at 1125–32. Berger had earlier argued in favor of immunity, though. *See* Freedman, *supra* note 2, at 11 n.12 (criticizing Berger).

42. 3 Joseph Story, Commentaries on the Constitution of the United States 418–19 (Boston, Hilliard, Gray, & Co. 1833); Turley, *supra* note 3, at 1068–69.

43. *See* H.R. Rep. No. 93-1305, at 362–72 (1974) (minority congressional argument for immunity); Don Van Natta, Jr., *Starr Is Weighing Whether to Indict Sitting President*, N.Y. Times, Jan. 31, 1999, at A1 (Clinton's pursuer advancing non-immunity argument); Dixon Memo, *supra* note 6 (Nixon administration argument for immunity); Moss Memo, *supra* note 8 (Clinton administration reaffirming Nixon memorandum in light of subsequent case law). The lack of a consensus has not

prevented claims of one. *See, e.g., Senate Hearing, supra* note 4, at 8 (statement of Edwin Meese III and Todd Gaziano) (asserting that during Watergate, "scholarly opinion at the time was that a sitting President could be indicted"); Vice-Presidential Immunity Memo, *supra* note 9, at 17 (stating that "[a]lmost all legal commentators agree" on temporary presidential immunity).

It is perhaps more precise to say that Leon Jaworski was prepared to argue that Nixon wasn't immune, but was unsure and avoided indicting Nixon for that reason (and for other political/strategic ones). *See* Freedman, *supra* note 2, at 10 n.7 (describing Jaworski's position); Carl Bernstein & Robert Woodward, *U.S. Panel Voted 19–0 in March,* Wash. Post, June 6, 1974, at A1 (indicating that Jaworski told grand jury "indictment of an incumbent President might not be legally possible").

44. *See Senate Hearing, supra* note 4 (testimony opposing immunity by Edwin Meese III and Todd Gaziano, Eric Freedman, and Jonathan Turley, and supporting immunity by Laurence Tribe, Lawrence Walsh, Akhil Reed Amar, and Susan Low Bloch); Charles L. Black, Jr., Impeachment: A Handbook 40–41 (1974) (for immunity); Freedman, *supra* note 2 (against immunity); Gormley, *supra* note 2, at 315–24 (for immunity); Isenbergh, *supra* note 40 (for immunity); *Ought a President of the United States to Be Prosecuted?*, 2 Nexus 1 (1997) (entire issue of journal, featuring articles for and against immunity by Akhil Reed Amar and me, Erwin Chemerinsky, Terry Eastland, Jay Bybee, Eric Freedman, and Scott Howe); Turley, *supra* note 3 (definitive critique of pro-immunity argument); *id.* at 1051 nn.10–11 (listing Profs. Akhil Reed Amar, Susan Low Bloch, Cass Sunstein, Paul Butler, and Joseph Isenbergh as immunity proponents); *cf. Senate Hearing, supra* note 4, at 198 (1998) (testimony of Jonathan Turley) (conceding despite anti-immunity position that immunity "remains one of the great unanswered questions of the Constitution"); Freedman, *supra* note 2, at 11 n.12 (criticizing Watergate-era scholarship on both sides).

45. *See* Howe, *supra* note 10, at 92–93 (exploring implications of Constitution not precluding immunity); Isenbergh, *supra* note 40, at 105–06 (proposing immunity legislation); Kavanaugh, *supra* note 10, at 2157 (proposing immunity legislation). Congress's necessary-and-proper power bolsters any federal powers—including executive ones—in the Constitution. *See* U.S. Const. art. I, § 8, cl. 18.

46. Sources discussing tolling the statute of limitations include: *Senate Hearing, supra* note 4, at 16 (statement of Lawrence E. Walsh); *id.* at 35 (statement of Eric M. Freedman); *id.* at 214–15 (statement of Akhil Reed Amar) (finding automatic tolling in Constitution but suggesting that clear legislation would be preferable); Dixon Memo, *supra* note 6, at 29; and Moss Memo, *supra* note 8, at 22, 32 n.34.

47. *See* Gormley, *supra* note 2, at 316 (opining that a "statutory solution to this unsettled question would go far toward correcting the awkward interrelationship between special prosecutors and legislators").

48. *See Senate Hearing, supra* note 4, at 92, 96 (statement of Eric M. Freedman) (suggesting independent-counsel preemption of state prosecution and special statute of limitations).

Chapter 2. The Presidential Self-Pardon Controversy

1. This chapter draws upon my student note (Brian C. Kalt, Note, *Pardon Me?: The Constitutional Case Against Presidential Self-Pardons*, 106 Yale L.J. 779 (1996)) in ways that are too cumbersome and subtle to cite point by point. In a few places, I use verbatim language from the note without putting it in quotation marks or citing it as such. In my note, I made the strongest case I could against the self-pardon power; by contrast, this chapter considers both sides. I still agree with most of what I wrote then, but not all of it.

2. *See, e.g., Impeachment Inquiry: William Jefferson Clinton, President of the United States, Presentation on Behalf of the President: Hearing Before the H. Comm. on the Judiciary*, 105th Cong. 450 (1998) [hereinafter *Clinton Impeachment*] (testimony of Charles Ruff, White House Counsel) (giving assurance that President Clinton would not pardon himself, in response to request from Rep. Chabot); Bob Woodward & Carl Bernstein, The Final Days 325–26 (1976) (discussing consideration of self-pardon by Nixon and his staff); Robert Nida & Rebecca L. Spiro, *The President as His Own Judge and Jury: A Legal Analysis of the Presidential Self-Pardon Power*, 52 Okla. L. Rev. 197, 198–99 & n.4, 200 & n.14, 212–16 (1999) (discussing Nixon, Bush, and Clinton); John M. Broder, *Clinton Is Said to Decide Against Pardon for Himself*, N.Y. Times, Apr. 13, 2000, at A24 (reporting President Clinton's decision not to pardon himself, implying that he could have); Frank J. Murray, *Clinton's Words Fuel Pardon Talk*, Wash. Times, Sept. 25, 1996, at A1 (discussing legality of potential Clinton self-pardon); Daniel Schorr, *Will Bush Pardon Himself?*, Balt. Evening Sun, Dec. 30, 1992, at 13A.

   P. S. Ruckman, probably the leading authority on American historical pardon practices, finds less meaning in this persistent self-pardon chatter: "The preemptive, self-pardon folks have been around for almost 40 years now and—by even the most generous estimate—they are 0 for 4. They were wrong during the administrations of Richard Nixon, Ronald Reagan, George H. W. Bush and Bill Clinton. Yes, they were very loud and wildly colorful, but no less wrong." Posting of P. S. Ruckman, Jr., *It Appears There Might Be a Possibility of Developing Plan!*, Pardon Power (July 24, 2008), http://www.pardonpower.com/2008/07/it-appears-there-might-be-possibility.html.

3. U.S. Const. art. II, § 2, cl. 1; *see Ex parte* Garland, 71 U.S. (4 Wall.) 333, 380 (1866) ("The power thus conferred is unlimited, with the exception stated.").

4. Proclamation No. 4311, 39 Fed. Reg. 32,601–02 (1974) (President Ford's pardon of President Nixon); *see Garland*, 71 U.S. (4 Wall.) at 380 (discussing expansiveness of pardon power); W. H. Humbert, The Pardoning Power of the President 63 (1941) (explaining that offense must be committed before it can be pardoned).

5. Harold J. Krent, *Conditioning the President's Conditional Pardon Power*, 89 Cal. L. Rev. 1665, 1716–18 (2001) (discussing courts' limited power to review pardons). Several scholars have assumed that presidents can pardon themselves. *See, e.g.,* William F. Duker, *The President's Power to Pardon*, 18 Wm. & Mary L. Rev. 475, 504 (1977); Eric

M. Freedman, *The Law as King and the King as Law: Is a President Immune from Criminal Prosecution Before Impeachment?*, 20 Hastings Const. L.Q. 7, 58 & n.159 (1992); Ken Gormley, *Impeachment and the Independent Counsel*, 51 Stan. L. Rev. 309, 323 (1999); Nida & Spiro, *supra* note 2; Stephen B. Presser, *The Legal Limits*, Chi. Trib., Nov. 17, 1996, at C21; Nelson Lund, *Why Ray Made the Deal: The Self-Pardon Card*, Nat'l Rev. Online (Jan. 20, 2001), http://www.nationalreview.com/comment/commentprint012001g.html. Nida and Spiro's article is the only article-length piece supporting the self-pardon power, but the actual argument is incomplete and occupies fewer than five pages. Lund's piece is more able and concise.

Those who support self-pardonability are apt to declare, without citing any data, that there is a consensus in their favor. *See, e.g., Clinton Impeachment, supra* note 2, at 74 (statement of Rep. Goodlatte) ("prevailing opinion"); *id.* at 358–59 (statement of Rep. Goodlatte); Richard A. Posner, An Affair of State: The Investigation, Impeachment, and Trial of President Clinton 108 (1999) ("generally been inferred"); *see also* John Dean, *President Clinton's Indictment and Pardon—Coming Soon*, Findlaw's Writ (Dec. 8, 2000), http://writ.news.findlaw.com/dean/20001208.html ("[W]hile a few scholars have concluded that the president cannot pardon himself, many more believe that he can.").

Nevertheless, plenty of people besides me have argued against the self-pardon power. *See, e.g.,* Kalt, *supra* note 1, at 779–81 nn.4–7, 20–21 (listing both proponents and opponents of self-pardon power); Peter M. Shane, *Presidents, Pardons, and Prosecutors: Legal Accountability and the Separation of Powers*, 11 Yale L. & Pol'y Rev. 361, 404 n.196 (1993) [hereinafter Shane, *Presidents*]; Peter M. Shane, *Who May Discipline or Remove Federal Judges?*, 142 U. Pa. L. Rev. 209, 230 n.72 (1993); Akhil Reed Amar, *Bringing Justice to Clinton*, N.Y. Times, Mar. 20, 2000, at A23; *Countdown* (MSNBC television broadcast, Nov. 17, 2008) (interview with Jonathan Turley) (transcript available at 2008 WLNR 21970716).

Still others are agnostic. *See, e.g., President Clinton's Eleventh Hour Pardons: Hearing Before the S. Comm. on the Judiciary*, 107th Cong. 56–57 (2001) [hereinafter *Clinton Pardon Hearings*] (statement of Ken Gormley) (suggesting that self-pardons may or may not be permissible, but that it would help to explicitly ban them); Erwin Chemerinsky, Constitutional Law: Principles and Policies 364 n.4 (3d ed. 2006) (characterizing self-pardon as unresolved "interesting issue" with arguments on both sides); Dale Keiger, *"Attack Politics" on Capitol Hill*, Johns Hopkins Mag., Nov. 1998, *available at* http://www.jhu.edu/~jhumag/1198web/policy.html#president (presenting argument by Joel Grossman that the Constitution does not preclude self-pardons, but that the Supreme Court might nonetheless rule against one); Bruce Gottlieb, *Can President Clinton Pardon Himself?*, Slate (Dec. 30, 1998), http://www.slate.com/id/1002012 (consulting Harold Bruff, Evan Caminker, Daniel Hays Lowenstein, and Louis Fisher on self-pardons, and concluding that "[n]o one knows the answer").

6. Schick v. Reed, 419 U.S. 256, 267 (1974); *see also Garland*, 71 U.S. (4 Wall.) at 380 ("The power thus conferred is unlimited, with the exception stated."); Posner,

supra note 5, at 107–08 (favoring expressio unius argument); Nida & Spiro, *supra* note 2, at 217, 221 (advocating textual argument against self-pardonability and citing *Schick*).

7. *But see* Joel B. Grossman & David A. Yalof, *The "Public" versus the "Private" President: Striking a Balance between Presidential Responsibilities and Immunities*, 28 Presidential Stud. Q. 821, 821 (1998) (criticizing use of "catchy slogans or mere rhetoric that obscures rather than illuminates important constitutional governance issues").

8. *See* Gottlieb, *supra* note 5 (presenting definitional argument). Jorge E. Souss has, in informal discussions with me, developed the definitional argument in more detail (and with more persistence) than anyone else.

9. *See* Posner, *supra* note 5, at 108 (discussing self-pardons and saying, of requirement that crime be committed before it can be pardoned, "This is a judge-made exception; others are conceivable").

10. 11 Oxford English Dictionary 218–19 (2d ed. 1989) ("pardon"); 6 *id.* at 718 ("grace"); 3 *id.* at 688 ("condone"); 4 *id.* at 951 ("donate").

11. United States v. Wilson, 32 U.S. (7 Pet.) 150, 160 (1833) (characterizing pardons as acts of grace); Biddle v. Perovich, 274 U.S. 480, 486 (1927) (characterizing pardons as policy decisions rather than acts of grace); Humbert, *supra* note 4, at 22–23 (discussing shift in Supreme Court definitions); Nida & Spiro, *supra* note 2, at 219 (noting possibility of self-pardon as policy judgment); *see also* Kalt, *supra* note 1, at 782–83 & n.26 (discussing function of fourteenth-century English pardons: raising money rather than extending mercy). The older, "act of grace" case law also treated the pardon as like a deed, which had to be offered by the president and accepted by the pardonee before it could be considered valid. *See, e.g.*, *Wilson*, 32 U.S. (7 Pet.) at 161. This further reinforces the inherently bilateral nature of pardons, at least before the Court moved toward its "policy judgment" language.

12. *See* Black's Law Dictionary 1137 (7th ed. 1999) ("pardon"); 2 Samuel Johnson, A Dictionary of the English Language (6th ed., London, W. Strahan et al. 1778) ("pardon"); 1 *id.* ("forgiveness"); Webster's Third New International Dictionary of the English Language, Unabridged 1641 (1981) ("pardon"). In Note, *Looking It Up: Dictionaries and Statutory Interpretation*, 107 Harv. L. Rev. 1437 (1994), *Black's* and *Webster's Third New International* were found to be the most frequently cited dictionaries by the Supreme Court during its 1988–94 terms. My research assistant Nathan Cortright did an updated survey in 2006 and found them still in the lead.

13. *See Wilson*, 32 U.S. (7 Pet.) at 160 (relying expressly on English pardon principles and rules to interpret American pardon power); Joseph Chitty, A Treatise on the Law of the Prerogatives of the Crown 5 (London, Joseph Butterworth and Son 1820) (discussing doctrine of royal legal infallibility); Humbert, *supra* note 4, at 34–35 (describing American courts' "considerable reliance" upon English precedent in pardon cases); Duker, *supra* note 5, at 508 (describing use of English

precedent in American pardon cases); *Ex parte* Wells, 59 U.S. (18 How.) 307, 318 (1855) (McLean, J., dissenting) (distinguishing English monarchy from American republican presidency in assessing American pardon power).

14. U.S. Const. art. I, § 4, cl. 1. The Supreme Court rejected the expressio unius reading of the Elections Clause in *Buckley v. Valeo*, when it held that Congress's election-regulating power did not allow it to usurp the president's appointment power by naming campaign regulators. Buckley v. Valeo, 424 U.S. 1, 132 (1976) (denying that Congress's authority to regulate elections "may be employed in such a manner as to offend well-established constitutional restrictions stemming from the separation of powers"). To be sure, the Supreme Court has used expressio unius readings in other contexts, such as interpretation of congressional qualifications, or the process for passing laws. Expressio unius readings make more sense in such cases, where the Court is reading things that purport to be enumerations ("a senator must be *X, Y,* and *Z,*" "a bill is passed by doing *A, B,* and *C*"). It is quite another to do it in places like the Elections Clause and the Pardon Clause. *See* Kalt, *supra* note 1, at 791–93 & n.83 (criticizing expressio unius reading with reference to numerous other analogous constitutional provisions).

15. Daniel Kobil has argued that the pardon power is subject to the Constitution's requirements of due process and equal protection. Daniel T. Kobil, *The Quality of Mercy Strained,* 69 Tex. L. Rev. 569, 617–18 & n.305 (1991); *see* Kalt, *supra* note 1, at 791 n.79 (discussing potential equal-protection limits on pardons); Mark Strasser, *Some Reflections on the President's Pardon Power,* 31 Cap. U. L. Rev. 143, 153–58 (2003) (classifying due-process and equal-protection challenges to pardon decisions as possible, though difficult).

16. Schick v. Reed, 419 U.S. 256, 267 (1974) (emphasis added).

17. *See* Biddle v. Perovich, 274 U.S. 480, 487 (1927) (explaining how pardon power means that no federal criminal punishment should proceed over presidential objections); Lund, *supra* note 5 (noting that president can refrain from prosecuting himself, suggesting Constitution does not contain any implicit prohibition on self-judging that would preclude a self-pardon).

18. *See* 28 U.S.C. § 455 (2006) (judicial recusal statute); Caperton v. A. T. Massey Coal Co., 129 S. Ct. 2252, 2259 (2009) (quoting precedents holding that while "most matters relating to judicial disqualification [do] not rise to a constitutional level," constitutional due process precludes judges ruling in cases in which they have a "direct" or "pecuniary interest," because of maxim that "[n]o man is allowed to be a judge in his own cause"); *Ex parte* Grossman, 267 U.S. 87, 121 (1925) ("Our Constitution confers this discretion on the highest officer in the nation in confidence that he will not abuse it."); Charles J. Bonaparte, *The Pardoning Power,* 19 Yale L.J. 603, 607 (1910) (discussing presidential accountability and responsiveness as basis for placing pardon power with him); Nida & Spiro, *supra* note 2, at 219 (answering self-dealing argument by noting that self-pardons could be justified as benefiting the country, not just the pardoner). *But see* Christopher E. Smith & Scott P. Johnson, *Presidential Pardons and Accountability in the Executive Branch,*

35 Wayne L. Rev. 1113, 1115–22 (1989) (discussing ways in which pardons can easily evade accountability).

Congress has recognized the president's special position in the executive branch. For instance, the federal conflict-of-interest law, which makes it a crime for other federal officers to make decisions in which they have a personal financial interest, exempts the president from its coverage. 18 U.S.C. §§ 202(c), 208 (2006). Even before Congress enacted this exemption, the Department of Justice considered the conflict law to be inapplicable to the president. *See* Letter from Laurence H. Silberman, Acting Attorney General, to Senator Howard W. Cannon 2–4 (Sept. 20, 1974).

Technically, someone else *could* pardon the president while he is president, if we distinguish between the office and its powers. The president could invoke the Twenty-Fifth Amendment to hand over power temporarily to the vice president, who could pardon him.

19. *But see Ex parte* Wells, 59 U.S. (18 How.) 307, 322–24 (1855) (McLean, J., dissenting) (discussing power of president, lacked by British monarchs, to commute a punishment to any lesser one of his choosing).

20. U.S. Const. art. I, § 6, cl. 2 (limiting other jobs for members of Congress); *id.* art. II, § 1, cl. 7 (restricting presidential emoluments and salary changes); *id.* amend. XXVII (restricting congressional pay raises); *see* Gottlieb, *supra* note 5 ("Since the Constitution makes it clear that avoiding conflicts-of-interest is important, it makes sense to assume that the Constitution never meant to allow the president to pardon himself."); *cf.* Akhil Reed Amar, *The Bill of Rights as a Constitution*, 100 Yale L.J. 1131 (1991) (arguing Bill of Rights is best understood as bulwark against congressional self-dealing).

21. *See* Lund, *supra* note 5 (noting how Constitution allows some conflicts of interest, suggesting it does not implicitly bar self-pardons).

22. U.S. Const. art. I, § 3, cl. 4 (making vice president Senate's president); *id.* at cl. 6 (assigning chief justice to preside only over presidential impeachment trials); *see* Michael Stokes Paulsen, *Someone Should Have Told Spiro Agnew*, in Constitutional Stupidities, Constitutional Tragedies 75 (1998) (arguing that Constitution mandates vice president presiding over his own impeachment trial); Joel K. Goldstein, *Can the Vice President Preside at His Own Impeachment Trial?*, 44 St. Louis U. L.J. 849 (2000) (arguing against power of vice president to preside over his own impeachment trial). The vice president has a conflict of interest when a president is on trial in the Senate because if the president is convicted, the vice president takes power.

The Constitution permits a serious conflict of interest when it assigns the vice president to preside over the electoral-vote count, since she will often be a candidate. In 2001, for example, Al Gore presided over his own count, and while he turned away attempts to contest the results that denied him victory, there was significant potential for mischief. Nevertheless, no one suggested that Gore's action was unconstitutional, because the Twelfth Amendment assigns the vice president this task explicitly and directly. *See also* Bruce Ackerman & David Fontana, *Thomas Jefferson Counts Himself into the Presidency*, 90 Va. L. Rev. 551 (2004) (noting questionable conduct of Thomas Jefferson in 1801 count).

23. *See* Kalt, *supra* note 1, at 796 & n.105 (discussing expulsion in additional detail). Dozens of members of Congress have faced expulsion votes, and none of them participated in roll-call votes in their own cases (though in many instances, such as the numerous expulsions of rebel sympathizers during the Civil War, they were absent). *See, e.g.,* 148 Cong. Rec. 14,318–19 (2002) (expulsion of Rep. Traficant); 126 *id.* at 28,977–78 (1980) (expulsion of Rep. Michael Myers); 88 *id.* at 3065 (1942) (failed expulsion of Sen. Langer); 65 *id.* at 9279 (1924) (failed expulsion of Sen. Wheeler); 57 *id.* at 1527 (1919) (failed expulsion of Sen. LaFollette); 41 *id.* at 3429–30 (1907) (failed expulsion of Sen. Smoot); Cong. Globe, 34th Cong., 1st Sess. 1628 (1856) (failed expulsion of Rep. Brooks); 17 Annals of Cong. 324 (1808) (failed expulsion—by one vote—of Sen. John Smith); 9 *id.* at 2973 (1799) (failed expulsion of Rep. Lyon); 7 *id.* at 44 (1797) (expulsion of Sen. Blount). *See generally* Anne Butler, United States Senate Election, Expulsion and Censure Cases, 1793–1990 (1995); Staff of Joint Comm. on Congressional Operations, 93d Cong., House of Representatives Exclusion, Censure and Expulsion Cases from 1789 to 1973 (1973).

Expulsion votes are generally not justiciable, so there is no case law and the pattern of non-voting in the record is the only precedent we can have. The House and Senate rules disfavor voting in these cases but do not forbid it outright. *See* Floyd M. Riddick & Alan S. Frumin, Riddick's Senate Procedure, S. Doc. No. 101-28, at 1398, 1409 (1992) (explaining how Senate Rule XII requires senators to vote as a general matter but excuses them if they have a conflict of interest); William Holmes Brown & Charles W. Johnson, House Practice: A Guide to the Rules, Precedents, and Procedures of the House §§ 8–9, at 887–88 (2003) (explaining same with regard to House Rule VIII); *cf.* Henry M. Robert et al., Robert's Rules of Order 402 (rev. ed. 1990) ("No member should vote on a question in which he has a direct personal or pecuniary interest not common to other members of the organization.").

Interestingly, out of the dozens more members of Congress who faced censure votes, only two participated in roll-call votes in their own cases. One of them, Representative Dan Crane, voted *against* himself. The other, Senator Thomas Dodd, voted in his own favor. However, censure has no legal effect, so these exceptions are distinguishable. *See* 129 Cong. Rec. 20,028–29 (1983) (censure vote on Crane); 113 *id.* at 17,011 (1967) (censure vote on Dodd). *See generally* Butler, *supra*; Staff of Joint Comm. on Congressional Operations, *supra*.

24. *See* Humbert, *supra* note 4, at 9–11 (describing history of English pardon power); Duker, *supra* note 5, at 476–87, 508 (describing history of English pardon power and its influence on interpretations of president's power); Nida & Spiro, *supra* note 2, at 203 (discussing English pardon history).

25. *See* Duker, *supra* note 5, at 487–97 (describing Danby case and its aftermath).

26. *See id.* at 497–501 (discussing colonial and early state pardon powers); Kobil, *supra* note 15, at 590 (discussing how several newly independent states shifted pardoning power away from their executives). The Constitution actually restricts presidents more than the Act of Settlement restricts English monarchs, because the queen can still reappoint officials whom Parliament had removed, while in the United States, the Senate can disqualify a convicted impeachee from ever again holding an office of honor, trust, or profit under the United States, and no presidential pardon can affect that. *See* Kalt, *supra* note 1, at 785 & nn.49–50 (discussing shifting language at Convention).

27. 2 The Records of the Federal Convention of 1787, at 626–27 (Max Farrand ed., 1911); *see* Kalt, *supra* note 1, at 784–87 (summarizing discussion and construction of pardon power at Convention). The ratification debates featured concerns similar to Randolph's, drawing retorts similar to Wilson's. *See, e.g.,* 3 The Debates in the Several State Conventions on the Adoption of the Federal Constitution 498 (Jonathan Elliot ed., Washington, 1836) (statement of James Madison); The Federalist No. 74, at 447–49 (Alexander Hamilton) (Clinton Rossiter ed., 1961); James Iredell, *Answers to Mr. Mason's Objections to the New Constitution, in* 2 Griffith J. McRee, Life and Correspondence of James Iredell 186, 199–202 (New York, D. Appleton & Co. 1858).

28. Wilson's comments are discussed in Chapter 1.

29. U.S. Const. art. III, § 3, cl. 1 (regulating treason charges). When they discuss the Randolph scenario, those who argue against the self-pardon power tend to focus on the fact that at the end of the day, the Framers allowed for the possibility of abuse and decided against restricting the pardon power. *See, e.g., Clinton Pardon Hearings, supra* note 5, at 61, 63 (statement of Christopher H. Schroeder); Nida & Spiro, *supra* note 2, at 218; Lund, *supra* note 5. As argued in the text, though, this misses the point that in reaching this decision, the Framers presupposed that the president himself could be prosecuted.

30. United States v. Klein, 80 U.S. (13 Wall.) 128, 147–48 (1871) ("It is the intention of the Constitution that each of the great co-ordinate departments of the government—the Legislative, the Executive, and the Judicial—shall be, in its sphere, independent of the others. To the executive alone is intrusted the power of pardon; and it is granted without limit. Now it is clear that the legislature cannot change the effect of such a pardon any more than the executive can change a law.") (emphasis in text added); *Ex parte* Garland, 71 U.S. (4 Wall.) 333, 380 (1866) ("The power thus conferred is unlimited, with the exception stated. This power of the President is not subject to legislative control. Congress can neither limit the effect of his pardon, nor exclude from its exercise any class of offenders. The benign prerogative of mercy reposed in him cannot be fettered by any legislative restrictions.") (emphasis in text added); *see* Kalt, *supra* note 1, at 803 n.138 (offering context for sweeping language in pardon cases).

31. Calder v. Bull, 3 U.S. (3 Dall.) 386, 388 (1798) (opinion of Chase, J.). Chase was referring to legislation that allowed for self-judging, but his principle also applies

to interpreting constitutional provisions. *The Federalist*, in its exposition of the new Constitution and the system it proposed to establish, offered similar evidence. In the famous Federalist No. 10, Madison justified the separation of powers by asserting that "No man is allowed to be a judge in his own cause, because his interest would certainly bias his judgment, and, not improbably, corrupt his integrity." The Federalist No. 10, *supra* note 27, at 79 (James Madison). The constitutional structure of the new Union was designed to prevent such pitfalls on a grand scale, and one can certainly argue that one should keep this general purpose in mind when interpreting the bounds of specific federal powers.

32. Gutierrez de Martinez v. Lamagno, 515 U.S. 417, 428 (1995) ("mainstay" case); Caperton v. A. T. Massey Coal Co., 129 S. Ct. 2252, 2259 (2009) (recusal case); *see also* Kalt, *supra* note 1, at 806–07 (discussing Supreme Court's treatment of self-judging); Presser, *supra* note 5 (citing *Calder* and anti-self-judging principles in opposition to self-pardons). Dissenting in *Gutierrez de Martinez*, Justice Souter (joined by Justices Scalia and Thomas) agreed that the anti-self-judging principle is "powerful" but disagreed that there was self-judging going on in the case and suggested that the principle should only be applied to a more direct conflict of interest. *Gutierrez de Martinez*, 515 U.S. at 448–49 (Souter, J., dissenting). Under that criterion, a self-pardon would give pause even to the dissenters.

33. Mass. Const. pt. I, art. XXX (originating phrase); United States v. Lee, 106 U.S. 196, 261 (1882).

34. *See* Kalt, *supra* note 1, at 808 (citing and discussing cases that refer to *Lee*).

35. *See* Lund, *supra* note 5 (making that argument).

36. Proclamation No. 6518, 57 Fed. Reg. 62,145 (1992) (text of Bush pardons); *see* Posner, *supra* note 5, at 108 (citing president's ability to indirectly self-pardon himself by pardoning his accomplices as evidence favoring self-pardon power); Kalt, *supra* note 1, at 799–800 & n.117 (discussing Bush case); *id.* at 786 (citing Framers' discussion of using pardon power to induce co-conspirators to testify against their leader); Nida & Spiro, *supra* note 2, at 214–16 & n.124 (detailing Bush's action, describing it as "constructive self-pardon," and citing others who agree); Shane, *Presidents, supra* note 5, at 403–04 ("[T]he Bush pardons violated the fundamental due process precept that people should not judge their own cause."). *But see* Proclamation No. 6518, *supra* (declaring that "no impartial person has seriously suggested that [Bush's] own role in this matter is legally questionable").

37. Gerald R. Ford, A Time to Heal 173 (1979); *see* Kalt, *supra* note 1, at 800 (discussing Nixon case); Mark J. Rozell, *President Ford's Pardon of Richard M. Nixon: Constitutional and Political Considerations*, 24 Presidential Stud. Q. 121, 134 (1994) (discussing political context and impact of President Ford's pardon of President Nixon); Bob Woodward, *Closing the Chapter on Watergate Wasn't Done Lightly*, Wash. Post, Dec. 28, 2006, at A5 (describing Ford's decision-making process in detail); *cf.* Kathleen Dean Moore, *The Power of the Pardon*, Oregonian, Dec. 7, 2008, *available at* 2008 WLNR 23550462 ("[A self-pardon] would be wrong. Even

if the legal standards are ambiguous, the moral standards and utilitarian considerations are not.").

38. *See Clinton Pardon Hearings, supra* note 5, at 18–19 (statement of Sen. McConnell)
(discussing prosecutability of pardons given in exchange for bribes); *id.* at 45
(statement of Benton Becker) (same); Strasser, *supra* note 15, at 159 (same); *cf.*
Duker, *supra* note 5, at 525 n.258 (discussing irrevocability of corrupt pardons);
Kobil, *supra* note 15, at 598 (citing *Hoffa v. Saxbe*, 378 F. Supp. 1221 (D.D.C. 1974)
for notion that corrupt pardons are "insulated from judicial review"). Nixon,
through his chief of staff Al Haig, tried to get Ford to agree in advance to pardon
Nixon. While Ford was sympathetic to Nixon's case, he made clear to Haig that
"there was no agreement, no decision and no deal." Ford's advisers pushed him to
eliminate any necessary connection between the resignation and the pardon. *See*
Woodward, *supra* note 37.

39. *See* Kalt, *supra* note 1, at 800–01 nn.128–29 (discussing possibility of prosecuting
or impeaching president for self-pardon).

40. *Cf.* Iredell, *supra* note 27, at 200 (declaring it "a remote and improbable danger"
that someone honorable enough to be elected president would risk "the damna-
tion of his fame to all future ages" by pardoning his fellow treasonous conspira-
tors). Abusing the pardon power would be a legitimate target for impeachment
and, as argued in Chapter 5, impeachment might proceed even against an
ex-president who issues his self-pardon on his way out of office. *See* Duker, *supra*
note 5, at 525 n.258 (discussing attempted impeachment of President Andrew
Johnson for his alleged misuse of the pardon power); Michael J. Gerhardt, *The
Perils of Presidential Impeachment*, 67 U. Chi. L. Rev. 293, 305–06 (2000)
(reviewing Posner, *supra* note 5) (discussing "the significance of impeachment as a
check on a president pardoning himself").

41. *See* Lund, *supra* note 5 (raising possibility of secret self-pardon).

42. The "suffered enough" phrase comes from President Ford's statement accompanying the Nixon pardon. 32 Cong. Q. 2455 (Sept. 14, 1974) (transcript of President
Ford's statement).

43. *But see* Posner, *supra* note 5, at 108 (suggesting that it would require a "bold"
Supreme Court to disallow a self-pardon "in the teeth of the constitutional
language").

44. *See Ex parte* Garland, 71 U.S. (4 Wall.) 333, 380 (1866) (declaring limits on Congress's
power to restrict pardons); Todd David Peterson, *Congressional Power over Pardon &
Amnesty*, 38 Wake Forest L. Rev. 1225 (2003) (discussing Congress's lack of power
here to regulate pardons); *cf.* Krent, *supra* note 5, at 1704 (discussing president's lack
of power to bind his successors with regard to individual conditional pardons).

45. *See* Nida & Spiro, *supra* note 2, at 221–22 (offering implausible, perfunctory constitutional amendment to solve self-pardon problem); Peter Ferrara, *Could President
Pardon Himself?*, Wash. Times, Oct. 22, 1996, at A14 (same). More conceivable
(though still unlikely) is that other events would lead Congress to consider
amending the pardon power in other ways, and that while it was at it, Congress

could explicitly ban self-pardons too. *See Clinton Pardon Hearings, supra* note 5, at 56 (statement of Ken Gormley) ("[I]f the Senate were to amend the existing pardon language of Article [II], section 2, it would make good sense to take the opportunity to make clear that the President cannot pardon himself or herself.").

46. *See* Strasser, *supra* note 15, at 144 (stating that costs of amending pardon power "would far exceed the benefits thereby gained"). The converse—a president trying to pardon himself, losing in court, and an outraged public amending the Constitution to allow self-pardons—is unimaginable. If the courts ruled that self-pardons are invalid, Congress might pass a law expanding the president's power beyond that which the Constitution (according to the courts) provides. It could also amend the federal criminal code to lift whatever criminal consequences the self-pardon purported to lift. Again, though, it is hard to imagine why Congress would ever do that. *But see* Daniel W. Weil, *Talking Politics: To Pardon or Not to Pardon? Why Clinton Has No Choice,* Crain's Chi. Bus., Mar. 9, 1998, at 13 (suggesting, approvingly, that President Clinton pardon himself).

Chapter 3. Removing a "Disabled" President

1. The names in this scenario are inspired by *The Caine Mutiny*: Captain Queeg (given name Philip Francis, feminized here to Frances Philips), Maryk (Merrick), Keefer (German for Cooper), and (in further facts later) Keith. *See* John D. Feerick, From Failing Hands 249 (1965) (discussing influence of *The Caine Mutiny* on 1964 ABA deliberations on presidential disability); *cf.* Birch E. Bayh, Jr., *The Twenty-Fifth Amendment: Its History and Meaning, in* Papers on Presidential Disability and the Twenty-Fifth Amendment 1, 38 (Kenneth W. Thompson ed., 1988) (using Captain Queeg example).

2. The uses of Section 4 in novels include John Calvin Batchelor, Father's Day (1994); Frederick Forsyth, The Negotiator (1990); Mario Puzo, The Fourth K (1990); and William Safire, Full Disclosure (1978). Films include Air Force One (Columbia Pictures 1997); Dave (Donner/Shuler-Donner Productions 1993); and The Enemy Within (Home Box Office 1994). Uses on television include episodes of 24 (Fox) and *Commander in Chief* (ABC).

  The behavior of our fictional President Philips is based on reported incidents involving Presidents Wilson, Coolidge, Nixon, and Reagan, among others. President Wilson remained president despite a serious stroke that was kept from the public, but which left him paralyzed and incapable of attending to his duties. *See* Feerick, *supra* note 1, at 167–74 (discussing Wilson cover-up). Even before the stroke, Wilson's poor health had led him to become "increasingly irascible," "petulan[t]," intransigent, forgetful, and sometimes incoherent. Bert E. Park, Ailing, Aging, Addicted: Studies of Compromised Leadership 103–07 (1993). In one episode at Versailles, "Wilson became obsessed with the arrangement of the furniture in his suite" and gibbered about the colors of the chairs until they were rearranged to his satisfaction. Kenneth R. Crispell & Carlos F. Gomez, Hidden Illness in the White House 63 (1988).

President Coolidge fell into a deep depression after his son died. He "withdrew almost completely from interaction with Congress and showed little inclination even to participate in the activities of the departments of his own government." Robert E. Gilbert, The Mortal Presidency 33–37 (1998).

President Nixon behaved erratically toward the end of his tenure, "drinking heavily and displaying paranoid and depressive symptoms." Jerrold M. Post, *Broken Minds, Broken Hearts, and the Twenty-Fifth Amendment, in* Managing Crisis: Presidential Disability and the Twenty-Fifth Amendment 111, 116–17 (Robert E. Gilbert ed., 2000); *see* Bob Woodward & Carl Bernstein, The Final Days 395 (1976) (quoting President Nixon's son-in-law as reporting that Nixon was drinking, "acting irrationally," and "walking the halls at night, talking to pictures of former Presidents").

President Reagan suffered a period of inattentiveness, indolence, and befuddlement later in his tenure, which led to serious internal discussions of invoking Section 4. *See* Herbert L. Abrams, "The President Has Been Shot": Confusion, Disability, and the 25th Amendment 218–19 (1992); Park, *supra*, at 219–20.

3. *See* 111 Cong. Rec. 3255 (1965) (statement of Sen. Bayh) (explaining one purpose of proposed amendment as providing certainty); *id.* at 15,587 (statement of Sen. Gore) (underlining importance of clarity and precision here).

4. U.S. Const. amend. XXV, § 4.

5. 111 Cong. Rec. 15,382 (1965) (statement of Sen. Kennedy) (worrying about earlier, but analogous, stage in Section 4 procedure); Henry B. Gonzalez, *The Relinquishment of Co-Equality by Congress*, 29 Harv. J. on Legis. 331, 349 (1992).

6. *See* Crispell & Gomez, *supra* note 2 (reviewing cover-ups of illnesses in Wilson, Roosevelt, and Kennedy presidencies); *id.* at 10–17 (describing numerous cover-ups of presidential disabilities); Robert E. Gilbert, *The Genius of the Twenty-Fifth Amendment, in* Managing Crisis, *supra* note 2, at 25, 26–29 (detailing twelve cases of concealed presidential disability). One example: When President Reagan was shot in 1981, he lost half of his blood volume and was minutes from death. The administration sugarcoated reports of his condition. Reagan was completely out of commission for days, and for several weeks afterward was able to work for only an hour or two a day. Neither Section 3 nor 4 was ever invoked. *See* Abrams, *supra* note 2, at 179–96 (relating reluctance to transfer power when Reagan was shot); *id.* at 61 (explaining how close to death Reagan had come); John D. Feerick, The Twenty-Fifth Amendment, at xiii–xv (2d ed. 1992) (discussing failure to invoke amendment when Reagan was shot).

7. U.S. Const. art. II, § 1, cl. 6; *see* S. Rep. No. 89-66, at 7–8 (1965) (explaining motive for amendment as rooted in uncertainty spawned by Article II); Akhil Reed Amar, America's Constitution 169 (2005) (mentioning Congress's unused power); Feerick, *supra* note 1, at 135–36 (analyzing implicit presidential and vice-presidential power to declare disability); *id.* at 118–38, 167–76 (discussing months-long near-complete disabilities of Presidents Garfield and Wilson, and reluctance of Vice Presidents Arthur and Marshall to assume power); Feerick, *supra* note 6, at 4–22

(describing serious disabilities of various presidents before Twenty-Fifth Amendment); Research and Policy Comm., Comm. for Econ. Dev., Presidential Succession and Inability 25 (1965) (discussing implicit presidential and vice-presidential power); Ruth Silva, Presidential Succession 100–02 (1951) (considering vice-presidential power).

8. *See* S. Rep. No. 89-66, at 13 (1965) (relying on good faith of parties); 111 Cong. Rec. 7942 (1965) (statement of Rep. Poff) (same); Feerick, *supra* note 6, at xxiii–xxiv (discussing decision to leave "disability" undefined in Twenty-Fifth Amendment); Feerick, *supra* note 1, at 250–51 (explaining benefits of having cabinet involved); Birch Bayh, *Reflections on the Twenty-Fifth Amendment as We Enter a New Century*, *in* Managing Crisis, *supra* note 2, at 55, 62–63 (justifying claim that the vice president and cabinet are best placed to evaluate whether an arguably disabled president should continue in power); Kenneth R. Crispell, *Presidential Disability*, *in* Papers on Presidential Disability and the Twenty-Fifth Amendment, *supra* note 1, at 43, 62 (stating, from medical perspective, that politics rather than medicine is the key issue in presidential disability situations); *see also* Gilbert, *supra* note 6, at 45; Joel K. Goldstein, *The Vice Presidency and the Twenty-Fifth Amendment*, *in* Managing Crisis, *supra* note 2, at 165, 193; Lawrence C. Mohr, *Medical Consideration in the Determination of Presidential Disability*, *in* Managing Crisis, *supra* note 2, at 97, 103.

9. *See* Jerrold M. Post & Robert S. Robins, When Illness Strikes the Leader 177–78 (1993) (describing power of White House staff, rather than vice president or cabinet, during periods of undeclared presidential disability); John D. Feerick, *The Twenty-Fifth Amendment: Its Origins and History*, *in* Managing Crisis, *supra* note 2, at 1, 6–7 (discussing reluctance of Vice Presidents Arthur and Marshall to act as president during the disabilities of Presidents Garfield and Wilson); Gilbert, *supra* note 6, at 45–46 (arguing that vice president and cabinet *should* be very reluctant to displace presidents and noting deleterious political effects of perceived presidential incapacity); Goldstein, *supra* note 8, at 194, 196 (discussing history and effect of vice-presidential loyalty and skittishness, and predicting that Section 4 would only be used for disabilities that are irrefutable or lengthy, or that occur when "some action urgently must be taken"); Herbert L. Abrams, *Can the Twenty-Fifth Amendment Deal with a Disabled President?*, 29 Presidential Stud. Q. 115, 116 (1999) (discussing incentives for inner circle to keep ailing president in office). *But see* Adam R. F. Gustafson, Note, *Presidential Inability and Subjective Meaning*, 27 Yale L. & Pol'y Rev. 459, 464–65 (2009) (suggesting that recent vice presidents are more assertive than those in the past).

10. *See* Abrams, *supra* note 2, at 187–89 (Reagan); Feerick, *supra* note 1, at 173–75 (Wilson); Silva, *supra* note 7, at 52–67 (Garfield and Wilson); Robert S. Robins, *The President's Spouse, the President's Health, and the Twenty-Fifth Amendment*, *in* Managing Crisis, *supra* note 2, at 125, 131–33 (Wilson); Herbert L. Abrams, *Shielding the President from the Constitution*, 23 Presidential Stud. Q. 533, 541 (1993) (noting that while President Reagan maintained power during his assassination

crisis, the White House communicated that Vice President Bush would step up "if a crisis occurred").

11. *See* S. Rep. No. 89-66, at 3 (1965) (conveying "additional stress to the interpreta-tion" that the vice president would be in control while the provisions of what became Section 4 were "being implemented"); Birch Bayh, One Heartbeat Away 345, 351 (1968) (describing process of drafting and passing amendment); Feerick, *supra* note 1, at 238–57 (discussing initial efforts leading to amendment); Presidential Disability 198 (James F. Toole & Robert J. Joynt eds., 2001) (statement of John Feerick) (characterizing Twenty-Fifth Amendment as the product of decades of careful thinking on the subject). *But see* 111 Cong. Rec. 7956 (1965) (statement of Rep. Randall) (stating that earlier version of Section 4 "is worded in such a way that all procedures are crystal clear," to avoid conflicting claims to the presidency). Section 4 was probably the most carefully debated and contentious part of the amendment. *See* H.R. Rep. No. 89-203, at 2 (1965) (noting how Sections 3 and 4 were the only ones still being worked on); Feerick, *supra* note 6, at 51–108 (describing genesis of amendment).

12. *Cf.* Feerick, *supra* note 1, at 176–79 (describing President Wilson's ouster of Secretary of State Lansing because of Lansing's attempts to continue the functions of government while Wilson was incapacitated).

13. Feerick, *supra* note 6, at 74, 246 (reproducing S.J. Res. 139 as introduced in 1963); *see* Bayh, *supra* note 11, at 283 (describing change in length of waiting period); 111 Cong. Rec. 7958 (1965) (statement of Rep. Love) (relating his effort to use "resume powers and duties after the waiting period" language instead of "resume power unless" language). This part of S.J. Res. 139 was lifted verbatim from S.J. Res. 28, 88th Cong. (1963), introduced by Senator Kefauver.

14. Feerick, *supra* note 6, at 246 (reproducing S.J. Res. 139 as introduced in 1963). The language here and in note 13, *supra*, was changed in committee, but Feerick does not explain the thinking behind these specific changes. *See* Feerick, *supra* note 6, at 76.

15. 111 Cong. Rec. 3285 (1965) (statements of Sens. Allott and Bayh); Bayh, *supra* note 11, at 272–73 (describing this part of debate and reasoning behind placing vice president in charge); *accord Presidential Inability: Hearings on H.R. 836 et al. Before the H. Comm. on the Judiciary*, 89th Cong. 58 (1965) (statement of Sen. Bayh) (expressing intention for vice president to be in charge during waiting period, in earlier but functionally identical version of Section 4); S. Rep. No. 89-66, at 3 (1965) (same); 111 Cong. Rec. 7939 (1965) (statement of Rep. Celler) (expressing conviction of Rep. Celler that vice president would be in control during waiting period, and quoting letter from Attorney General Katzenbach stating that this was "entirely clear"); *see* Bayh, *supra* note 11, at 217 (describing effort to make original language more concise); Feerick, *supra* note 6, at 74–75 (detailing changes made to waiting-period language by Senate committee).

16. *See* 111 Cong. Rec. 7963–66 (1965) (debating and rejecting, by 58–122 vote, Rep. Moore's proposal to place president in charge during waiting period and

congressional deliberations); *id.* at 7949–50 (statement of Rep. Moore) (explaining basis of proposal); Feerick, *supra* note 6, at 102–03 (summarizing debate on Moore's proposal); *cf.* 111 Cong. Rec. 7948 (1965) (statement of Rep. Lindsay) (describing Lindsay's failed attempt in committee to put president in charge during waiting period and congressional deliberations).

17. *See* S. Rep. No. 89-66, at 3 (1965) (explaining incentive); *see also* Goldstein, *supra* note 8, at 189–90; Gustafson, *supra* note 9, at 472 & n.52. President Philips could point out that Section 3 has incentives even under her reading of Section 4. For instance, if she uses Section 3, she is the sole arbiter of her abilities and does not need to worry about the matter being referred to Congress. *Cf.* Gustafson, *supra* note 9 (arguing that Sections 3 and 4 require different levels of "inability").

18. Abrams, *supra* note 2, at 117–18; *see* Abrams, *supra* note 10, at 539 (describing Reagan administration study and planning); Robert E. Gilbert, *The Contemporary Presidency: The Twenty-Fifth Amendment*, 33 Presidential Stud. Q. 877, 883 (2003) (describing contingency planning by presidents since Reagan).

19. Gregory F. Jacob, 25, 7 Green Bag 2d 23, 26–27 (2003); Posting of Reed Hundt (for Peter M. Shane), *25th Amendment Revisited via TV's 24*, TPM Café (Apr. 7, 2007), http://tpmcafe.talkingpointsmemo.com/2007/04/07/25th_amendment_revisited_via_t; *see supra* text accompanying note 15 (displaying Sen. Allott's apparent confusion); 111 Cong. Rec. 3268 (1965) (statement of Sen. Dirksen) (expressing uncertainty over who has power during waiting period); *id.* at 7939 (statement of Rep. Duncan of Oregon) (inquiring about "ambiguity," which "ought to be cleared up," over who would have control during waiting period); *id.* at 7958–59 (statement of Rep. Love) (expressing initial confusion over "unless" language). One authority states that Section 4 leaves it unclear who is in control while Congress deliberates. John R. Vile, A Companion to the United States Constitution and Its Amendments 219 (4th ed. 2006). At least one scholar (writing after this chapter was drafted) has noted and refuted the incorrect reading. Gustafson, *supra* note 9, at 469 & n.41.

20. *See* William Eskridge, *The New Textualism*, 37 UCLA L. Rev. 621 (1990). Eskridge contrasted the earlier practice, in which "even an apparently plain meaning can be rebutted by legislative history," with Scalia's new textualism, in which legislative history is ignored. *Id.* at 623–24. Eskridge noted in 1990 that Scalia's approach had already made inroads. *Id.* at 656–61; *see also* Jonathan T. Molot, *The Rise and Fall of Textualism*, 106 Colum. L. Rev. 1, 38–39 (2006) (noting, more recently, that judges use legislative history less often than they used to).

21. As Bayh put it on the Senate floor, "Any interpretation of the Constitution, as the Senator knows, includes reference to the record of the debate, the record of the hearings, and specific interpretations placed upon the measure by the Senator in charge of the bill [i.e., Bayh]." 111 Cong. Rec. 15,384 (1965) (statement of Sen. Bayh); *see also* Bayh, *supra* note 11, at 223, 230–31 (showing similar confidence in usefulness of placing in the legislative record his intentions about ambiguous text). Current legislators and their staffs are aware of the Scalia critique but continue to value legislative history—in part in defiance of Scalia, and in part for

other institutional reasons. *See* Victoria F. Nourse & Jane S. Schacter, *The Politics of Legislative Drafting*, 77 N.Y.U. L. Rev. 575, 606–10, 620 (2002) (discussing legislative drafting in wake of Scalia critique).

22. III Cong. Rec. 3285 (1965) (statement of Sen. Bayh) (asserting ability of vice president to hand power back before expiration of waiting period); *accord Presidential Inability and Vacancies in the Office of Vice President: Hearing on S.J. Res. 1 et al. Before the Subcomm. on Constitutional Amendments of the S. Comm. on the Judiciary*, 89th Cong. 10 (1965) [hereinafter *Hearing*] (statement of Att'y Gen. Katzenbach); S. Rep. No. 89-66, at 18–20 (1965) (individual views of Sen. Dirksen) (quoting statement by attorney general); III Cong. Rec. 7939 (1965) (statement of Reps. Duncan of Oregon and Celler); *id.* at 15,214 (statement of Rep. Poff); *see* Gustafson, *supra* note 9, at 475 & n.67 (listing additional sources and rejecting "rigidly textualist" anti-waiver reading). In other legislative history, Bayh contradicted the waiver theory. *See* text accompanying note 15 ("[I]t would be 7 days before he could possibly resume the office of President.").

   In fairness to Senator Bayh, it should be noted that he was responsible for the earlier version of the Twenty-Fifth Amendment that would have circumvented all the problems in this chapter. *See* Bayh, *supra* note 11, at 345, 351; *supra* text accompanying notes 13–14 (quoting earlier draft). The intent lurking behind less-than-clear clauses was probably clear to him because he still recalled his original language, and because the changes to it had been meant to add clarity without changing the substance (though it didn't work out quite that way). *See* Bayh, *supra* note 11, at 217 (stating intended nature of changes); *see also supra* note 13 (discussing Bayh's initial language and changes to it).

23. *See Hearing, supra* note 22, at 20 (statement of Sen. Hruska) (cautioning Sen. Bayh).

24. III Cong. Rec. 15,587 (1965) (statement of Sen. Gore); *see* Feerick, *supra* note 6, at 104–06 & n.* (describing conference committee). The Bayh-Gore debate appears at III Cong. Rec. 15,382–87, 15,584–96 (1965). It is recounted more colorfully in Bayh, *supra* note 11, at 311–33.

25. *See* III Cong. Rec. 15,380 (1965) (statement of Sen. Kennedy of New York) (worrying about president firing cabinet preemptively); Gonzalez, *supra* note 5, at 353 (noting that Section 4 requires cabinet members to plot in secret, to avoid being fired before they can displace president); Jacob, *supra* note 19, at 25–26 (noting president's ability to fire cabinet members during vote on an initial Section 4 declaration).

26. *See Hearing, supra* note 22, at 17–18 (statement of Sen. Bayh) (noting drive to simplify power transfers and limit their number); *see also* III Cong. Rec. 3284 (1965) (statement of Sen. Bayh); *id.* at 7966 (statement of Rep. McClory).

27. *See* S. Rep. No. 89-66, at 18–20 (1965) (individual views of Sen. Hruska) ("Every sensible and sympathetic construction favoring [the president's] continued performance of presidential duties should be accorded him."); III Cong. Rec. 7964 (1965) (statement of Rep. Moore) (proposing to keep president in control during

Section 4 proceedings on these grounds); *id.* at 3284 (statements of Sens. Hart and Bayh) (arguing in favor of keeping vice president in charge); Feerick, *supra* note 9, at 14 (noting ABA recommendation that vice president "serve in the interval").

28. *See* Bayh, *supra* note 11, at 273 (worrying foremost about "a President gone berserk"); Feerick, *supra* note 1, at 175 (noting fecklessness of stricken President Wilson); James F. Childress, *Presidential Illness, in* Papers on Presidential Disability and the Twenty-Fifth Amendment, *supra* note 1, at 123, 134–35 (discussing, with commenters, ways in which subordinates can disregard inappropriate orders from mentally unbalanced leaders); Gustafson, *supra* note 9, at 474 (noting role, and presumptive loyalty, of cabinet). Thomas G. Wicker, *The Public's Right to Know, in* Presidential Disability, *supra* note 11, at 118, 124 (describing President Nixon's "very sudden and sometimes outlandish orders," which he would retract days later, indicating that his subordinates were not carrying them out in the meantime).

29. *See* Silva, *supra* note 7, at 100–09 (discussing relative authority of presidents, vice presidents, Congress, and courts to determine presidential disability under Article II). If the courts decided first, Congress would have no reason to reject the decision, since the losing party in Congress could litigate that result and presumably get the courts to reaffirm themselves. If Congress decided first, the courts would likely defer under the political-question doctrine, as discussed next.

30. Chapter 5 discusses a similar divide in a late-impeachment case, between a majority-rule jurisdictional question (debated for a month) and a two-thirds majority question on the merits.

31. U.S. Const. art. I, § 3, cl. 6 (Senate Impeachment Clause); *id.* § 5, cl. 1 (Elections Clause); *see* Baker v. Carr, 369 U.S. 186, 217 (1962) (providing typology of political questions, including textual commission).

32. *See Baker*, 369 U.S. at 217 (providing typology of political questions).

33. *See generally* Rachel E. Barkow, *More Supreme Than Court?: The Fall of the Political Question Doctrine and the Rise of Judicial Supremacy*, 102 Colum. L. Rev. 237 (2002).

34. The impeachment would best be structured as directed at the president's inappropriate seizure of power—not at her being disabled, since that is not a "high crime or misdemeanor." *See* Feerick, *supra* note 1, at 241 (discussing inaptness of impeachment in disability cases); Gustafson, *supra* note 9, at 468 (same).

35. *See* Antonin Scalia, *The Twenty-Fifth Amendment Needs Clarification in Regard to Presidential Succession, in* Amendment XXV: Presidential Disability and Succession 109 (Sylvia Engdahl ed., 2010) (noting problematic gaps left by amendment). Those arguing that no amendment could be perfect, and that any cure for the Twenty-Fifth Amendment would be worse than the disease, include Bayh, *supra* note 8, at 63; Gilbert, *supra* note 6, at 46; Tom Wicker, *The Imperfect but Useful Twenty-Fifth Amendment, in* Managing Crisis, *supra* note 2, at 215, 221; Gustafson, *supra* note 9, at 495–96; Richard E. Neustadt, *The Twenty-Fifth Amendment and Its Achilles Heel*, 30 Wake Forest L. Rev. 427, 433 (1995).

36. Feerick, *supra* note 6, at 246 (reproducing S.J. Res. 139 as introduced in 1963, which designated cabinet in place at time of president's declaration of fitness); *see*

111 Cong. Rec. 3284 (1965) (statements of Sens. Hart and Bayh) (discussing possibility of acting president entrenching himself by replacing disabled president's
cabinet); *Hearing, supra* note 22, at 16–17, 28 (statements of Sen. Bayh, Sen.
Hruska, and Att'y Gen. Katzenbach) (discussing ability of acting president to fire
cabinet members). Of course, if the vice president stacks the second vote,
Congress can still rule against him on the merits; the bigger problem is when the
president stacks the vote, because that prevents Congress from getting the case.

37. *See* S. Rep. No. 89-66, at 9 (1965) (explaining that when constitutional provisions
on power transfer are unclear, legislation to clarify them will necessarily be subject
to attack); 111 Cong. Rec. 3255 (1965) (statement of Sen. Bayh) (same).

38. *See* Presidential Disability, *supra* note 11 (recommending—albeit for medical rather
than constitutional details—that presidents prepare Twenty-Fifth Amendment
contingency plans and make the unclassified portions public); Gilbert, *supra* note
18, at 883 (describing recent contingency planning by presidents since Reagan); *cf.*
Gustafson, *supra* note 9, at 496 (suggesting that Department of Justice's Office of
Legal Counsel issue public opinion on similar issue).

Chapter 4. The Line of Succession Controversy

1. *Presidential Succession Act: Hearing Before the Subcomm. on the Constitution of the H.
Comm. on the Judiciary,* 108th Cong. 37 (2004) [hereinafter 2004 House Hearing]
(statement of M. Miller Baker) ("most dangerous"); *id.* at 49 (statement of Sen.
Cornyn) ("intolerable"); *Ensuring the Continuity of the United States Government:
The Presidency: Joint Hearing Before the S. Comm. on the Judiciary and Comm. on
Rules and Admin.,* 108th Cong. 7 (2003) [hereinafter 2003 Senate Hearing] (statement of Akhil Amar) ("disastrous," "accident waiting to happen"); *accord
Presidential Inability and Vacancies in the Office of Vice President: Hearings on S.J.
Res. 13 et al. Before the Subcomm. on Constitutional Amendments of the S. Comm. on
the Judiciary,* 88th Cong. 217 (1964) [hereinafter 1964 House Hearings] (statement of Clinton Rossiter) (calling current law "one of the poorest ever to emerge
from this stately and distinguished body," doubting its constitutionality, and
concluding that "soon[e]r or later it will have to be amended, if not scrapped"); *cf.*
The Constitution of the United States of America: Analysis and Interpretation 387
(Edward S. Corwin ed., 1953) (stating that "[i]t is unlikely that Congress ever
passed a more ill-considered law" than the 1792 succession act, given its constitutional defects, which current law shares).

    Dramatic uses of the line of succession include novels (Tom Clancy, Debt of
Honor (1994); Tom Clancy, Executive Orders (1996); Clive Cussler, Deep Six
(1984); Pat Frank, Alas, Babylon (1959)), films (By Dawn's Early Light (Home Box
Office 1990); Mars Attacks! (Warner Bros. 1996); and My Fellow Americans
(Warner Bros. 1996)), and television programs (*Commander in Chief* (ABC); *Jericho*
(CBS); and *The West Wing* (NBC)).

    Politicians criticizing legislative succession include Senators Trent Lott and
John Cornyn, and Representative Brad Sherman. *See* 2004 House Hearing, *supra,*

at 43–48 (statement of Rep. Sherman); 2003 Senate Hearing, *supra*, at 3 (statement of Sen. Lott); *id.* at 4 (statement of Sen. Cornyn).

The definitive article arguing that the current succession law is unconstitutional is Akhil Reed Amar & Vikram David Amar, *Is the Presidential Succession Law Constitutional?*, 48 Stan. L. Rev. 113 (1995); *see* Seth Barrett Tillman, *Legislative Officer Succession: Part I and Part II*, at 3–4 (working paper 2008), *available at* http://works.bepress.com/seth_barrett_tillman/29 (according Amars' article canonical status and noting prominent citations of it). Some others include Ruth C. Silva, Presidential Succession (1951); and John C. Fortier & Norman J. Ornstein, *Presidential Succession and Congressional Leaders*, 53 Cath. U. L. Rev. 993 (2004).

Not everyone is so sure. *See, e.g.*, Steven G. Calabresi, *The Political Question of Presidential Succession*, 48 Stan. L. Rev. 155 (1995) (arguing that Constitution precludes legislative officials from being in line of succession, but that it is a nonjusticiable question); John F. Manning, *Not Proved: Some Lingering Questions About Legislative Succession to the Presidency*, 48 Stan. L. Rev. 141, 153 (1995) (conceding "substantial constitutional concerns" but preferring deference to Congress on this ambiguous question); Tillman, *supra*, at 3–4 (disagreeing with Amars outright); Howard M. Wasserman, *Structural Principles and Presidential Succession*, 90 Ky. L.J. 345 (2002) (assuming that current law is constitutional, though arguing that it violates structural principles).

2. H.R. Rep. No. 49-26, at 1 (1886).
3. U.S. Const. art. II, § 1, cl. 6.
4. Act of Mar. 1, 1792, ch. 8, § 9, 1 Stat. 239, 240 (repealed 1886). For discussion of the political and legislative history of the 1792 act, see John D. Feerick, From Failing Hands 57–62 (1965) [hereinafter Feerick, Hands]; John D. Feerick, The Twenty-Fifth Amendment 37–39 (2d ed. 1992) [hereinafter Feerick, Amendment]; Silva, *supra* note 1, at 113–15; Amar & Amar, *supra* note 1, at 132.
5. Letter from James Madison to Edmund Pendleton (Feb. 21, 1792), *in* 14 The Papers of James Madison 235, 235 (Robert A. Rutland et al. eds., 1983); *see* 3 Annals of Cong. 402 (1792) (recording House vote to replace PPT and Speaker with secretary of state); *id.* at 90 (recording Senate rejection of House amendment); *id.* at 417 (recording House's 31–24 vote to recede from its amendment); Feerick, Hands, *supra* note 4, at 58–61 (discussing congressional debates, anti-Jefferson impetus, and lack of record of Senate proceedings); Silva, *supra* note 1, at 113–14 (describing how Senate opposition to Jefferson trumped constitutional concerns); *id.* at 131–33 (describing constitutional objections to legislative succession in First and Second Congresses); Ruth C. Silva, *The Presidential Succession Act of 1947*, 47 Mich. L. Rev. 451, 458 & n.28 (1949) (explaining lack of record of Senate debate).

In the House, there were seven Convention delegates: Baldwin, Dayton, Fitzsimons, Gerry, Gilman, Madison, and Williamson. When the House first considered the Senate bill, four (Baldwin, Fitzsimons, Madison, and Williamson) opposed legislative succession, although the record does not specify the extent to which their preferences were based on constitutional concerns. Gerry—who had refused to sign the Constitution—and Gilman approved the use of the PPT. Dayton did not vote. When the Senate held firm, four (Baldwin, Gilman, Madison, and Williamson) voted to oppose the Senate version; the other three voted to accede to it. An eighth Convention delegate, John Mercer, had joined the House by this point, but he did not participate in the vote. *See* Feerick, Hands, *supra* note 4, at 59–60 (listing votes); Silva, *supra* note 1, at 132–33 (listing votes); *see also* 3 Annals of Cong. 281 (1791) (including constitutional objections by Reps. Sturges, White, and Giles, with defenses by Reps. Sedgwick and Gerry); *id.* at 417–18 (recording final vote).

The previous year, the First Congress had debated succession, and a proposal to use the Speaker and PPT spurred strong constitutional objections. *See* 2 *id.* at 1854–55 (1791).

6. *See* Silva, *supra* note 1, at 177 (listing ten vacancies between 1792 and 1886, totaling over twenty-two years); *id.* at 117 (discussing Wade's conflict of interest).

7. Feerick, Hands, *supra* note 4, at 118, 130–32 (Garfield and Arthur); *id.* at 141 (Cleveland); Silva, *supra* note 1, at 117–20 (Arthur and Cleveland); Richard C. Sachs, Cong. Research Serv., RL 30960, The President Pro Tempore of the Senate 5–7 (2003) (discussing temporary and ad hoc procedures for selecting PPTs before 1890, which often led to vacancies). President Arthur, who was in New York when he became president, secretly mailed a letter to himself in Washington that called the Senate into special session, to be opened in case he died. Once he arrived alive in Washington, he called a special session, and the Senate selected a PPT. *See* Feerick, Hands, *supra* note 4, at 130–32 & n.†; Silva, *supra* note 1, at 118.

8. Act of Jan. 19, 1886, ch. 4, 24 Stat. 1, 1–2 (repealed 1947); *see* H.R. Rep. No. 49-26, at 2–3 (1886) (supporting cabinet succession and leading with constitutional objections to 1792 act); Charles S. Hamlin, *The Presidential Succession Act of 1886*, 18 Harv. L. Rev. 182, 182–90 (1905) (describing motivations of 1886 act, and history of proposals from 1881 to 1886); *see also* Feerick, Hands, *supra* note 4, at 142–46; Silva, *supra* note 1, at 121–23, 133–34; Amar & Amar, *supra* note 1, at 134; *cf.* David A. McKnight, The Electoral System of the United States 345–47 (Phila., J. B. Lippincott & Co. 1878) (criticizing 1792 act on constitutional grounds).

9. *See* Act of July 18, 1947, 61 Stat. 380, 380–81; 91 Cong. Rec. 6272 (1945) (message from President Truman to Congress); Silva, *supra* note 1, at 123–30 (describing legislative history of 1947 act, including Truman's role). The aversion to presidents appointing their successors had come up in the 1792 and 1886 debates as well. *See* Feerick, Hands, *supra* note 4, at 59, 146; Lindsay Rogers, *Presidential Inability*, 2 Review 481 (1920) (discussing other problems with 1886 act).

10. Act of July 18, 1947, 61 Stat. 380, 380–81; Silva, *supra* note 1, at 126–29; *accord* 91 Cong. Rec. 7020 (1945) (statement of Rep. Graham) (comparing several days of consideration of succession in 1886 with House Judiciary Committee's forty-five minutes of consideration in 1945); Feerick, Hands, *supra* note 4, at 206–09 (describing 1945 bill's death in Senate "probably because of doubts about its

constitutionality," followed by passage in 1947 after the Senate "largely ignored" constitutional questions); Amar & Amar, *supra* note 1, at 134 & n.131 (characterizing constitutional analysis of Acting Attorney General McGregor, on which Congress relied, as "shoddy").

Examples of the unavailing constitutional arguments against Speaker succession include 91 Cong. Rec. A3639–41 (1945) (statement of Sen. Green); *id.* at 7015–16 (statement of Rep. Hancock); *id.* at 7017–18 (statement of Rep. Gwynne); and *id.* at 8272–74 (statement of Sen. Hatch). Despite all this, in his opening statement on June 26, 1947, the bill's sponsor, Senator Wherry, spoke at great length without mentioning the constitutional problems. He discussed the motivations of the 1886 act but left out the constitutional concerns with Speaker and PPT succession. 93 *id.* at 7691–700 (1947) (statement of Sen. Wherry). Later, in response to a serious inquiry and presentation by Senator Hatch, Wherry cursorily addressed the "officer" problem and suggested that further discussion was pointless. *See id.* at 7698, 7712–13, 7766–72 (statements of Sens. Hatch and Wherry); *see also id.* at 8628 (statement of Rep. Gwynne) (pressing on with constitutional objections).

11. *See* Silva, *supra* note 1, at 126–30 (describing legislative history). Two important new practical problems are the resignation requirement (anyone in the line of succession acting as president must resign her previous post) and the "bumping" provision (if there is no qualified Speaker or PPT and power passes to a cabinet secretary, a Speaker or PPT can later qualify and "bump" the secretary). One important practical problem with the 1792 act has gone away, though. The Twentieth Amendment, passed in 1933, reconfigured Congress's schedule and eliminated the problem of long congressional recesses in which there was no Speaker or PPT. *See* U.S. Const. amend. XX; Silva, *supra* note 1, at 173 (describing effect of Twentieth Amendment on succession). Having the cabinet in line provides a further backstop.

12. U.S. Const. amend. XXV; *cf.* 1964 House Hearings, *supra* note 1, at 53 (statement of Sen. Javits) (complaining that vice-presidential appointment provision—similar to the one later enacted in the Twenty-Fifth Amendment—would clash with 1947 act).

13. *See supra* note 1 (listing critics of law). *See generally* 2004 House Hearing, *supra* note 1; 2003 Senate Hearing, *supra* note 1.

14. U.S. Const. art. II, § 1, cl. 6. If a court struck down only the offending portion of the statute, the secretary of state would be next in line. If, as is less likely, the court struck down the entire statute, the law would arguably revert back to the 1886 statute, which would also put the secretary of state next in line.

15. *Id.* art. I, § 6, cl. 2; *see* 2004 House Hearing, *supra* note 1, at 57–58 (statement of Rep. Hostettler) (supporting executive succession instead of "parliamentary" system); Amar & Amar, *supra* note 1, at 115, 118–19 (discussing implications of Incompatibility Clause); *see also supra* note 10 (listing some unsuccessful uses of this argument in debate over 1947 act).

16. U.S. Const. art. II, § 1, cl. 2 (emphasis added); U.S. Const. amend. XIV, § 3 (emphasis added); *see* Amar & Amar, *supra* note 1, at 117–18 & n.28 (discussing

clauses); *see also supra* note 10 (listing some unsuccessful uses of this argument in debate over 1947 act). Three other examples are U.S. Const. art. I, § 6, cl. 2 (Emoluments Clause); *id*. art. VI, cl. 3 (Oath Clause); *id*. amend. XIV, § 2 (regulating state elections). Seth Tillman has made a good case that officers "under the authority of the United States" in the Emoluments Clause are not the same set as officers "under" or "of" the United States, and that people should be careful about treating these different phrasings as though they are necessarily identical. *See* Tillman, *supra* note 1, at 11–23.

17. U.S. Const. art. II, § 2, cl. 2 (appointments); *id*. § 3 (commissions); *id*. § 4 (impeachment); *see* Amar & Amar, *supra* note 1, at 115–16 (discussing clauses); *see also supra* note 10 (listing some unsuccessful uses of this argument in debate over 1947 act). The non-impeachability of members of Congress is discussed further in Chapter 5.

18. *See* U.S. Const. art. I, § 9, cl. 8 (restricting foreign gifts); *id*. art. II, § 2, cl. 1 (empowering president to request opinions from cabinet members); *id*. art. VI, § 3 (banning religious tests); *id*. amend. XXV (referring to cabinet).

19. *See Succession to the Presidency: Hearings Before the S. Comm. on Rules and Admin. on S. Con. Res. 1 et al.*, 80th Cong. 63 (1947) [hereinafter 1947 Senate Hearings] (statement of Sen. Wherry) (proposing "solution" to officer controversy); *accord Hearing on H.R. 2749 et al. Before Subcomm. No. 1 of the H. Comm. on the Judiciary*, 80th Cong. 13 (unpublished May 5, 1947) (statement of Rep. Reed).

20. *See* 93 Cong. Rec. 7694–95 (1947) (reproducing House report concluding law was constitutional because of precedent of 1792 act and "long-continued acquiescence" to it); *id*. at 8627 (statement of Rep. Kefauver) (denying, inaccurately, that opponents of 1792 act raised any constitutional objections to designation of PPT and Speaker as "officers"); 91 *id*. at 7016 (1945) (statement of Rep. Kefauver) (same); *id*. at 7010 (statement of Rep. Michener) (stating, inaccurately, "Yes, the succession was changed by the Congress [in 1886], but not because the former law was considered unconstitutional"); Silva, *supra* note 1, at 133 (citing reliance of 1947 act's supporters on constitutional judgment of Second Congress); *supra* notes 4–5, 8, and accompanying text (describing partisan motivations of 1792 act, constitutional arguments against it, and 1886 act's reaction to the latter); *cf*. H.R. Rep. No. 79-829, at 4 (1945) (presuming constitutionality of products of Second Congress, but arguing that resignation requirement, which 1792 act lacked, is constitutionally mandated); 14 Cong. Rec. 690 (1882) (statement of Sen. Edmunds) (defending 1792 act as product of "utmost care" by Founding generation); *id*. at 914 (statement of Sen. Maxey) (refuting—persuasively—Edmunds's characterization of 1792 proceedings).

The 1947 act's supporters also relied on an 1856 Senate Judiciary Committee report concluding that PPT and Speaker succession was constitutional. *See, e.g.*, 1947 Senate Hearings, *supra* note 19, at 44 (statement of Sen. Wherry). But the 1856 report never addressed the question. *See* S. Rep. No. 34-260 (1856).

The Supreme Court decision improperly relied upon is *Lamar v. United States*, 240 U.S. 60, 65 (1916) (Lamar I), 241 U.S. 103, 112–13 (1916) (Lamar II); *see* 93 Cong. Rec. 7712–13 (1947) (statement of Sen. Wherry) (relying on *Lamar* to support constitutionality of 1947 act); *id.* at 8629 (statement of Rep. Gwynne) (explaining *Lamar*'s irrelevance in House debate, unavailingly); *id.* at 8631 (statement of Rep. Springer) (quoting *Lamar*, ignoring its explicit distinction between the statute and the Constitution). The Court in *Lamar* made clear that it was interpreting only a statute, not the constitutional term "officer." *Lamar I*, 240 U.S. at 65; *see Lamar II*, 241 U.S. at 112 (reiterating this); Silva, *supra* note 1, at 135 & n.98 (discussing reliance on *Lamar*).

21. *See* 3 Annals of Cong. 281 (1791) (statement of Rep. Gerry) (noting Constitution establishes Speaker as officer of the House); Manning, *supra* note 1, at 143 (rejecting reading of "officers" as including ordinary members of Congress). Interestingly, in his next breath Elbridge Gerry opposed legislative succession, on policy grounds. For other uses of the "officer of the House" argument, see 3 Annals of Cong. 281 (1791) (statement of Rep. Sedgwick); 14 Cong. Rec. 881 (1883) (statement of Sen. Jones of Florida); 91 *id.* at 7016 (1945) (statement of Rep. Kefauver); 93 *id.* at 8627 (1947) (statement of Rep. Kefauver); 2003 Senate Hearing, *supra* note 1, at 76 (statement of Howard M. Wasserman); *cf.* 17 Cong. Rec. 671–72 (1886) (statement of Rep. Peters) (arguing that Speaker and PPT are officers of the United States).

22. U.S. Const. art. I, § 2, cl. 6; *id.* § 3, cl. 5; *see* Feerick, Hands, *supra* note 4, at 144 n.§ (citing argument in consideration of 1886 act that PPT is not an officer of the Senate); Silva, *supra* note 1, at 136 (arguing PPT is not an officer of the Senate); Manning, *supra* note 1, at 143 n.16 (arguing PPT is an officer in this situation).

23. 2 The Records of the Federal Convention of 1787, at 185–86 (Max Farrand ed., 1911) (showing Framers' changes to nature of presidency); *id.* at 573, 599 (showing Committee of Style's changes); *see* Silva, *supra* note 1, at 8, 131 (discussing role of Committee of Style); *id.* at 7, 137 (describing Convention's creation of vice presidency); Amar & Amar, *supra* note 1, at 116 (describing drafting history of Succession Clause); *id.* at 124–25 (emphasizing Congress's limited constitutional role in presidential elections, and independence of electoral college from Congress). *But see* Manning, *supra* note 1, at 144 (arguing that Framers' failure to say "officers of the United States" is meaningful, and that Committee of Style might have made a substantive change even if it was not supposed to, since the final text is binding and earlier drafts and contents of Convention debates were unknown to ratifying conventions).

24. *See* 1 Asher Hinds, Hinds' Precedents of the House of Representatives of the United States § 187, at 110, 113 (1907) (listing officers of House "in addition to the Speaker" as "Clerk, Sergeant-at-Arms, Doorkeeper, Postmaster, and Chaplain," and noting Speaker is only House officer who is also a member); 1 Lewis Deschler, Deschler's Precedents of the United States House of Representatives, ch. 6, § 15, at 574 (1974) (similar); U.S. Senate: Officers and Staff, http://www.senate.gov/

reference/reference_index_subjects/Officers_Staff_vrd.htm (Dec. 18, 2010) (listing Senate officers—including secretary of the Senate, sergeant at arms and doorkeeper, and chaplain—and linking to articles about them). Congress did not have majority and minority leaders until its second century. *See* Wasserman, *supra* note 1, at 387 (noting that minority leader might be better choice for succession but is not arguably an officer). For arguments that the Succession Clause does not allow state officers, see Amar & Amar, *supra* note 1, at 117 & nn.25–26; Wasserman, *supra* note 1, at 357 n.48.

When Vice President Agnew resigned, President Nixon chose House Minority Leader Ford as his new vice president. Note that while Nixon chose a legislator, he didn't choose an "officer"; the Republican Nixon would not have picked the Democratic Speaker or PPT—let alone the Senate doorkeeper. *But see* James M. Cannon, Time and Chance 204 (1998) (describing Nixon's offer of vice presidency, apparently insincerely, to Speaker Carl Albert).

25. *See* Silva, *supra* note 1, at 138–39 (explaining common understanding that acting president would retain prior office); *see also* 91 Cong. Rec. 7026 (1945); Amar & Amar, *supra* note 1, at 120.

26. U.S. Const. art. I, § 6, cl. 2; *see* H.R. Rep. No. 79-829, at 4 (1945) (arguing resignation requirement is constitutional necessity); Feerick, Hands, *supra* note 4, at 208 (noting criticism in 1947 of resignation provision because of effect on Speakers when president's disability is very short); Silva, *supra* note 1, at 138–39 (discussing Incompatibility Clause and separation-of-powers issues); Amar & Amar, *supra* note 1, at 118–21 (noting incompatibility-resignation conundrum); Calabresi, *supra* note 1, at 163–66 (discussing separation-of-powers problems); Wasserman, *supra* note 1, at 354, 365–69 (stating that resignation is required to avoid incompatibility problem, and criticizing current law because of its violence to separation of powers). *But see* Manning, *supra* note 1, at 147–48 (arguing that a Speaker or PPT serving as acting president would only be a de minimis violation of separation of powers, especially if the service were only until a special election, as in the 1792 act).

To be sure, the current law requires everyone in the line of succession, including cabinet members, to resign their posts before acting as president. But if it didn't, there would be no constitutional problem with cabinet members not resigning; the Constitution does not preclude holding multiple executive offices simultaneously. And if cabinet members do resign they can get their old jobs back much more quickly than House members can. *See* Amar & Amar, *supra* note 1, at 119–20, 135–36 (making these points). Executive officers also need not worry about their cabinet terms expiring; by contrast, a sitting Speaker's House term might expire if she acted as president around midterm without resigning. *See* 17 Cong. Rec. 221 (1885) (statement of Sen. Beck) (raising same issue with regard to PPT acting as president).

27. Letter from James Madison to Edmund Pendleton, *supra* note 5, at 235–36; *see* Feerick, Hands, *supra* note 4, at 61–62 (quoting Madison's statement of the

Catch-22); Amar & Amar, *supra* note 1, at 134 n.131 (discussing Catch-22). The Catch-22 was a key argument in support of the 1886 act. *See* Feerick, Hands, *supra* note 4, at 145 (discussing debate); Silva, *supra* note 1, at 138–39 (discussing debate). *But see* Calabresi, *supra* note 1, at 165–66 (contending that there would be no incompatibility problem, because acting presidents are not officers).

28. *See* 2004 House Hearing, *supra* note 1, at 43 (statement of Rep. Sherman) (calling for succession law to be redrafted with "continuity" and "legitimacy" as goals); Calabresi, *supra* note 1, at 155 (stressing importance of certainty).

29. *See* Amar & Amar, *supra* note 1, at 121–23, 128–29 (discussing conflict-of-interest problem in contexts of impeachment and Twenty-Fifth Amendment proceedings); Calabresi, *supra* note 1, at 155 (advocating succession rules that minimize incentives to kill or remove presidents); Manning, *supra* note 1, at 145 n.27 (responding to conflict-of-interest concerns). The Twenty-Fifth Amendment provides procedures for a temporarily disabled president to hand power to the vice president, not to anyone else in the line of succession, but it doesn't forbid the latter.

30. Feerick, Amendment, *supra* note 4, at xii; *see* Herbert L. Abrams, "The President Has Been Shot": Confusion, Disability, and the 25th Amendment 106–11 (1992) (describing Haig episode).

31. *See* U.S. Const. amend. XXV, § 1; Silva, *supra* note 1, at 14–28 (discussing Tyler's case and its use as precedent).

32. *See* 2003 Senate Hearing, *supra* note 1, at 70 (statement of Howard M. Wasserman) (refuting Truman's claims).

33. *See* Amar & Amar, *supra* note 1, at 130–31 (discussing relative representativeness of congressional leaders and cabinet secretaries); Calabresi, *supra* note 1, at 173 (noting national constituency of cabinet). Professor Amar concedes, however, that it is suboptimal to have appointees become president. *See* Akhil Reed Amar, *Presidents Without Mandates (with Special Emphasis on Ohio)*, 67 U. Cin. L. Rev. 375, 386 (1999).

34. *See* Sachs, *supra* note 7, at 4, 7–9 (describing historical criteria for PPT selection); Wasserman, *supra* note 1, at 405 (discussing PPT); *supra* note 24 (discussing non-officer status of majority leaders).

35. U.S. Const. amend. XXV, § 2; *see* 2 Annals of Cong. 1866 (1790) (statement by Rep. Sedgwick) (speaking against presidents naming their successors); 2003 Senate Hearing, *supra* note 1, at 24 (statement of Akhil Amar) (explaining how "Truman's vision" is "undercut" by Twenty-Fifth Amendment); Feerick, Hands, *supra* note 4, at 59, 146 (citing appearances of anti-democratic argument in 1792 and 1886); Robert S. Rankin, *Presidential Succession in the United States*, 8 J. Pol. 44, 51–52 (1946) (making distinction between successor and stand-in); Wasserman, *supra* note 1, at 407–08 (discussing presidents' role in choosing vice presidents, before and after Twenty-Fifth Amendment). *But see* 93 Cong. Rec. 7703 (1947) (featuring debate over presidential nominees' role in selecting vice-presidential nominees).

36. *See* 93 Cong. Rec. 7777 (1947) (statement of Sen. Fulbright) (recognizing doubt over whether Speaker and PPT are "officers," but arguing that it would matter much less if they served only until a special election); Silva, *supra* note 1, at 123–26, 145–49 (explaining fate of special-election provisions); Feerick, Hands, *supra* note 4, at 146 (discussing optional special-election provision in 1886 act); Amar & Amar, *supra* note 1, at 137–38 & n.144 (advocating special elections but noting serious practical and constitutional objections); Hamlin, *supra* note 8 (opposing special elections and discussing constitutional and policy ramifications); Arthur M. Schlesinger, Jr., *On the Presidential Succession*, 89 Pol. Sci. Q. 475 (1974) (advocating special elections); Wasserman, *supra* note 1, at 410–12 (praising democratic benefits of special elections).

37. *See* S. Rep. No. 34-260, at 3 (1856) (noting lack of democratic mandate for anyone in line of succession after vice president); Feerick, Hands, *supra* note 4, at 145 (relating continuity arguments in debate over 1886 act); Silva, *supra* note 1, at 158 (praising continuity of cabinet succession); Wasserman, *supra* note 1, at 368–69, 406–07 (noting secretary of state's institutional closeness to presidency, and noting how 1947 act's framers ignored it).

38. *See* Amar & Amar, *supra* note 1, at 130 (examining congressional versus executive experience of presidents). Constitutionally, the vice president has only legislative powers. Speaking more practically, though, he has long been in the president's cabinet and, more recently, has had an office in the White House and a significant executive role. It is this experience, not the legislative role, that gets touted when vice presidents run for president.

39. *See* 17 Cong. Rec. 224 (1886) (statement of Sen. Call) (explaining support for cabinet succession on continuity grounds, despite belief that senators and representatives are "officers of the United States"). On the party-switch problem, see 2003 Senate Hearing, *supra* note 1, at 8 (statement of Akhil Amar); 2004 House Hearing, *supra* note 1, at 58 (statement of Rep. Sherman); Silva, *supra* note 1, at 154–56; Schlesinger, *supra* note 36, at 503; Wasserman, *supra* note 1, at 377–88 (noting potential for succession law to flout electorate's choice of divided government). *But see Hearing on H.R. 1121 Before Subcomm. No. 1 of the H. Comm. on the Judiciary*, 80th Cong. 8–9 (unpublished Apr. 23, 1947) (statement of Rep. Chelf) (stating as a Democrat that if President Truman died and the Republican Speaker of the House took over, it would be fair "democracy in action").

40. *See* Presidential Succession: Ford, Rockefeller & the 25th Amendment 41–46, 207–16 (Lester A. Sobel ed., 1975) (recounting Ford and Rockefeller confirmations); Silva, *supra* note 1, at 156 (raising conflict-of-interest issue); Amar & Amar, *supra* note 1, at 128–29 (discussing Rockefeller confirmation); Thomas Vinciguerra, *Least Likely Ladder to the Presidency*, N.Y. Times, July 31, 2005, at C2 (describing Albert's promise); *see also* 17 Cong. Rec. 676 (1886) (statement of Rep. Cowles) (noting that Republican-controlled Senate acted against its own advantage in 1886 by removing PPT from line of succession during Democratic presidency).

41. *See* William F. Brown & Americo R. Cinquegrana, *The Realities of Presidential Succession*, 75 Geo. L.J. 1389, 1445 n.187 (1987) (discussing who would resolve a succession dispute).

42. *But see* Calabresi, *supra* note 1, at 168–69. Calabresi argues that while Speaker succession is unconstitutional, cabinet succession is illegitimate without a special-election provision. Therefore, he says, there is no way for the Supreme Court to take appropriate action that reinforces democratic legitimacy, and thus there are no "judicially discoverable and manageable standards"—a factor in political-question analysis that I have subsumed into the category of "mere policy versus actual legal questions." Calabresi says further that the case would consist "mainly [of] political arguments dressed up in legal trappings," but I see it as a case with real legal issues that happen to have political overtones. This points to a larger issue about the Court's general role in constitutional cliffhangers, a matter covered in Chapter 7. Calabresi further argues that it would be "unthinkable" for the Supreme Court to order a Speaker to stand down as acting president, and that the Court would run the risk of being ignored by the Speaker and by Congress. *See id.* at 169–70. I agree with regard to "ordinary" cases, in which the government and nation generally accept the Speaker, and the challenge comes from a disgruntled but isolated secretary of state, or from a pointy-headed third party like me. But if the Speaker's political position is weaker, and the secretary of state has significant institutional backing, I maintain that it may *only* be the Court that can settle the issue.

43. Presidents Arthur, Truman, and Ford had the chief justice administer their oaths when they succeeded to the presidency, though Arthur had previously had a state-court judge administer his.

44. 1964 House Hearings, *supra* note 1, at 214 (statement of Clinton Rossiter); *see* 2003 Senate Hearing, *supra* note 1, at 7 (statement of Akhil Amar) (noting potential legitimacy problems current law poses); Amar & Amar, *supra* note 1, at 136 (defining the problem as the potential crisis, not the potential unconstitutional result); Manning, *supra* note 1, at 153 (supporting constitutionality of Speaker succession as "reasonable implementation of ambiguous language" but noting "substantial constitutional concerns" and suggesting that "a law for times of exigency should be free of doubt").

45. *See* 93 Cong. Rec. 786 (1947) (communication from President Truman) (renewing request for new law putting Speaker and PPT in line of succession); Feerick, Hands, *supra* note 4, at 265–66 (noting critics of 1947 act but explaining why Congress is unlikely to respond); Silva, *supra* note 1, at 115–20 (detailing unsuccessful reform proposals between 1792 and 1886); Thomas H. Neale, Cong. Research Serv., RL 34692, Presidential Succession: Perspectives, Contemporary Analysis, and 110th Congress Proposed Legislation 15–21 (2008) [hereinafter Neale 2008 Report] (listing then-current legislative proposals, none of which passed); Thomas H. Neale, Cong. Research Serv., RL 32969, Presidential Succession: An Overview with Analysis of Legislation Proposed in the 109th Congress 15–18 (2005) (same); Thomas H. Neale, Cong. Research Serv., RL 31761,

Presidential and Vice Presidential Succession: Overview and Current Legislation 14–19 (2004) (same).

For a striking example of defensiveness about the prerogatives of the Speaker and House, see 111 Cong. Rec. 7961 (1965) (statement of Rep. Dingell) (saying proposal to fill vice-presidential vacancies, which became Section 2 of the Twenty-Fifth Amendment, was "a slap at the Members of the House of Representatives, a slap at our elected leadership, and it in effect says that [the Speaker is] not capable to succeed to the high Office of the Presidency"); *see also* Birch Bayh, One Heartbeat Away 40–41, 48 (1968) (describing Speaker McCormack's prickliness over Speaker succession).

46. *See* Amar & Amar, *supra* note 1, at 135 (describing practical problems with current law's "bumping" provision and lack of special-election provision); Fortier & Ornstein, *supra* note 1, at 1006–10 (describing problems with multiple vacancies on Inauguration Day); Paul Taylor, *Proposals to Prevent Discontinuity in Government and Preserve the Right to Elected Representation,* 54 Syracuse L. Rev. 435, 465–71 (2004) (describing practical problems with bumping, geography, and acting secretaries); Neale 2008 Report, *supra* note 45, at 9–24 (listing issues with current succession law and noting proposed fixes).

Chapter 5. Impeaching an Ex-President

1. Large parts of this chapter are taken from my article, Brian C. Kalt, *The Constitutional Case for the Impeachability of Former Federal Officials,* 6 Tex. Rev. L. & Pol. 13 (2001). While I use a lot of the article here, including some unmarked and uncited quotations from it, I also cite the article in the endnotes to direct readers to parts of it that I *don't* quote or use in the text. The article contains mounds of evidence, arguments, and nuances at every turn; there simply is no room for all of them in this chapter.

Discussions opposing late impeachability include *President Clinton's Eleventh Hour Pardons: Hearing Before the Senate Judiciary Comm.,* 107th Cong. 91–92 (2001) (statement of Ken Gormley); Eleanore Bushnell, Crimes, Follies, and Misfortunes: The Federal Impeachment Trials 16 (1992); 2 Joseph Story, Commentaries on the Constitution of the United States 271 (Boston, Hilliard, Gray, & Co. 1833); Robert C. Stelle, Note, *Defining High Crimes and Misdemeanors: A Call for Stare Decisis,* 15 J.L. & Pol. 309, 358 (1999); Mark R. Levin, *Arlen Specter, the Constitution, & UFOs,* Nat'l Rev. Online (Feb. 12, 2001), http://www.nationalreview.com/contributors/levin021201a.shtml; Jorge E. Souss, *Impeach Clinton? Why Not Impeach O.J.?,* Jurist (Mar. 1, 2001), http://jurist.law.pitt.edu/pardonop4.htm. *See also* Peter Charles Hoffer & N. E. H. Hull, Impeachment in America, 1635–1805, at 257 (1984) (seeming to assume that late impeachability is inappropriate). *But see* 2 Story, *supra,* at 273 (issuing strong caveat weakening conclusion on late impeachment).

Commentary in favor of late impeachability, besides my own, includes Memorandum from Robert G. Dixon, Jr., Assistant Attorney General, Office of

Legal Counsel 4–5 (Sept. 24, 1973) [hereinafter Dixon Memo]; Michael J. Gerhardt, *The Federal Impeachment Process* 79–81 (2d ed. 2000); William Rawle, *A View of the Constitution of the United States* 213 (Da Capo Press 1970) (2d ed. 1829); Arthur Bestor, *Impeachment*, 49 Wash. L. Rev. 255, 277–81 (1973) (book review); Edwin Brown Firmage & R. Collin Mangrum, *Removal of the President: Resignation and the Procedural Law of Impeachment*, 1974 Duke L.J. 1023, 1089–94; Jonathan Turley, *The Executive Function Theory, the Hamilton Affair, and Other Constitutional Mythologies*, 77 N.C. L. Rev. 1791, 1827 (1999); C. S. Potts, *Impeachment as a Remedy*, 12 St. Louis L. Rev. 15, 23 (1927); Victor Williams, *Pardongate: Another Impeachment after the Investigations Conclude?*, Findlaw's Writ (Feb. 27, 2001), http://writ.news.findlaw.com/commentary/20010227_williams.html. Also seemingly in favor are Akhil Reed Amar, *Attainder and Amendment 2*, 95 Mich. L. Rev. 203, 214 n.36 (1996); Ronald D. Rotunda, *An Essay on the Constitutional Parameters of Federal Impeachment*, 76 Ky. L.J. 707, 716–18 (1988).

2. Gerhardt, *supra* note 1, at 192.
3. *See* U.S. Const. art. I, § 2, cl. 5 (House); *id.* § 3, cl. 6 (Senate).
4. *Id.* cl. 7 (punishment); *id.* art. II, § 2, cl. 1 (pardons).
5. *Id.* § 4.
6. *See* Congressional Record Containing the Proceedings of the Senate Sitting for the Trial of William W. Belknap, Late Secretary of War 48 (Washington, Government Printing Office 1876) [hereinafter Belknap Trial] (argument by House managers) (touting flexibility of punishment in a late impeachment); Bestor, *supra* note 1, at 281 (noting benefit of having removal off the table in late impeachment).

If Congress were interested in expressing its disapproval of an ex-officer without actually leveling punishment, it could simply censure him. But this provides a perfect example of the special essence of impeachment. Censure reflects the desire of a bare majority of a chamber in Congress to make a political statement with no legal effect. It is congressional froth, as significant as a resolution declaring National Toothpick Week. Some even question its constitutionality. *See* Michael J. Klarman, *Constitutional Fetishism and the Clinton Impeachment Debate*, 85 Va. L. Rev. 631, 649–50 & nn.73–74 (1999) (citing differing opinions on the constitutionality of censuring presidents); *see also* Gerhardt, *supra* note 1, at 186–87 (refuting notion that censure is unconstitutional). Impeachment, by contrast, requires a majority in the House and a two-thirds majority in the Senate, which essentially requires bipartisan agreement. The very difficulty of obtaining an impeachment conviction casts it as a sober and momentous decision rather than a cynical political one. If the Senate determines that conviction is not worthwhile in a case, this reflects its judgment rather than the inevitable limits of impeachment itself.

7. *See* 3 U.S.C. § 102 (2006) (statutory notes); *Fox News Sunday* (Fox News Channel television broadcast, Feb. 11, 2001) (interview with Sen. Specter). One could argue that making the punishment on conviction include such a severe financial penalty would violate the constitutional provision that "Judgment in Cases of Impeachment shall not extend further than to removal from Office, and

disqualification to hold and enjoy any Office of honor, Trust or Profit under the United States." If this is true, however, it makes the current presidential benefits law unconstitutional as well. But the benefits law operates independently of the impeachment process—loss of the pension would be based on the operation of the pension law, not on the "judgment" of the Senate in the impeachment case.

8. Belknap Trial, *supra* note 6, at 64 (statement of Rep. Knott).

9. Cong. Globe, 29th Cong., 1st Sess. 641 (1846) (statement of Rep. Adams); *see id.* at 636–41 (Webster); 3 Reg. Deb. 574–75, 1123–24, 1143 (1827) (Calhoun). Because Calhoun was vice president at the time, he also would have been subject to impeachment under the Protective interpretation of the impeachment power (discussed later), which rejects late impeachment.

10. The ex-presidents who saw the other party take a majority of the House and two-thirds of the Senate are John Adams (1803–26), Martin Van Buren (1861–62), Franklin Pierce (1861–68), James Buchanan (1861–69), Andrew Johnson (1869–75), Herbert Hoover (1935–43), and Dwight Eisenhower (1965–67).

11. *Cf.* Gerhardt, *supra* note 1, at 180–81 (discussing extent to which impeachment of President Clinton failed because of Clinton's popularity).

12. Belknap Trial, *supra* note 6, at 71 (argument of defense counsel); *see id.* at 132 (opinion of Sen. Boutwell) (making similar argument); Souss, *supra* note 1 ("The word 'President' appears 14 other times in Article II, and in every single case it is undisputed that it refers to the person serving as President, not to a former President."). Seth Tillman has argued to me privately that it is inconsistent to say that "officers" include ex-officers here, but not to say so in the Succession Clause, where some people say (as discussed in Chapter 4) that the "officer" acting as president must not be forced to resign from the previous office.

13. *See* Charles L. Black, Jr., Impeachment: A Handbook 39–40 (1974). Black's view does not rule out late impeachment; Congress could make its judgment about the impeachability of an offense more generally, and with an eye toward setting precedent, rather than limiting it to just the case at hand. Another point: if someone returns to office many years after committing his offenses, the evidence might have degraded, making it harder to impeach him successfully.

For more on the removability argument, see Belknap Trial, *supra* note 6, at 82, 85, 115, 124 (opinions of Sens. Morton, Frelinghuysen, Eaton, and McMillan); 2 Story, *supra* note 1, at 271; Souss, *supra* note 1. On impeachment as non-punitive, see Jonathan Turley, *"From Pillar to Post": The Prosecution of American Presidents*, 37 Am. Crim. L. Rev. 1049, 1052 (2000); Souss, *supra* note 1.

14. *See, e.g.*, Belknap Trial, *supra* note 6, at 26, 100, 115, 127 (argument of defense counsel, and opinions of Sens. Cameron, Howe, and Eaton); Souss, *supra* note 1.

15. Technically this may be incorrect, as the Constitution distinguishes the president and vice president from civil officers. Article II, Section 4, does not say "all *other* civil officers," after all. The distinction appears to be that the president and vice president are elected, *see* U.S. Const. art. II, § 1, cl. 1, while civil officers are appointed, and are commissioned by the president, *see id.* § 2, cl. 2; *id.* § 3. On the

other hand, the Constitution refers repeatedly to the president and vice president as holding "office." *See, e.g., id.* art. I, § 3, cl. 5; *id.* art. II, § 1, cls. 1, 5, 8; *id.* amend. XII; *see also* Seth Barrett Tillman & Steven G. Calabresi, Debate, *The Great Divorce: The Current Understanding of Separation of Powers and the Original Meaning of the Incompatibility Clause,* 157 U. Pa. L. Rev. PENNumbra 134 (2008) (debating whether president is an "officer under the United States").

16. *See* Kalt, *supra* note 1, at 58–63 (considering and dismissing Radical interpretation, and narrow view of Article II, Section 4, in more detail). In a debate over an actual late impeachment, several senators espoused the Radical interpretation, arguing that the only limits on Congress's impeachment powers were those inherent in the definition of "impeachment." *See* Belknap Trial, *supra* note 6, at 34, 49–50, 80, 86, 88, 136 (argument of House impeachment managers and Sens. Wallace, Sherman, Edmunds, and Saulsbury); *see also* Seth Barrett Tillman, *The Originalist Who Came in from the Cold: A Response to Professor Josh Chafetz's Impeachment and Assassination* 17 n.34 (Oct. 11, 2010) (unpublished manuscript), *available at* http://ssrn.com/abstract=1622441 (noting how Senate Impeachment Trial Clause speaks of "person[s]" and not officers). More recently, Joseph Isenbergh has argued that impeachment is not limited to removals for high crimes and misdemeanors; to him, Article II, Section 4, merely requires that *if* the impeachment is for a high crime or misdemeanor, the target must leave office if convicted. *See* Joseph Isenbergh, *Impeachment and Presidential Immunity from Judicial Process,* 18 Yale L. & Pol'y Rev. 53 (1999).

17. The Federalist No. 65, at 396 (Alexander Hamilton) (Clinton Rossiter ed., 1961); *accord* 1 The Works of James Wilson 426 (Robert Green McCloskey ed., 1967); *see* Belknap Trial, *supra* note 6, at 154 (opinion of Sen. Kernan) (making this argument); Gerhardt, *supra* note 1, at 79–80 (same).

18. *See* Gerhardt, *supra* note 1, at 80 (citing possibility of disqualification as evidence of late impeachability).

19. For examples of such clear language, see Vt. Const. ch. 2, § 58 (specifying late impeachability of ex-officers who resigned or were removed); N.J. Const. art. VII, § 3, cl. 1 (making state officers impeachable for two years after leaving office).

20. 4 The Debates in the Several State Conventions on the Adoption of the Federal Constitution 32 (Jonathan Elliot ed., Washington, 1836) [hereinafter Elliot's Debates]; *accord* The Federalist No. 64, *supra* note 17, at 396 (John Jay); *id.* No. 65, at 397 (Alexander Hamilton) (expressing sense of impeachment as check on other branches by Congress); John R. Labovitz, Presidential Impeachment 198–99 (1978) (noting Framers' concern with deterrence, though noting that "major purpose of impeachment" is removal); Emily Field Van Tassel & Paul Finkelman, Impeachable Offenses 3 (1999); Jonathan Turley, *Congress as Grand Jury: The Role of the House of Representatives in the Impeachment of an American President,* 67 Geo. Wash. L. Rev. 735, 769 (1999).

21. *Cf.* Akhil Reed Amar, *The Two-Tiered Structure of the Judiciary Act of 1789,* 138 U. Pa. L. Rev. 1499, 1500 & n.3 (1990) (making similar point about presidential vetoes,

and noting that "[t]he framers well understood this political science law of antici-
pated response"). The possibility of a president abusing power to get reelected was
even more problematic under the original Constitution, which did not limit presidential terms; this made removability more important to the Framers, and late
impeachability correspondingly less prominent.

22. *See* Belknap Trial, *supra* note 6, at 129 (opinion of Sen. Bayard) ("The train could
be laid and the slow-match lighted with close calculation, and the incendiary retire
to the place of safety outside the jurisdiction charged with his punishment.");
Bestor, *supra* note 1, at 277 (arguing that impeachment serves both "to render the
perpetrator incapable of further wrongdoing and to make his punishment serve as
a warning to his successors"). Even opponents of late impeachment have noted
strongly that impeachment is a "curb upon the exercise of power in the possession
of those subject to impeachment." Belknap Trial, *supra* note 6, at 40 (argument of
defense counsel).

23. The Federalist No. 65, *supra* note 17, at 399 (Alexander Hamilton) ("ostracism");
Belknap Trial, *supra* note 6, at 92–93 (opinion of Sen. Maxey) ("infamy"); *see also*
State v. Hill, 55 N.W. 794, 796 (Neb. 1893) (rejecting late impeachability in state
case but stating that "[a]ll will concede that disqualification to hold office is a
punishment much greater than removal"); Mitchell Franklin, *Romanist Infamy
and the American Constitutional Conception of Impeachment*, 23 Buff. L. Rev. 313
(1974) (emphasizing extent to which impeachment is about "infamy"). Further
evidence of the significance of disqualification to the Framers' generation is the
fact that all but one of the state constitutions in 1787 that provided specific
impeachment penalties included disqualification. *See* Del. Const. of 1776, art.
XXIII; Mass. Const. of 1780, pt. II, ch. 1, § 2, art. VIII; N.H. Const. of 1784, pt. II,
art. XXXIX; N.Y. Const. of 1777, art. XXXIII; Va. Const. of 1776, art. XVI; *see also*
N.J. Const. of 1776, art. XII (not providing for disqualification). Also notable is that
the First Congress made disqualification a penalty for officials convicted of bribery.
See Act of Apr. 30, 1790, ch. 9, § 21, 1 Stat. 112, 117.

24. *See* Bushnell, *supra* note 1, at 6 (noting that the Senate had only disqualified two
convicts, Judges West Humphreys and Robert Archbald); *id.* at 39 (noting that
"[m]ore than fifty federal judges have resigned while under investigation or after
their impeachment had been recommended to the House of Representatives");
Firmage & Mangrum, *supra* note 1, at 1094 ("Resignation need not represent the
defeat of the impeachment process but instead may be just one aspect of its
successful operation."). Judge Thomas Porteous was impeached, convicted, and
disqualified on December 8, 2010, as this chapter was being edited.

25. *See* Richard A. Posner, An Affair of State: The Investigation, Impeachment, and
Trial of President Clinton 101 n.21 (1999) (stating that possibility of evading
disqualification renders it "unclear whether resignation moots an impeachment
proceeding").

26. Belknap Trial, *supra* note 6, at 359 (opinion of Sen. Norwood). *Cf.* Josh Chafetz,
Leaving the House, 58 Duke L.J. 177, 227–30 (2008) (positing limits on ability of

House members to resign given that resignation could preempt House's use of expulsion power).

27. *See* Belknap Trial, *supra* note 6, at 83 (opinion of Sen. Frelinghuysen) (arguing that resignation cannot end a trial, once begun); *id.* at 101 (opinion of Sen. Christiancy) (hinting at same).

28. Souss, *supra* note 1. One possible response to Souss is that his hypothetical pre-inaugural robber could be impeached if he covers up the crime while in office. For crimes committed and covered up earlier, he could be impeached for committing fraud against the voters to get into office. *Cf.* Gerhardt, *supra* note 1, at 108 (discussing fact that nobody has ever been impeached for private pre-office conduct).

29. *See* Bushnell, *supra* note 1, at 37, 189 (discussing Blount's and Belknap's subsequent careers); Jonathan Turley, *Senate Trials and Factional Disputes: Impeachment as a Madisonian Device*, 49 Duke L.J. 1, 56 (1999) ("At a time of lost public confidence in the integrity of the government, the conduct of a former official can demand a political response. This response in the form of an impeachment may be more important than a legal response in the form of a prosecution.").

30. The Federalist No. 65, *supra* note 17, at 397 (Alexander Hamilton); *see* Gerhardt, *supra* note 1, at 104–05 (expounding on official, political nature of impeachable offenses); Richard M. Pious, *Impeaching the President*, 43 St. Louis U. L.J. 859, 862 (1999) (explaining meaning of "high").

31. 4 William Blackstone, Commentaries *260–61 (discussing impeachment of public officers); *accord* 1 The Works of James Wilson, *supra* note 17, at 426; *see* Raoul Berger, Impeachment: The Constitutional Problems 3–4, 217 (1973) (describing English influences on American impeachment); The Federalist No. 65, *supra* note 17, at 397 (Alexander Hamilton) (referring to British impeachment as "model" for American impeachment); Hoffer & Hull, *supra* note 1, at 8 (describing two "well-defined" categories into which all English impeachments fell after early 1700s); *id.* at 268 (arguing colonial and state impeachment influenced federal law more than English impeachment did); Labovitz, *supra* note 20, at 110–11 (highlighting use of English impeachment cases as "procedural model" in Congress); Gordon S. Wood, The Creation of the American Republic, 1776–1797, at 141 (1969) (describing English Whig roots of American impeachment); Kalt, *supra* note 1, at 24 (discussing decline of English practice of impeaching private citizens).

32. *See* Hoffer & Hull, *supra* note 1, at 3 (describing English impeachment punishments); Kalt, *supra* note 1, at 26–27 (discussing continued use of late impeachment even as punishments weakened).

33. *See* 16 Thomas Bayly Howell, A Complete Collection of State Trials 767–68 (London, T. C. Hansard 1816) (Macclesfield); A. Mervyn Davies, Strange Destiny: A Biography of Warren Hastings 335, 373–74, 377–83, 411–12 (1935) (Hastings). There was one other impeachment during that period: Jacobite conspirator Lord Lovat was impeached, convicted, and executed in 1746 for high treason. Lovat was a peer, not a private citizen, but he was not a minister of government. *See* 18

Howell, *supra*, at 529–858. The only English impeachment since Hastings's was Lord Melville's, in 1806. It too was a late impeachment. *See* Kalt, *supra* note 1, at 27 (discussing Melville case).

34. *See* Hoffer & Hull, *supra* note 1, at 268 (arguing that colonial and state precedents "were far more important in influencing federal law than English examples"). This point pervades Hoffer and Hull's book.

35. *See* Del. Const. of 1776, art. XXIII; Pa. Const. of 1776, ch. 2, § 22; Vt. Const. of 1777, ch. 2, § 20; Va. Const. of 1776, art. XVI; Hoffer & Hull, *supra* note 1, at 84–86 (describing Jefferson case); Kalt, *supra* note 1, at 35 (analyzing these state-constitutional texts to conclude that accountability was stressed over removal).

36. *See* Mass. Const. of 1780, pt. II, ch. 1, § 2, art. VIII; N.H. Const. of 1784, pt. II, art. XXXVIII; N.Y. Const. of 1777, art. XXXIII; S.C. Const. of 1778, art. XXIII; *see also* N.C. Const. of 1776, art. XXIII (providing for impeachment only, not trial, and shedding no light on late impeachability); Kalt, *supra* note 1, at 36–37 (offering further basis for conclusion that failure to mention late impeachment amounted to endorsement of it). The tenth state, New Jersey, wrote its constitution before every state mentioned here besides Virginia. Like the federal constitution, it provides only a mandatory punishment provision and does not speak directly to impeachability. *See* N.J. Const. of 1776, art. XII.

37. *See* Belknap Trial, *supra* note 6, at 363 (discussing familiarity of Framers with state-constitution impeachment provisions); Berger, *supra* note 31, at 91 n.160 (describing American familiarity with English impeachment law); Hoffer & Hull, *supra* note 1, at 96, 266–70 (discussing familiarity of Framers with state impeachment law and cases, downplaying English influence, and criticizing Berger's assumptions). For a general reckoning of the deliberation over impeachment at the Convention, see Labovitz, *supra* note 20, at 2–16.

Hastings's case was mentioned at the Convention in a way that bolsters the notion that the Framers accepted late impeachment. *See* 2 The Records of the Federal Convention of 1787, at 550 (Max Farrand ed., 1911) [hereinafter Farrand] (referring to Hastings, in statement by George Mason); Kalt, *supra* note 1, at 46–48 (analyzing significance, and sloppiness, of Mason's mention of Hastings); *see also* Belknap Trial, *supra* note 6, at 98 (opinion of Sen. Howe) (noting that Hastings's "case was present to all minds, and was debated by all lips" at the Convention); Bestor, *supra* note 1, at 284 (noting timing of Hastings's trial vis-à-vis state constitutional ratifying conventions).

38. 2 Farrand, *supra* note 37, at 64; Gerhardt, *supra* note 1, at 80 (noting focus of convention discussion on presidential impeachment *while* in office); Kalt, *supra* note 1, at 43–46 (highlighting evidence from the debate of the Framers' concern for accountability and deterrence). For the evolution of the relevant impeachment provisions at the Convention, see 1 Farrand, *supra* note 37, at 22, 78; 2 *id.* at 53, 64–69. Another item that indirectly touched upon late impeachment was John Rutledge and Gouverneur Morris's unsuccessful proposal to suspend impeached officers pending their trial and acquittal. This might suggest that impeachment could only involve

sitting officers. Then again, it might just mean that Rutledge and Morris wanted to consider suspension in those cases that did. 2 *id.* at 612–13.

39. The Federalist No. 69, *supra* note 17, at 416 (Alexander Hamilton). To take another example from *The Federalist,* James Madison noted that "The President of the United States is impeachable at any time during his continuance in office," which might sound like a statement against late impeachment. But Madison wrote this in a discussion of the length of congressional and presidential terms, and was simply noting the possibility that the president might leave office early. *Id.* No. 39, at 242 (James Madison).

40. 4 Elliot's Debates, *supra* note 20, at 32–35.

41. *See* Gerhardt, *supra* note 1, at 79 (offering similar argument).

42. 3 Asher C. Hinds, Hinds' Precedents of the House of Representatives 307 & n.3 (1907) (describing "nature of impeachment"); *see id.* § 2007, at 310–21 (discussing Belknap case); Gerhardt, *supra* note 1, at 49 (discussing congressional prerogative to revisit constitutional precedents); Kalt, *supra* note 1, at 103–04 (discussing use of Belknap precedent in Archbald impeachment); Neal Kumar Katyal, *Impeachment as Congressional Constitutional Interpretation,* Law & Contemp. Probs., Spring 2000, at 169, 183–88 (arguing that rationales for following precedent are not compelling in legislative context).

43. David P. Currie, The Constitution in Congress: The Federalist Period, 1789–1801, at 278–81 (1997); *see* Francis Wharton, State Trials of the United States During the Administrations of Washington and Adams 200–07, 250–317 (Burt Franklin 1970) (1849) (Blount's case); Bushnell, *supra* note 1, at 27–38 (discussing Blount). This is the conventional understanding of *Blount,* but the record does not formally indicate the reason why each senator voted as he did.

44. *See* Bushnell, *supra* note 1, at 166–67, 171 (describing Belknap's conduct and intentions).

45. Belknap Trial, *supra* note 6, at iii, 2; *see* 4 Cong. Rec. 1433 (1876) (approving resolution of impeachment); *id.* at 1431 (statement of Rep. Bass) (arguing that it was for the Senate to decide jurisdiction); Belknap Trial, *supra* note 6, at 14–15 (indicating political climate); Bushnell, *supra* note 1, at 166–67 (describing political climate in Congress in 1876); Michael F. Holt, By One Vote 67–68 (2008) (describing Democratic election-year strategy of aggressively investigating Grant administration).

46. *See* Belknap Trial, *supra* note 6, at 6, 15–72, 77–158 (debating Senate's jurisdiction from April 28 to May 29).

47. *See id.* at 38–39, 53, 57–58, 98–99, 118–20, 156 (Constitutional Convention); *id.* at 120–21, 150 (state ratification debates); *id.* at 28, 36–37, 42 (Blount); *id.* at 30, 40, 42, 152 (Story); *id.* at 111–12 (Rawle and Adams); *see also* Kalt, *supra* note 1, at 97–99 (recounting, indexing, and cross-referencing arguments more extensively); note 1, *supra* (citing Rawle).

48. *See* Belknap Trial, *supra* note 6, at 76 (recording vote); Bushnell, *supra* note 1, at 176 (breaking down vote by party). One of those counted as a Republican here, Newton Booth, was technically elected as a member of the Anti-Monopoly Party.

49. *See* Bushnell, *supra* note 1, at 186 (describing and tallying votes); Gerhardt, *supra* note 1, at 52 (discussing mixed precedential signals sent by Senate); Van Tassel & Finkelman, *supra* note 20, at 193 (describing and tallying votes).

50. *See* Belknap Trial, *supra* note 6, at 158 (opinion of Sen. Cragin) (relying on Belknap's potential criminal liability); *cf.* Gerhardt, *supra* note 1, at 79 (stating that Congress has failed to successfully late-impeach for political, not constitutional, reasons); Van Tassel & Finkelman, *supra* note 20, at 12 ("As a practical matter, the fact that the Senate did not convict Belknap, suggests that except in extraordinary circumstances, resignation will bring the impeachment process to a close.").

51. *Proceedings of the United States Senate in the Trial of Impeachment of George W. English, District Judge of the United States for the Eastern District of Illinois*, S. Doc. No. 69-177, at 80–81 (1926) [hereinafter *English Trial*] (House resolution); *id.* at 91–92 (speech of Sen. Fletcher) ("distinctly understood"); Staff of House Comm. on the Judiciary, 93d Cong., Impeachment: Selected Materials on Procedure 891 (Comm. Print 1974) (reproducing House managers' communication); *see English Trial, supra*, at 76–78 (showing timing of trial and resignation); *id.* at 81–93 (debating legality and desirability of proceeding); *id.* at 91 (speech of Sen. King) (speaking, alone, against late impeachability when House wants case dismissed).

52. *See* H.R. Rep. No. 79-1639, at 38–39 (1946) (recommending against proceeding with impeachment of Judge Albert Johnson, because he had resigned and relinquished his pension, but specifically reaffirming that he *could* be impeached); *id.* at 45 (views of Rep. Cravens) (dissenting from committee's conclusion favoring late impeachability); Bushnell, *supra* note 1, at 39 (noting dozens of judicial resignation cases).

53. *See* Nixon v. United States, 506 U.S. 224 (1993).

54. *See* Powell v. McCormack, 395 U.S. 486 (1969).

55. *See* Gerhardt, *supra* note 1, at 125 (suggesting justiciability of a challenge to impeachment of someone arguably not subject to impeachment).

56. Nixon-era commentary includes Dixon Memo, *supra* note 1, at 4–5; Bestor, *supra* note 1, at 277–81; Firmage & Mangrum, *supra* note 1, at 1089–94. All these sources supported late impeachability. Clinton-era commentary was more mixed. Support for late impeachability included *President Clinton's Eleventh Hour Pardons, supra* note 1, at 86 (colloquy between Sen. Specter and Benton Becker) (assuming late impeachability); Brian Kalt, ". . . And Stay Out!": *The Constitutional Case for Post-Presidential Impeachment*, Jurist (Mar. 1, 2001), http://jurist.law.pitt.edu/pardonop3.htm; Williams, *supra* note 1. Opposition included *President Clinton's Eleventh Hour Pardons, supra* note 1, at 91–92 (statement of Ken Gormley); Levin, *supra* note 1; Souss, *supra* note 1.

57. *See* Kalt, *supra* note 1, at 133–34 (worrying about potential for Congress to abuse late impeachment); *cf.* Gerhardt, *supra* note 1, at 53–58 (discussing Congress's historical lack of abuse of its impeachment powers).

Chapter 6. The Third-Term Controversy

1. A good accounting and analysis of dozens of term-limit evasions appears in a working paper by Zachary Elkins, Tom Ginsburg, and James Melton, "On the Evasion of Term Limits" (Jan. 15, 2010, draft on file with author). The paper finds that when term limits are challenged, they usually fall. Sometimes they are repealed, sometimes they are ignored, and sometimes they are worked around as in this chapter.

2. For reviews of the origins of, and proposed changes to, constitutional treatment of presidential terms, see 93 Cong. Rec. 1952–54 (1947); Alan P. Grimes, Democracy and the Amendments to the Constitution 115 (1978); 2 Proposed Amendments to the U.S. Constitution, 1787–2001, at 657–66 (John R. Vile ed., 2003); Charles W. Stein, The Third-Term Tradition (1943); Earl Spangler, Presidential Tenure and Constitutional Limitation (1977); Bruce G. Peabody & Scott E. Gant, *The Twice and Future President*, 83 Minn. L. Rev. 565, 570–93 (1999) (tracing development of two-term tradition, such as it was, and of proposals to constitutionalize term limits); Stephen W. Stathis, *The Twenty-Second Amendment*, 7 Const. Comment. 61, 62–65 (1990). Stein notes that, along with Presidents Grant (who was nearly nominated for a third term in 1880 after being elected in 1868 and 1872) and Theodore Roosevelt (who ran for a third term in 1912 after succeeding to the presidency in 1901 and being elected in 1904), the era's other two-term presidents (Cleveland, McKinley, Wilson, and Coolidge) all spurred discussion of third terms.

3. *See* Stein, *supra* note 2, at 317–40 (discussing 1940 campaign); Stathis, *supra* note 2, at 65 (same); Philip Kinsley, *Hits "3d Term Dictator,"* Chi. Daily Trib., Oct. 15, 1940, at 1 (noting Willkie's rhetoric).

4. *See* 93 Cong. Rec. 48 (1947) (introducing H.R.J. Res. 27 on January 3, 1947); Grimes, *supra* note 2, at 113–22 (discussing congressional debate and action on the amendment); Stathis, *supra* note 2, at 65–68 (same).

5. *Cf.* 93 Cong. Rec. 1947 (1947) (statement of Sen. Lucas) (worrying about inability under term-limit regime to cope properly with "an atomic emergency"); Stein, *supra* note 2, at 12–15 (citing Charles Cotesworth Pinckney, George Washington, James Madison, and Alexander Hamilton for notion that term limits could cause dangerous lack of continuity during crises); Peabody & Gant, *supra* note 2, at 570 n.20, 634 n.284 (agreeing that third-term scenarios are plausible).

6. *See Presidential Terms of Office: Hearing Before the Subcomm. on Constitutional Amendments of the S. Comm. on the Judiciary*, 86th Cong. 3 (1959) (statement of Sen. Kefauver) (arguing that repeal might take too long in a crisis); 93 Cong. Rec. 2391 (1947) (statement of Rep. Rankin) (arguing, in favor of amendment, that "the Constitution can be amended at any time"); Stathis, *supra* note 2, at 87 (discussing difficulty of repealing an amendment quickly, even in an emergency). The fastest-ever amendment—the Twenty-Sixth, lowering the voting age to eighteen—still took more than three months to ratify. The next fastest, the Twelfth, took over six months.

7. *See* Richard Albert, *The Evolving Vice Presidency*, 78 Temp. L. Rev. 811, 857 & nn.314–15 (2005) (collecting six sources that declare President Clinton eligible for vice presidency in 2000 or 2004); Peabody & Gant, *supra* note 2, at 602–10 (summarizing repeal proposals, from Truman era through Clinton era); Stathis, *supra* note 2, at 76–77 (noting months of discussion of possibility of President Eisenhower running for vice president in 1960); *id.* at 78–81 (discussing campaign to repeal term limits and allow President Reagan to run for president in 1988); George Dixon, *Ike's Right to V.P. Spot*, Wash. Post & Times-Herald, Jan. 21, 1960, at A23 (offering opinion of Democratic senator that President Eisenhower could run for vice president and succeed to the presidency); James Jackson Kilpatrick, *The Ike Plan Cometh*, Nat'l Rev., June 16, 1964, at 483 (arguing in detail for same).

8. David A. Strauss, *The Irrelevance of Constitutional Amendments*, 114 Harv. L. Rev. 1457, 1496 (2001).

9. *See* Peabody & Gant, *supra* note 2. Among many others advancing the same basic argument, in less detail, are Kilpatrick, *supra* note 7, at 483; Peter Baker, *VP Bill? Depends on Meaning of "Elected,"* Wash. Post., Oct. 20, 2006, at A19 (citing Prof. Kathleen M. Sullivan and bipartisan group of former White House lawyers); Michael C. Dorf, *The Case for a Gore-Clinton Ticket*, Findlaw (July 31, 2000), http://writ.news.findlaw.com/dorf/20000731.html; Jack Shafer, *Vice President Bill Clinton? Take 3*, Slate (Sept. 7, 2000), http://www.slate.com/id/1006013.

10. U.S. Const. amend. XXII; *see* Peabody & Gant, *supra* note 2, at 613.

11. 93 Cong. Rec. 870 (1947) (statement of Rep. Michener); *see* H.R.J. Res. 27, 80th Cong. (1947) (emphasis added) (as introduced by Rep. Michener); H.R. Rep. No. 80-17, at 1 (1947) (emphasis added) (as approved by House Judiciary Committee); 93 Cong. Rec. 841–72 (1947) (House debate); *see also* Peabody & Gant, *supra* note 2, at 593–99 (describing House and Senate processes, including original and amended texts); Kilpatrick, *supra* note 7, at 484 (recounting language changes). The House language tracked that of a proposed amendment from 1927. *See* 93 Cong. Rec. 1954 (1947) (quoting 1927 amendment).

12. *See* S. Rep. No. 80-34, at 1–3 (1947) (emphasis added) (discussing changes made by Senate Judiciary Committee to House-passed resolution, to preclude future service as acting president); Peabody & Gant, *supra* note 2, at 613, 616 & n.224 (stating significance of contrast between Senate Judiciary Committee language and final amendment).

13. *See* 93 Cong. Rec. 1863 (1947) (statement of Sen. Magnuson); Peabody & Gant, *supra* note 2, at 595 & n.145 (discussing Magnuson proposal); Kilpatrick, *supra* note 7, at 485 (same).

14. *See* U.S. Const. amend. XXII; 93 Cong. Rec. 1938 (1947) (statement of Sen. Wiley) (introducing and discussing compromise language, which was eventually adopted); Peabody & Gant, *supra* note 2, at 597–600 (discussing Senate proceedings); Kilpatrick, *supra* note 7, at 484–85 (noting effect of Senate's changed language).

15. Those writing against the loophole theory include Albert, *supra* note 7, at 858–59; James R. Whitson, *Can a Two-Term President Be Vice President?*, President Elect (Aug. 19, 2000), http://www.presidentelect.org/art_preztoveep.html. Citations connected to the Eisenhower and Clinton cases are in note 7, *supra*.

16. One example of the presumption against the loophole, strongly expressed, appeared in a blog post by Professor John Eastman excoriating Professor Stephen Gillers for his *New York Times* op-ed advancing the loophole theory. *See* John Eastman, The Claremont Institute: The Remedy (Mar. 4, 2004), http://www. claremont.org/weblog (blog now defunct; on file with author) ("The contention is so preposterous, and so obviously wrong, that one wonders how a nationally renowned law professor at one of the top law schools in the nation could make such a mistake. Professor Gillers . . . quite obviously knows little about the Constitution.").

17. *See* 93 Cong. Rec. 1863–67 (1947) (Senate debate over Magnuson proposal); *id.* at 2389 (statement of Rep. Michener) (labeling Senate's treatment of partial terms as only material change from House version, and characterizing Senate bill as limiting "serv[ic]e" to ten years); Peabody & Gant, *supra* note 2, at 600 (presuming that loophole was created "unwittingly"). Notably, Senator Tydings referred to Senator Magnuson's language as providing for "two elected terms" but said in the very next sentence that he wanted "to see the Presidency limited to two terms," unmodified. 93 Cong. Rec. 1863 (1947). As a general matter, Peabody and Gant note that the debate on the amendment was surprisingly thin, both in Congress and in the ratifying states. *See* Peabody & Gant, *supra* note 2, at 615 & n.223.

    One statement was close to a "peep." Later in the debate, Magnuson amended his language to bar only two *consecutive* terms. Senator Revercomb noted that this would allow a person to serve as president for twelve years minus one day (by succeeding to the office on the second day of the term), leave office and allow a term to elapse, and then return to serve another twelve years minus one day. *See* 93 Cong. Rec. 1938–39, 1946 (1947). Revercomb thus foresaw the possibility of a former president reentering office through succession. But it appears that he set the second period as twelve years minus one day (instead of eight years) in order to inflate the total amount of time a person could serve, rather than to make a point about reentering office through succession.

18. *See* Albert, *supra* note 7, at 857–59 (declaring that, properly read, Twenty-Second Amendment makes presidents "ineligible" to the office of president); Peabody & Gant, *supra* note 2, at 601 (expressing confidence that legislative intent does not support the loophole theory); *cf. id.* at 629–31 (considering extent to which avoiding term limits through succession violates "spirit" of Twenty-Second Amendment). Peabody and Gant conclude that invocations of the "spirit" of the Constitution are not as prominent as they once were, but they do not offer much general discussion of "purposive" interpretations.

19. *See* Henry M. Hart, Jr. & Albert M. Sacks, The Legal Process 1374 (William N. Eskridge, Jr. & Philip P. Frickey eds., 1994) (explaining, albeit for statutes and not

constitutional provisions, that an interpretive approach should operate "so as to carry out the [legislative] purpose as best it can, making sure, however, that it does not give the words either (a) a meaning they will not bear, or (b) a meaning which would violate any established policy of clear statement"); John F. Manning, *The Eleventh Amendment and the Reading of Precise Constitutional Texts*, 113 Yale L.J. 1663, 1668–70 (2004) (criticizing notion of using intent to venture beyond a precisely written text); *cf.* Miranda McGowan, *Do as I Do, Not as I Say: An Empirical Investigation of Justice Scalia's Ordinary Meaning Method of Statutory Interpretation*, 78 Miss. L.J. 129, 188–89 (2008) (arguing that even purportedly textualist Justice Scalia, "if statutory purpose requires it, . . . is willing to adopt second-best textual interpretations"). Manning's argument is rooted in the Supreme Court's Eleventh Amendment sovereign-immunity jurisprudence, in which the Court goes far beyond the text of the amendment in order to vindicate the broader purposes and understandings of the original Constitution's Framers. But the Twenty-Second Amendment doesn't even do that—it cannot be construed as a manifestation of a broader underlying principle resident in the Constitution.

20. *See* Lawrence C. Marshall, *Fighting the Words of the Eleventh Amendment*, 102 Harv. L. Rev. 1342, 1345 (1989) ("[A]t times the originalist will disregard the plain meaning of the text in favor of a history-based theory of what the framers and supporters must have intended."); *see also* Whitson, *supra* note 15 (arguing against two-termers' eligibility because Supreme Court often considers legislative intent).

21. Professor Richard Hasen has identified what he calls the "Democracy Canon," under which the courts interpret provisions in a way that errs on the side of allowing more people to vote and run for office. *See* Richard L. Hasen, *The Democracy Canon*, 62 Stan. L. Rev. 69 (2009). Reading the word "elected" in the Twenty-Second Amendment narrowly would be an example of this.

    The only amendment that restricted rights as directly as the Twenty-Second was the Eighteenth, which established Prohibition, and which was repealed. *See Presidential Terms of Office*, *supra* note 6, at 2, 10, 12 (statements of Sen. Kefauver) (making this point).

22. *See* Peabody & Gant, *supra* note 2, at 618 (discussing initial lack of need to specify vice-presidential qualifications). The legislative history of the Twelfth Amendment shows that, while the other provisions of the amendment were hotly contested, the clause on vice-presidential qualifications was uncontroversial and was barely discussed. *See* 13 Annals of Cong. 84 (1803) (introducing clause). The only exception came obliquely, in a long speech by Senator Uriah Tracy. In one passage, he criticized the House's cursory approach to the amendment process, noting that it had overlooked the need for a qualification requirement, twice passing a version of the amendment that lacked one. Tracy complained that "for aught that they had guarded against, we might have had a man [succeeding to] the Chief Magistracy from Morocco, a foreigner, who had not been in the country a month." *Id.* at 178 (statement of Sen. Tracy); *see also id.* at 170 (statement of Sen. Tracy) (noting that original Constitution spoke only of qualifications for president, not for vice

president). *See generally id.* at 372–85, 646–777 (House debate on Twelfth Amendment); *id.* at 16–27, 81–210 (Senate debate).

23. U.S. Const. art. II, § 1, cl. 5 (citizenship, age, and residency); *id.* amend. XIV, § 3 (loyalty); *see* Peabody & Gant, *supra* note 2, at 619 (drawing this connection between Twelfth Amendment and Article II).

24. For examples of the "easy" answer, see, e.g., Albert, *supra* note 7, at 858–59; Arthur Krock, *"Ike for V.P." Idea Perished 160 Years Ago*, N.Y. Times, Oct. 10, 1963, at 40; Eastman, *supra* note 16 (rejecting loophole theory as sophistry because "[o]ne who legally cannot be elected to the office is ineligible for the office").

25. *See* Eugene Volokh, *Clinton as VP?*, The Volokh Conspiracy (Mar. 8, 2004), http://volokh.com/2004_02_29_volokh_archive.html#107833460411712131 ("I think that as a matter of common usage, 'eligible' in the 12th Amendment should be interpreted as meaning 'eligible in the ordinary course of things,' not 'eligible in a small subset of cases, though ineligible in the ordinary course of things.'"). The electable/eligible synonym argument is typically based on Twelfth Amendment– era dictionaries or on the two words' common origin from the Latin ēligĕre (to choose). *See, e.g.,* Eugene Volokh, *Bill Clinton for Vice-President?*, The Volokh Conspiracy (June 19, 2006), http://volokh.com/2006/06/19/bill-clinton-for-vice-president (citing *Bouvier's Law Dictionary*); *id.,* comment of Mike S., http://volokh.com/2006/06/19/bill-clinton-for-vice-president/#comment-144465 (noting common Latin origin). One should be especially careful with the Latin-origin argument. Left-handed people can still be dextrous, right-handed people can still be sinister, and a dilapidated building needn't be made of stone. The eligible/electable link is not as easy to dismiss as these examples, but neither is it as obviously correct as its proponents would have it.

26. This appears to be the interpretation reached by President Eisenhower's attorney general, when asked whether the two-term president could run for vice president. *See* Peabody & Gant, *supra* note 2, at 605 & n.185 (citing President Eisenhower's statement at a press conference and Vice President Nixon's statement to the *New York Times*). *But see* Felix Belair, Jr., *Nixon Is His Choice, President Indicates*, N.Y. Times, Jan. 14, 1960, at 1 (suggesting that president's "inner circle" had determined that Eisenhower could not succeed to the presidency). Others suggesting the interpretation include Peabody & Gant, *supra* note 2, at 619–20; Dorf, *supra* note 9.

27. Baker, *supra* note 9, at A19 (quoting e-mail from Judge Posner).

28. *See* Sarah Helen Duggin & Mary Beth Collins, *"Natural Born" in the USA,* 85 B.U. L. Rev. 53, 61–62, 109 & n.293 (2005) (asserting that presidential and vice-presidential qualification disputes would be resolved in court); *id.* at 112–14 (analyzing potential plaintiffs); Daniel P. Tokaji, Commentary, *The Justiciability of Eligibility,* 107 Mich. L. Rev. First Impressions 31 (2008), www.michiganlawreview.org/assets/fi/107/tokaji.pdf (discussing difficulty in bringing a justiciable challenge to presidential candidate's eligibility, but concluding that state-court challenges would work, especially if plaintiff was a major-party candidate). Courts have ruled

that a citizen's general interest in having the Constitution followed is not suffi-cient to give that citizen standing to sue. The citizen must have some distinct injury of a different nature than his or her fellow citizens. *See, e.g.,* Jones v. Bush, 122 F. Supp. 2d 713 (N.D. Tex.) (rejecting, for lack of standing, citizens' challenge to Texas casting electoral votes for Texan George W. Bush and alleged Texan Dick Cheney), *aff'd* 244 F.3d 134 (5th Cir. 2000).

29. *See* Duggin & Collins, *supra* note 28, at 117–18 (noting advantages of resolving qualifications disputes sooner rather than later).

30. U.S. Const. art. I, § 5, cl. 1 (emphasis added) (congressional election disputes); *see* Vasan Kesavan, *Is the Electoral Count Act Unconstitutional?*, 80 N.C. L. Rev. 1653, 1703–04 (2002) (discussing congressional power to count and adjudge validity of electoral votes); Stephen A. Siegel, *The Conscientious Congressman's Guide to the Electoral Count Act of 1887*, 56 Fla. L. Rev. 541, 551–66 (2004) (discussing nine-teenth-century perspectives on this congressional power). A good history of the political-question doctrine, including its recent decline, is Rachel E. Barkow, *More Supreme Than Court?: The Fall of the Political Question Doctrine and the Rise of Judicial Supremacy*, 102 Colum. L. Rev. 237 (2002).

The Electoral Count Act of 1887, 24 Stat. 373, codified at 3 U.S.C. §§ 5, 6, 15 [here-inafter 1887 Act], governs the resolution of electoral-vote disputes in Congress on Counting Day. The legislative history of the act, discussed by Justice Breyer in *Bush v. Gore*, includes relevant statements by the sponsor: "The power to judge of the legality of the votes is a necessary consequent of the power to count," and "Under the Constitution who else could decide?" Bush v. Gore, 531 U.S. 98, 154 (Breyer, J., dissenting) (quoting 18 Cong. Rec. 30–31 (1886) (remarks of Rep. Caldwell)).

31. 1887 Act, *supra* note 30. For a helpful summary of this era, including another controversy over electoral votes from 1868, see Barkow, *supra* note 30, at 287–92.

32. Barkow, *supra* note 30, at 302; *see Bush*, 531 U.S. at 153–58 (Breyer, J., dissenting) (discussing political-question argument, joined by Justices Stevens and Ginsburg); *id.* at 153 (speaking only of congressional authority over resolving disputes over electoral votes—disputes that arise only after elections); Elizabeth Garrett, *Leaving the Decision to Congress, in* The Vote: Bush, Gore, and the Supreme Court 38 (Cass R. Sunstein & Richard A. Epstein eds., 2001) (lamenting Court's and public's unwarranted and damaging lack of faith in Congress's ability to resolve *Bush*); Barkow, *supra* note 30, at 298 ("To be sure, having a politically determined outcome might have taken far longer and involved more openly partisan debate."); *see also* Peter Berkowitz, *One Year Later: The Continuing Controversy over* Bush v. Gore, Nat'l Rev. Online (Dec. 12, 2001), http://old.nationalreview.com/comment/comment-berkowitz121201.shtml (collecting political-question commentary on *Bush v. Gore*).

33. *See* Duggin & Collins, *supra* note 28, at 123–25 (making similar points about polit-ical questions for an analogous scenario). Duggin and Collins have a lengthy treat-ment of justiciability issues—who can bring a suit, in what forum, and

when—surrounding challenges to a presidential candidate's citizenship. *Id.* at 112–26. Their analysis is very helpful and analogous to justiciability in the term-limit context. Other justiciability issues (such as standing and ripeness) are not quite as knotty.

34. *See* 3 U.S.C. § 15 (2006); Siegel, *supra* note 30, at 554 & n.66, 619 & n.474 (explaining original understanding of "regularly given," which allowed Congress to reject otherwise valid and certified votes cast for constitutionally disqualified candidates). Vasan Kesavan makes a fairly exhaustive argument that the 1887 Act is unconstitutional and that Congress has no authority to regulate so thoroughly in this area. *See* Kesavan, *supra* note 30. Of particular interest here, he argues that the electors get the last word, not Congress, so that a congressional declaration that a bona fide electoral certificate was not "regularly given" would be unconstitutional. *Id.* at 1774. Kesavan argues that the Framers apparently understood that the president of the Senate would be the counter, not the House and Senate, but that the interpretation evolved into the latter. *See id.* at 1706–08. Some people, including some members of Congress, consider the counting function to be merely ministerial. *See id.* at 1713–17.

35. *See* Siegel, *supra* note 30, at 619 & n.474 (giving broad view of congressional power under Electoral Count Act of 1887 to reject votes cast for constitutionally unqualified candidates). Even in the two most serious disputes, Congress decided both cases in a passive way, deferring to the state courts and executive officials in the first case, and to the elector in the second. *See* Kesavan, *supra* note 30, at 1691–94.

36. *See* Cong. Globe, 42d Cong., 3d Sess. 1296–99 (1873) (debating Greeley electoral votes); Siegel, *supra* note 30, at 554 & n.66, 619 & n.474 (describing intent of 1887 law). After accepting their power to judge, many more members of Congress voted to count Greeley's votes than to void them. The vote in the Senate was 44–19 to count them, while the vote in the House was a narrow 101–99 against counting them. Under the rule in place at the time, though, challenged electoral votes did not count unless both houses agreed that they were valid. *See* Kesavan, *supra* note 30, at 1676, 1688 (describing and criticizing vote and both-house rule).

37. *See* 3 U.S.C. § 15 (2006) (requiring objection from at least one senator and one representative); Berkowitz, *supra* note 32 (distinguishing Congress's final authority from exclusive authority, and noting lack of latter).

38. *See* S. Res. 511 (2008) (declaring John McCain a "natural born Citizen"); Duggin & Collins, *supra* note 28, at 124 (describing post-election intervention by Congress as "not inconceivable"); *cf.* Sanford Levinson, Bush v. Gore *and the French Revolution*, Law & Contemp. Probs., Summer 2002, at 7, 26 (noting Congress's acceptance of Supreme Court supremacy in 2000 election).

39. *See* 93 Cong. Rec. 858 (1947) (statement of Rep. Mundt) (advocating for Twenty-Second Amendment on anti-incumbent grounds); *id.* at 1939 (statement of Sen. Magnuson) (stating core purpose of amendment as avoiding incumbent using his leverage to win successive terms); Dorf, *supra* note 9 (contending that it would not violate Twenty-Second Amendment's spirit for two-termer to run for vice

president with intention of actually serving in that capacity); Kilpatrick, *supra* note 7, at 486 (arguing that Twenty-Second Amendment's spirit concerned only consecutive terms); *cf.* Peabody & Gant, *supra* note 2, at 622–24 (positing that having a placeholder run for president with open intention of stepping aside would be less constitutionally problematic than covert plan to do so; latter would conflict with constitutional notions of republican government).

40. *See* Peabody & Gant, *supra* note 2, at 568–69 (discussing succession from further down the line).

41. *See* 3 U.S.C. § 19(e) (2006); *cf.* Peabody & Gant, *supra* note 2, at 619 (surmising that vice presidents barred from succeeding to the presidency could still constitutionally act as president).

42. U.S. Const. amend. XX, § 3 (stating that "Congress may by law provide for the case wherein neither a President elect nor a Vice President elect shall have qualified, declaring who then shall act as President," and that "such *person* shall act accordingly") (emphasis added); *see* Edward S. Corwin, The President: Office and Powers, 1787–1984, at 62 (Randall W. Bland et al. eds., 5th rev. ed. 1984) (noting that Congress implemented Section 3 simply by including "failure to qualify" in 1947 succession law).

43. Stephen Gillers, *Who Says the Election Has a Dec. 12 Deadline?*, N.Y. Times, Dec. 2, 2000, at A19. Along the same lines, Congress could put former presidents in the regular line of succession as well. *See* Peabody & Gant, *supra* note 2, at 634 (making this suggestion). As argued in Chapter 4, ex-presidents might need to be "officers" to be eligible, but Congress could create an "office" of president emeritus (perhaps with an age limit or a restriction to those of the same party as the current president), whose duty would be to prepare to retake power in an emergency.

44. *See* Strauss, *supra* note 8, at 1495 (offering "spouse" and "crony" options, as evidence of Twenty-Second Amendment's irrelevance). The Alabama Constitution's language also precluded Wallace from becoming lieutenant governor, because it precluded him from any state office for a year after his term as governor expired. *See* Ala. Const. § 116, *amended by* Ala. Const. amend. 282. When Alabama replaced its one-term limit with a two-term limit in 1968, it used language that allows a "Lurleen" subterfuge, and also a "President Frederick" subterfuge. *See* Ala. Const. amend. 282. After his hiatus, Wallace was elected to two terms in 1970 and 1974, stepped aside in respect of the new limit, and was elected to one more term in 1982.

45. 49 Cong. Rec. 2259 (1913) (statement of Sen. Lodge).

46. 3 U.S.C. § 19(e) (2006).

47. *See Larry King Live* (CNN television broadcast, June 27, 2004) (interview with President Clinton).

48. *See* Stephen L. Carter, *Constitutional Improprieties*, 57 U. Chi. L. Rev. 357 (1990); Peabody & Gant, *supra* note 2, at 632–33 (invoking Carter).

49. Dixon, *supra* note 7, at A23 (characterizing comments of Dean Acheson).

Chapter 7. Getting Out of Trouble

1. *See* Clinton v. Jones, 520 U.S. 681 (1997); United States v. Nixon, 418 U.S. 683 (1974). The decision against Nixon was 8–0; Nixon appointed three of the eight. A fourth Nixon appointee, Justice Rehnquist, recused himself.

2. Bush v. Gore, 531 U.S. 98 (2000); *cf.* Frank B. Cross, *Political Science and the New Legal Realism*, 92 Nw. U. L. Rev. 251, 324 (1997) (admonishing Congress to find ways of drafting that prevent politicized judges from ignoring congressional intent). Cass Sunstein offers a very helpful understanding of the politicized nature of *Bush v. Gore*, and of politicized cases in general, in Cass R. Sunstein, *Introduction: Of Law and Politics, in* The Vote: Bush, Gore, and the Supreme Court 1, 4–6 (Cass R. Sunstein & Richard A. Epstein eds., 2001). The rest of the volume is a good compendium of insights about politicized cases in general, and *Bush v. Gore* in particular. One article in it makes a strong but lonely case, countering the "perfectly politicized" perception of *Bush v. Gore*, that the justices' divisions in *Bush v. Gore* tracked their divisions in other, nonpartisan cases concerning the law of democracy. *See* Richard H. Pildes, *Democracy and Disorder, in* The Vote, *supra*, at 140.

3. *Cf.* Neal Kumar Katyal, *Legislative Constitutional Interpretation*, 50 Duke L.J. 1335, 1389 (2001) (noting impact in Congress, not court, of the potential application of current decisions to an unknown future); Adrian Vermeule, *Veil of Ignorance Rules in Constitutional Law*, 111 Yale L.J. 399, 416–19 (2001) (noting that politicians' current interests loom much larger than their future ones).

4. *See* Richard A. Posner, How Judges Think 289 (2008) (discussing why judges believe they are following law, even though—to Posner—it is clear that they merely make political choices); Richard A. Posner, The Federal Courts 311–12 (1996) (explaining that "professional opinion" constrains judges to be consistent and to draw from a limited set of acceptable legal arguments, or else be labeled "unprincipled").

5. *See* William N. Eskridge, Jr. & Sanford Levinson, *Introduction, in* Constitutional Stupidities, Constitutional Tragedies 1, 5 (1998) (noting that constitutional "stupidities" tend to be structural provisions and not open-ended provisions that are easier to optimize through loose interpretation). Political scientists tend to be adamant that judges do little more than pursue their political preferences. (I have been ridiculed by more than one of them for asserting otherwise.) Lawyers generally don't deny that politics can matter—in the Supreme Court, in hard cases, etc.—but they generally defend the role of legal doctrine as well. My own beliefs and opinions on this debate comport with those in Cross, *supra* note 2. Cross notes two main things: that lawyers ignore the hard data that political scientists have amassed to back up their "attitudinal model," but that political scientists ignore some very important flaws and limitations in the attitudinal model. (My admiration for Cross's article might reflect the extent to which it reinforced beliefs I already had.) *See generally* Jeffrey A. Segal & Harold J. Spaeth, The Supreme Court

and the Attitudinal Model Revisited (2002) (providing leading account of attitudinal model).

6. *See* Elizabeth Garrett, *Leaving the Decision to Congress, in* The Vote, *supra* note 2, at
38; *see also* Samuel Issacharoff, *Political Judgments, in* The Vote, *supra* note 2, at 55
(offering further criticism of Court's recent unwillingness to defer to Congress
and states in election cases); Frank I. Michelman, *Suspicion, or the New Prince, in*
The Vote, *supra* note 2, at 123 (same).

7. *See* Roger H. Davidson, *The Lawmaking Congress*, Law & Contemp. Probs.,
Autumn 1993, at 99, 118 (noting tendency of Congress to "interpret[] constitutional language in terms of its impact on specific constituency interests"); Neal
Devins, *Reanimator: Mark Tushnet and the Second Coming of the Imperial Presidency*,
34 U. Rich. L. Rev. 359, 366 (2000) (depicting congressional committees as seeing
"constitutional arguments as simply another roadblock"); Sanford Levinson, Bush
v. Gore *and the French Revolution*, Law & Contemp. Probs., Summer 2002, at 7,
17–28 (describing Supreme Court's "monarch-like" credibility with public, and
assertiveness in constitutional matters).

8. *See* Josh Chafetz, *Executive Branch Contempt of Congress*, 76 U. Chi. L. Rev. 1083,
1146–56 (2009) (arguing that courts do great damage by preempting congressional constitutional decision making); Garrett, *supra* note 6, at 38–39 (praising
Congress's ability to resolve constitutional disputes and noting damage caused by
denying it the opportunity); Ronald J. Krotoszynski, Jr., *An* Epitaphios *for Neutral
Principles in Constitutional Law*, 90 Geo. L.J. 2087, 2136 (2002) ("When judges
become politicians, the rule of law dies."); Michelman, *supra* note 6, at 133 (preferring, in *Bush v. Gore*, potential party-line vote in Congress to actual one in Supreme
Court); Keith E. Whittington, *The Death of the Legalized Constitution and the Specter
of Judicial Review, in* Courts and the Culture Wars 27, 38 (Bradley C. S. Watson ed.,
2002) (same); Michael J. Gerhardt, *Judging Congress*, 89 B.U. L. Rev. 525, 536–37
(2009) (noting difference between Congress's constitutional "construction" and
courts' constitutional "interpretation").

9. *See* Jane S. Schacter, *Political Accountability, Proxy Accountability, and the
Democratic Legitimacy of Legislatures, in* The Least Examined Branch 45, 73–75
(Richard W. Bauman & Tsvi Kahana eds., 2006) (concluding that legislative
accountability is "thin, sporadic, and unequal," such that it is unrealistic simply to
label Congress as accountable and courts as not); Katyal, *supra* note 3, at 1382–85
(advocating consideration of "popular views and beliefs" when Congress interprets constitutional provisions, but noting need for role of politics in process to be
"open, unabashed, and honest"). My list of problems with even well-meaning
Congresses is drawn from Sanford Levinson, Our Undemocratic Constitution
25–77 (2006).

10. *See* Mark V. Tushnet, Taking the Constitution Away from the Courts 9–12 (1999)
(suggesting that populist constitutionalism is not well suited for interpreting the
"thick constitution," by which Tushnet means narrow procedural provisions);
Katyal, *supra* note 3, at 1379–81 (noting but disagreeing with Tushnet).

11. *See* Gordon S. Wood, The Creation of the American Republic, 1776–1787, at 319–28 (1969) (discussing role of "people out-of-doors" in Revolutionary era); Sanford Levinson & Jack Balkin, *Constitutional Crises*, 157 U. Pa. L. Rev. 707, 741 (2009) (discussing precedents for, and importance of, public demonstrations and "mass civil disobedience" in constitutional crises). Levinson and Balkin note the historically remarkable lack of such demonstrations during the 2000 recount. *See id.* at 744. *See generally* Larry D. Kramer, The People Themselves (2004) (noting important role of ordinary citizens in constitutional government).

12. Levinson & Balkin, *supra* note 11, at 714.

13. S. Rep. No. 68-170, at 4 (1924).

14. *See* Levinson, *supra* note 7, at 33–35 (attempting to explain national tendency to ignore dangerous constitutional structural defects, even after they have caused real problems).

15. *See* Birch Bayh, One Heartbeat Away (1968) (describing dogged leadership of Sen. Bayh in passage of Twenty-Fifth Amendment); David E. Kyvig, Explicit and Authentic Acts 269–74 (1996) (recounting dogged leadership of Sen. George Norris in passage of Twentieth Amendment); Levinson, *supra* note 9, at 21 (citing comparative study by Donald Lutz on difficulty of amending constitutions); *cf.* Davidson, *supra* note 7, at 112 (noting relative ease of overriding judicial decisions by passing statutes, as opposed to using constitutional amendments).

16. *See* Garrett, *supra* note 6, at 51–52 (highlighting benefit of creating proactive, and thus neutral, processes); Sanford Levinson, *Why It's Smart to Think About Constitutional Stupidities*, 17 Ga. St. U. L. Rev. 359, 372 (2000) (noting disinclination of Congress to act in ways that threaten its members' prerogatives); Vermeule, *supra* note 3, at 416–18 (noting that politicians' focus on present interests dampens neutralizing effect of future uncertainty). *But see* Mark Tushnet, *Interpretation in Legislatures and Courts, in* The Least Examined Branch, *supra* note 9, at 355, 362 (asserting that following Constitution might be an important interest for constituencies to whom Congress is responsive).

17. *See* Elizabeth Garrett & Adrian Vermeule, *Institutional Design of a Thayerian Congress*, 50 Duke L.J. 1277, 1300 (2001) (discussing importance of "elicit[ing] strong and competing interest-group activity"); Levinson, *supra* note 16, at 371 (noting difficulty in getting Congress to pay attention to issues with no political payoff); Vermeule, *supra* note 3, at 430–31 (noting "activity-dampening effects" of any constraint on self-interest).

18. *See also* Kyvig, *supra* note 15, at xvi (noting that most constitutional amendments come in bursts); George W. Norris, Fighting Liberal 342 (1945) (depicting Twentieth Amendment Sections 3 and 4 as afterthoughts, in autobiography of amendment's main proponent). In 1924, working on an earlier version of the Twentieth Amendment, Senator Norris explained the need to add a revision of a hardwired date in the Twelfth Amendment, concerning presidential elections thrown into the House. "[W]hile we were proposing to amend the Constitution . . . ," he said, "we might just as well provide for that contingency." 65 Cong. Rec. 4142

NOTESTOPAGES171–177

(1924). Senator Fess chimed in with "another contingency that might arise," and which he and others had long worried about, namely, the death of the president-elect. *Id.* The draft amendment did not address Fess's concern until a House Committee added a provision in 1926, along with what became Section 4 of the amendment. *See* H.R. Rep. No. 69-311, at 5–9 (1926) (discussing additions, motivated by desire to avoid "doubt" and "chaos" that then-current Constitution could cause, and discussing other such issues consciously left unaddressed). The Senate version kept excluding these provisions until almost the bitter end. *See* H.R. Rep. No. 72-633, at 3–4 (1932) (Conf. Rep.) (recording Senate's final acceptance of House's approach); 69 Cong. Rec. 953 (1928) (statement of Sen. Norris) (announcing intention to add House language, but only if and when House passed amendment).

19. *See* Senate Rule 25.1(n)(1) (describing jurisdiction of Senate Rules Committee); Davidson, *supra* note 7, at 107–10 (noting lack of moderates in judiciary committees and relevant subcommittees in both houses); Garrett & Vermeule, *supra* note 17, at 1290 (noting existence and effects of Congress's "severely constricted agenda"); *id.* at 1321 (discussing ideological extremity of judiciary committee members); Abner J. Mikva, *How Well Does Congress Support and Defend the Constitution?*, 61 N.C. L. Rev. 587, 610 (1983) (noting factors that prevent "meaningful" attention to the Constitution in committees); The Constitution, http://judiciary.senate.gov/about/subcommittees/constitution.cfm (July 19, 2010) (describing jurisdiction of Senate Judiciary Committee's Subcommittee on the Constitution).

    One study showed that between 1971 and 2000, only 10 percent of committee hearings on constitutional issues were to consider actual constitutional amendments. *See* Keith E. Whittington et al., *The Constitution and Congressional Committees, in* The Least Examined Branch, *supra* note 9, at 396, 399.

20. *Cf.* Lawrence E. Filson & Sandra L. Strokoff, The Legislative Drafter's Desk Reference 251 (2d ed. 2008) (advising legislative drafters to "clarify the meaning in the statute itself" rather than rely on statements in legislative history).

21. *See* John R. Vile, A Companion to the United States Constitution and Its Amendments 213 (4th ed. 2006) (noting Congress's failure to implement Section 4 of the Twentieth Amendment).

22. *See* Bayh, *supra* note 15 (Twenty-Fifth Amendment); William J. Keefe & Morris S. Ogul, The American Legislative Process 16 (6th ed. 1985) (noting how process of converting ideas into law often entails multiple failures and several years); Norris, *supra* note 18, at 329–43 (Twentieth Amendment); Kyvig, *supra* note 15, at 389–90 (describing failure of direct-election amendment despite overwhelming passage in House, support from president, and strong support in Senate).

23. For an excellent summary of the difficulties Congress faces, see Barbara Sinclair, *Question: What's Wrong with Congress? Answer: It's a Democratic Legislature*, 89 B.U. L. Rev. 387, 389 (2009).

24. *See* Bayh, *supra* note 15 (describing creation of Twenty-Fifth Amendment).

25. *See* Victoria F. Nourse & Jane S. Schacter, *The Politics of Legislative Drafting*, 77 N.Y.U. L. Rev. 575, 592–93 (2002) (discussing dangers of drafting on Senate floor); *id.* at 594–95 (discussing time pressure as source of unclear drafting); *cf.* Eric J. Gouvin, *Truth in Savings and the Failure of Legislative Methodology*, 62 U. Cin. L. Rev. 1282 (1994) (observing that poor legislative drafting often results when a solution is proposed, and the debate around it is organized, before there is agreement on what the problem to be addressed is).

26. Beth Simone Noveck, Wiki Government (2009).

27. *See* Beth Simone Noveck, *The Electronic Revolution in Rulemaking*, 53 Emory L.J. 433 (2004) (distinguishing effectiveness of public participation and collaboration from ineffectiveness of "one-off commenting"); Cary Coglianese, *Citizen Participation in Rulemaking*, 55 Duke L.J. 943 (2006) (detailing disappointing results of regulatory e-rulemaking); Jacob Ewerdt, *Open Legislation Development*, 7 Nw. J. Tech. & Intell. Prop. 63 (2008), http://www.law.northwestern.edu/ journals/njtip/v7/n1/5 (explaining benefits of open-source software, applying its principles to designing legislation, and noting some successful preliminary uses); Roberto Casati & Gino Roncaglia, *The Anatomy of a Collaborative Writing Tool for Public Participation in Democracy* (Oct. 31, 2007), http://jeannicod.ccsd.cnrs.fr/ ijn_00184564/en (exploring various types of collaborative technologies for drafting legislation).

28. James Surowiecki, The Wisdom of Crowds (2004) (exploring nature of collective wisdom); *see* Noveck, *supra* note 26, at 40, 180 (discussing "'Digg-style' tools for submitting and rating the quality of others' submissions"); Sanford Levinson, *Constitutional Engagement "Outside the Courts" (and "Inside the Legislature")*, *in* The Least Examined Branch, *supra* note 9, at 378, 381–82 (noting ability of non-lawyers to contribute to constitutional deliberation); *see also* Garrett & Vermeule, *supra* note 17, at 1304 (calling for legislative processes that encourage broad, transparent input from experts and the public).

29. Wikis work poorly when participants have opposing viewpoints. This is why I have limited my proposal to achieving a common goal: a text that best achieves a policy design on which there is already consensus. *See* Michael Allan, *Recombinant Text* § 6.5 (2007), http://zelea.com/project/textbender/d/overview.xht (discussing limits of wikis and proposing alternative "recombinant" model for collaborators with significant disagreements); Casati & Roncaglia, *supra* note 27, at 9 (theorizing about designs of collaborative software to allow for diverging drafts).

INDEX

Act of Settlement, 51–52, 198n26
acting presidents, 4, 65n, 93, 96,
 103n; pardons by, 196n18;
 qualifications of, 154; succession
 and, 98, 102, 105; Twenty-Fifth
 Amendment disability and, 68–69,
 81, 92–93, 96
acting secretaries, 74n
Adams, John, 33
Adams, John Quincy, 112–13, 128, 141
Agnew, Spiro, 87, 100, 214n24
Albert, Carl, 88, 100
Albright, Madeline, 154
Allott, Gordon, 70, 72
amendments. *See* constitutional
 amendments
appointment power, 67n, 77, 87,
 89–90, 119
Appointments Clause, 67n, 89–90
Arthur, Chester, 4, 86, 104, 210n7,
 217n43
assassination, 5, 86, 96

Balkin, Jack, 166
Barkow, Rachel, 150
Bayh, Birch, 70, 72–74, 80, 171–72, 177,
 205n21, 206n22

Belknap, William, 110n, 113, 122,
 127–29, 168n
Black, Charles, 114
Black Swans, 2
Black's Law Dictionary, 44
Bloomberg, Michael, 135
Blount, William, 122, 126–28, 168,
 225n43
Bradley, Joseph, 162n
Breyer, Stephen, 150, 232n30
Burr, Aaron, 4, 9, 168
Bush, George H. W., 12, 40, 48, 56–58
Bush, George W.: criminal record of,
 41n; election of, 152, 159; potential
 impeachment of, 111; potential
 prosecution of, 12; self-pardon
 speculation about, 40, 192n2; term
 limits and, 136
Bush v. Gore, 79, 150, 159–60, 162–63,
 232n30, 235n2
Byrd, Robert, 182n3

cabinet, 16, 18, 23, 67n, 100; as
 pathway to presidency, 99;
 presidential disability determinations
 and, 22, 23n, 63–66, 68–69, 71,
 73n, 75–76, 80–81, 176; succession